November 18, 1984

Sport Aviation Series/Book No.7

ARV

*To Dr. Tom & Ginnie,
With many thanks for all your help
and continue interest in my endeavors.
Fondly,
Mike & Roberta*

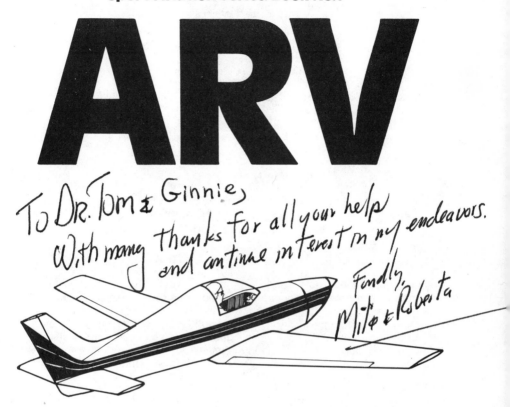

Michael A. Markowski

THE ENCYCLOPEDIA OF AIRCRAFT RECREATIONAL VEHICLES

AViation Publishers

**One Aviation Way ● Lock Box 234
Hummelstown, PA 17036 USA**

ARV —
The Encyclopedia Of
Aircraft Recreational Vehicles

Michael A. Markowski

Copyright © 1984 by Michael A. Markowski

FIRST EDITION
First Printing — May 1984

Published by:
Aviation Publishers Division
Ultralight Publications, Inc.
Post Office Box 234
Hummelstown, PA 17036

Books by the Author

THE HANG GLIDER'S BIBLE, The Complete Pilot's and Builder's Guide
THE ENCYCLOPEDIA OF HOMEBUILT AIRCRAFT, including Powered Hang Gliders
ULTRALIGHT AIRCRAFT, The Basic Handbook of Ultralight Aviation
ULTRALIGHT FLIGHT, The Pilot's Handbook of Ultralight Knowledge
ULTRALIGHT TECHNIQUE, How to Fly and Navigate Ultralight Air Vehicles

Library of Congress Cataloging in Publications Data

Markowski, Michael A.
ARV — The Encyclopedia Of Aircraft Recreational Vehicles
(Sport Aviation Series/Book No. 7)

1. Airplane, Home-built.   I. Title
TL671.2.M327   1984   629.133'343   83-51822
ISBN   0-938716-10-7 (paperback)

On The Cover

The Brown "Starlite" was the first place winner of the Great 1983 ARV Competition and Fly-Off, held at Wittman Field, Oshkosh, WI. It features a mixture of composite and wooden construction in a sleek, sophisticated shape. Powered by a 28 hp engine, it cruises 100 mph while burning 1.2 gal/hr. It can be trailered, and field assembled in ten minutes by one person. Courtesy Starlite Aircraft Co., 2219 Orange Blossom, San Antonio, TX 78247, (512) 494-9812.

Acknowledgement

Special thanks go out to the following individuals, organizations, and manufacturers, who all made this work possible. Through their efforts, we will all benefit with aircraft of higher performance from less power and for less expense.

AB RADAB, Hal Adkins, AmEagle Corp., J.W. Batter of *WWI AERO*, Bensen Aircraft Corp., Mark Brown, Catto Aircraft, CGS Aviation, Bill Chana, Devore Aviation Corp., Diehl AeroNautical, Inc., the EAA, Eipper Aircraft, Inc., the FAA, Fishercraft, Inc., *Flying*, Goldwing, Ltd., Monty Groves, Headberg Aviation, R.W. Hovey, Morry Hummel, Mike Kimbrel, Light Aero, Inc., Light Miniature Aircraft, Lockheed Aircraft Corp., Fred Quarles, Rand/Robinson Engineering, Inc., Rutan Aircraft Factory, Inc., Kevin Renshaw, Sather Enterprises, Dave Sclair of the Flyer Newspapers, Smithsonian Institution, Sorrell Aviation, Inc., Don Stewart, Mrs. J.F. Taylor, Molt Taylor, Dick Tichenor of *R/C Modeler*, John Underwood, Viking Aircraft, Inc., Gary Watson, Zenair, Ltd, and all the great aviation pioneers that contributed to the advancement of the ARV concept.

About The Author

Mike Markowski's life literally revolves around flight. He is a graduate aeronautical engineer (specialized in low speed aerodynamics) and FAA licensed private pilot who, since 1971, has devoted his life to the development of sport aviation. He was instrumental in initiating hang gliding in the eastern regions of the United States, and began his writing career as editor of the original *Skysurfer* magazine. Prior to that, he was employed as an advanced research engineer for Douglas and Sikorsky aircraft companies, working in the areas of advanced designs and new concepts. Since then, he has built and flown many ultralights of his own design, founded two manufacturing firms, ran a flight school, taught ultralight flight theory at the university level (M.I.T. and others), and is considered an authority on sport aviation.

He has lectured to numerous organizations and groups, including the International Symposium on the Technology and Science of Low Speed and Motorless Flight held at M.I.T. He was also responsible for the Forum on Foot-Launched Flight held at the Annual Convention and Fly-In of the Experimental Aircraft Association during the mid-seventies. He has made "star" appearances on national television shows, is sought after for speaking engagements by various groups, and he is aften quoted in books, magazines, and newspapers around the world.

Mike is a widely read author, having five books (The Hang Glider's Bible, The Encyclopedia of Homebuilt Aircraft, Ultralight Aircraft, Ultralight Flight, Ultralight Technique, and The Encyclopedia of Aircraft Recreational Vehicles) to his credit—classics in their fields—as well as numerous magazine articles.

In addition to writing and flying, Mike is a consultant to the ultralight industry for engineering design, as well as marketing, advertising, and public relations. He is also listed as the nation's only Technical Expert in Ultralight Aviation by Attorneys in the Products Liability and Transportation Legal Directory and, as such, is active in legal cases. He holds memberships in the Experimental Aircraft Association, Soaring Society of America, United States Hang Gliding Association, the Aircraft Owners and Pilots Association, and the National Association of Sport Aircraft Designers.

It is hoped that this book will foster safety through education as ARVs develop and grow into recreational flying of the future.

Contents

Introduction

Something very exciting is happening in general aviation. A new "class" of aircraft is emerging, bridging the gap between ultralights and traditional lightplanes. These new aircraft are known as ARVs — Aircraft Recreational Vehicles. They should foster a tremendous resurgence in sport flying and flying in general.

For the first time in aviation history, airplanes are being developed and sold solely for recreational purposes, and successfully at that. Until recently, flying machines have always had to justify their existence either through military employment or by serving the needs of commerce and industry. With ARV's recreation is first. They are as inexpensive as ultralights to own and operate yet offer reasonably fast, efficient cross-country transportation, and, some real utility. It's the logical class for ultralighters to progress to and, offers a viable flight alternative to licensed pilots. Some are two-seaters, enabling you to share your flying experiences with a friend — something many ultralighters would like to do.

The rising popularity of ultralights, has proven the public is very interested in fulfilling the age old dream of flying. Yet, they probably represent only the "tip-of-the-proverbial-iceberg." With the streamlining of amateur-built rules, more appropriate certification requirements, and the release of the long awaited Recreational Pilots License, flying should experience a growth unparalleled in all of aviation history.

Since the time of Otto Lilienthal (1896), engineers have strived to develop inexpensive sportsplanes the average working man could afford. Today, that goal is alive and well. . . stronger than ever. At various times since the turn of the century, individuals, groups, and organizations have tried to make it happen. Men like Santos Dumont, Ed Heath, Henry Mignet, Paul Poberezny, Ray Stits and Burt Rutan come to mind. They stirred the imagination and got people flying.

In the early 20s, 1923 to be exact, the Lympne Lightplane Trials took place — the first such event in history. Many light and ultralight designs resulted. In 1953, Paul Poberezny organized the EAA (Experimental Aircraft Association), which now has over 70,000 members in over 600 chapters throughout the world. The EAA is, in fact, the backbone of the sport flying movement, and works with the FAA in aiding its orderly, sensible development.

In 1962, the wooden Bower's Fly Baby won the EAA's design contest. In 1981, the *Flyer Newspapers,* in conjunction with the EAA, DuPont and Cuyuna Engine Company, sponsored the great ARV design competition. It attracted 126 entries in two categories: 44 ultralights and 82 lightplanes. The fly-off was held at the EAA's 1983 Oshkosh convention. Never before was there so much interest in new aircraft designs.

So what is an ARV? Basically, it is a single or two-place machine that looks like an airplane (as opposed to a powered hang glider). It features conventional three-axis aerodynamic controls, and has a partially or totally enclosed cabin. As this book is concerned with the lightplane category of ARVs, they are also fast enough to provide decent cross-country performance. They are not as gust sensitive as ultralights, and offer more creature comforts to pilot and passenger. They are also built like conventional aircraft.

The light ARV must be inspected and registered as amateur-built, and the operator must possess a pilot's license. Hopefully, it would be used as a recreational vehicle, away from large airports and TCAs (Terminal Control Areas). It is powered by a smaller engine and carries less fuel than a Cessna 152, for instance, and is lighter as well. The modern ARV is an inspiration of the ultralight and the potential it uncovered. It's the embodiment of new thinking, and the application of new powerplants and materials, spurred on by sensible FAA rules. This developed in large part, due to the success of the EAA movement and its concern for education, safety and practicability in flying.

What began as powered hang gliders in the mid-70s, had evolved into "proper little aeroplanes" by the mid-80s. Cable braced, bolt-together tubular constructions gave way to welded steel tubing, heliarced aluminum, and composites. Open-air seating yielded to nose fairings, cockpits, and totally enclosed cabins with heat and other amenities. Also, the airplane was more-or-less "re-invented" and "re-discovered" by a new generation of designers and would-be aviators. They had discovered the joys of flight in an ultralight and awoke to flying's potential as a fast, efficient form of transportation. Out of frustration with conventional aviation, these men were bound and determined to make aircraft that were both affordable and fun to fly.

Several designs existed before the ARV competition, while some were introduced during it, but not entered. They broke new ground without realizing the "iceberg" they were chipping away at. New blood had entered mainstream aviation by the "backdoor," and the public was eager to support it.

This book chronicles the development of the ARV, reviews the various designs you can build and fly today, and takes a look at the future. Presented are things like: performance and dimensional specifications, flight characteristics, pilot reports, three-view drawings, inboard profiles, cutaways, photographs, and more. Information is also included on the requirements, parts, tools, shop facilities, and the construction details and techniques associated with building and flying each aircraft.

In these pages, you'll probably find an ARV suited to your wants, needs and skills. It is hoped that Aircraft Recreational Vehicles can help guide you to your dream machine. Perhaps it will enable you to fulfill your desires for flight, and the joy and utility it can provide. In your own way, you'll be a part of a revolution in flying.

The FAA has recognized and even embraced the EAA's philosophy of guiding sport aviation along the lines of safety and practicability above and beyond minimum standards. As a result, the designer's creativity and the needs of regulations are met on a common ground, insuring orderly development and growth.

The EAA's philosophy of guiding sport aviation along the lines of safety and practicability above and beyond minimum standards, has allowed the FAA to embrace it.

Indeed, the FAA looks to the EAA for guidance.

WARNING—A WORD OF CAUTION

Flight, in and of itself, is not necessarily dangerous, however it is most unforgiving of errors, sloppiness and misjudgement on the parts of the designer, manufacturer, and pilot. Whenever a man flys, he accepts the risk that he may be injured or even killed. It is each individual's decision to either accept or reject this risk in light of its potential hazards, challenges and rewards. Flying can be, and is done safely every day of the year by paying strict attention to the details involved.

This book is not intended as a do-it-yourself guide, but merely as a source of information to be used as a reference. If there is anything you don't understand, don't hesitate to ask your flight instructor and other pilots. All of the aircraft featured in this volume are homebuilt, and as such, are governed by the FAA's Advisory Circular No. 20-27C — Certification And Operation Of Amateur-Built Aircraft (see the Appendix of this book for complete details). ARVs are real airplanes, and you must possess at least a student pilot's license before you fly one. And, always remember to treat any aircraft with due respect.

Section I
Experimental Aircraft And The Development Of The ARV

In his age old quest for simple, affordable flight, man has conceived, built and flown all manner of flying machines. This section will show you some of the interesting minimum aircraft that have been developed since the early part of the century.

To gain a better understanding of and appreciation for today's ARV, it is useful to go back in time to look at what has already been done. It is important to study the development of the ARV concept so that we can avoid repeating dangerous mistakes. Furthermore, in light of the scientific and technological advances that have occurred, we may find it desirable to resurrect an old concept and refine it. An idea or configuration that might have been impractical only a few short years ago, may be revolutionary today because of new methods, materials and aerodynamics.

Contrary to its modern "coinage," the ARV has been in existence since the first decade of this century. Many designers and visionaries were far ahead of their time. Many tried to popularize the ARV concept, and some even met with limited success from time to time. But, intervening events, like wars and the great depression, took their toll. The great dream of "an airplane in every garage" wasn't even remotely possible until mid-century.

But we digress. Let's go back to the beginning — to the time of the Wright Brothers — to see how it all started. Let's trace the development of the ARV and discover the many "false starts" the popularization of recreational flying had to experience before today's success could be realized.

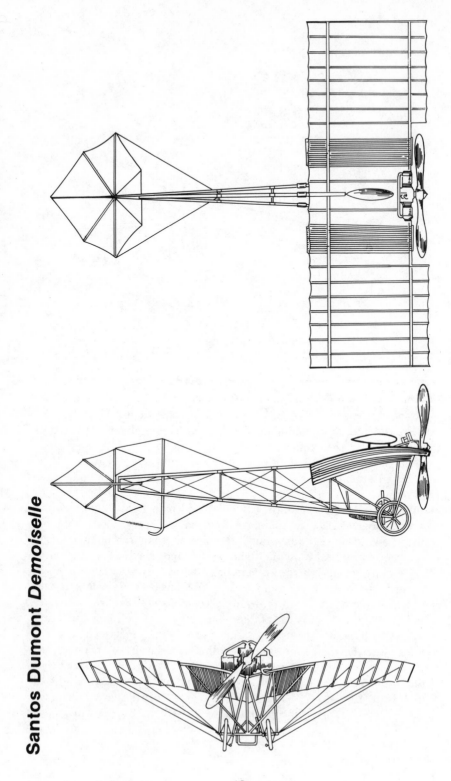

Santos Dumont Demoiselle

1

SANTOS DUMONT
DEMOISELLE

Alberto Santos-Dumont probably deserves more credit than anyone else of his time for getting recreational aviation started. After spending several years building and flying dirigibles, this little Brazilian living in Paris turned his thoughts towards aircraft. In 1906, he became the first man in Europe to fly. Three years later, he came out with his diminutive "Demoiselle." It cruised at 56 mph, and could lift its 260 pounds plus pilot off the ground in only about 200 feet.

True to form and unlike his contemporaries, Santos released his drawings to the general public. In fact, *Popular Mechanics* published a complete set of working drawings in their June and July, 1910 issues. The magazine made the following statement:

"From time to time vague descriptions of the manner of constructing aeroplanes have been given to the public. All over the United States there are thousands of persons who are intensely interested in the subject of aerial flight, but until now nothing of a tangible nature has been presented on which work could be started with a reasonable prospect of success. It is a great satisfaction therefore, to be able to present the working drawings of the wonderful monoplane invented by M. Santos-Dumont. However, it

Fig. 1-1. Santos Dumont takes to the air in the spring of 1909 at St. Syr, France. His Demoiselle was the first popular ARV. Courtesy Smithsonian Institution.

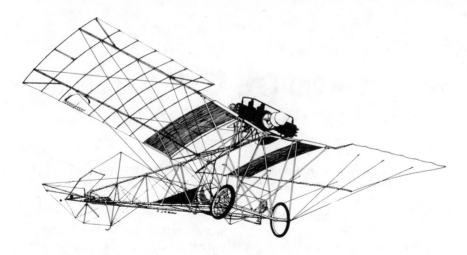

Fig. 1- 2. Cutaway of Demoiselle shows intricate lightweight structure. Fuselage longerons were bamboo. Copyright J.W. Batter, "WWI Aero" magazine.

would be useless for anyone not possessed of some mechanical skill, and plenty of common sense, to attempt to construct a copy of the famous flyer, even with such detailed drawings and instructions."

Excerpts from the *Popular Mechanics* feature follow:

"Following the announcement, made some months ago by Alberto Santos-Dumont that he intended to give the plans of his latest aeroplane, the Demoiselle, to the world in the interest of aeronautics, great interest has been centered in the wonderful monoplane. It is the lightest and smallest of all heavier-than-air machines, yet is thoroughly practical.

"It would be well, of course, for the prospective aviator to make himself acquainted with the subject of the atmosphere as it applies to aeronautics, to have a good knowledge of gasoline motors, and to study the properties and qualities of the different materials which enter into construction of the monoplane.

"The greatest items of expense will be the motor and the propeller. Santos-Dumont used a Darracq motor of 30 hp. There are American motors which will do just as well, probably. We advise that the propeller be purchased.

"A good place to start would be the vertical rudder, plate iii. the thickness of the bamboo there given is the maximum. The heavier and stronger portions are used for the centers where the strain is heaviest. Drawing C on this plate shows the manner in which the cloth is attached to the framework by No. 21 piano wire, as it should be done throughout.

"After having sewn the piano wire into the outer edge of the cloth, the wire should be stretched to get it to the extremity, and then dropped into a slot made for it to rest in on the outer end of the bamboo. Thus the pieces of cloth are well stretched, and are held firmly in place, adding to the strength of the machine. This applies to the wings also, where every added bit of strength and firmness adds to the successful completion.

Fig. 1-3. Demoiselle featured a universal jointed all-moving tail and wing warping. Twin-cylinder opposed Duthell-Chalmers engine produced 20 hp directly to prop. Pilot here is a young lady. Courtesy Smithsonian Institution.

"Slots are made at the ends of the bamboos for the wires to slip into. It is a good idea to put a cork into the hollow end and cut the slots in both at the same time. Brass wire, gauge No. 25, should be wound around the rod just below the end of the slot to prevent its splitting. In later models, Santos-Dumont used metal caps over the ends of the bamboo rods.

"The cloth used by Santos-Dumont was a very finely woven silk. It has the greatest objection of expense, however, and it would probably be as well to use percale or muslin of the best grade.

"Plate IV shows the details of the horizontal rudder which governs the altitude of the machine 'Gouvernail de Profondeur' is the French term for it. It should be constructed in the same manner as the vertical rudder. The method of attaching the rudders to the frame is shown on Plate IV. This is practically a universal joint, allowing the steering device to be turned in any direction by the controlling wires shown on Plate I. These wires should be very carefully selected and tested, for a great deal depends upon their strength. It would be very imprudent to use ordinary piano wire. The U-joint should be made of the best steel tubing procurable; good bicycle tubing is excellent.

"Having finished the steering arrangement, it would be wise to take up construction of the wings next. These are made entirely of bamboo rods with bamboo or ash spars as shown in Plate V. However, Clement Bayard, at whose factory in France these monoplanes are being manufactured, makes the spars of poplar or ash. Aluminum tubes also have been used. It would be advisable, however, to stick to the bamboo rods which served Santos-Dumont so well.

"In order to secure the ribbing curves as shown at the top of Plate V, it would be sufficient to bend the rods over a form by force. They may also be bent by means of a string tied to the ends, drawing them together, and then plunging them into boiling water for about 15 minutes. They will retain their shape if given time to dry before the strings are removed. If the builder desires to use wood, he may proceed in like manner. The curve is almost the true arc of a circle. The whole plane structure is kept rigid by guide wires running to the frame as shown in Plate I.

"The wings completed, it would be well next to undertake construction of the frame. The wheels are easily made, for, save that they have a longer hub, they are very similar in construction to the ordinary bicycle wheel.

"It would be well to use strong spokes, for at times, when the machine strikes the ground suddenly, great stress is put upon them. Santos-Dumont settled on a wheel hub length of six inches. These hubs are simply slipped on over the axle tubes and fastened with a cotter pin. It is not necessary to provide any special bearings for the wheels, as it is intended they should work with a slight friction. The wheels are inclined toward one another at the top, to prevent their being broken when subjected to a light jar. Details of construction of the joints, where the landing gear tubing is attached to the bamboo frame, are shown in Detail of Assembly A on Plate VII. It would be imprudent and dangerous to make a hole in any of the three main bamboo rods which constitute the frame of the machine, for this would detract from their strength.

"The machine thus far completed, we may proceed to attach the piano wire stretchers, and then the wires controlling the horizontal and vertical rudders and governing the warping of the planes. The rudder controls may be installed in accordance with the builder's ideas, and the motor controls will vary, of course, with the type of motor used.

"In Santos-Dumont's Demoiselle, the wire regulating the horizontal rudder is attached to a lever within easy reach of the pilot's right hand. The vertical rudder is controlled by a wheel at the pilot's left hand.

"The lever which controls the warping of the planes is placed behind the pilot's seat. Santos-Dumont operated this by bending his body to the right or left, the lever fitting into a tube fastened to his coat in the rear. A side movement pulls the rear end of the wing opposite to the side to which the pilot leans. The balancing of the whole apparatus is, therefore, in a manner, automatic. The pilot has but to bend over to one side in order to balance the machine.

"Springs are introduced on the wires which control the rudders of some of the machines, so as to bring the rudder back to its normal position without effort on the part of the operator. The seat is a piece of canvas or leather stretched across the two lower bamboo rods just behind the wheels.

"Santos-Dumont had his motor control so arranged that he could regulate the supply of gasoline by his foot. The spark switch may be placed on the steering lever, or may be arranged differently with other motors. It is of prime importance that the motor should be perfectly balanced, direct-connected to the axle holding the propeller. The gasoline reservoir is

Fig. 1-4. Reproduction of a Demoiselle advertisement from a 1910 issue of *Popular Mechanics*.

located behind the pilot's seat, the fuel being forced up into a smaller one
just above the motor.

"In his remarkable flight from St. Cyr to Buc, the inventor of the
monoplane used a two-cylinder Darracq of 30 hp which gave the propeller
1000 rpm. It weighed just over 99 pounds. The entire machine weighed 260
pounds without the pilot. . ."

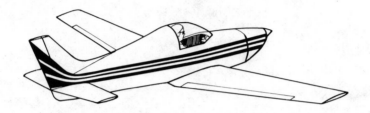

2

LYMPNE SINGLE-SEATER COMPETITION

After the cessation of the hostilities of WWI, there was a great deal of interest in gliding. It wasn't before long that some enterprising individuals mounted small engines to their gliders, freeing them from a ground crew and the worries of landing off field. The idea was wildly accepted all across Europe, but there was no organization.

By April 1923, the once booming British aircraft industry was at a virtual standstill. Most companies manufacturing aircraft had to depend on other sources of income to survive. Fortunately, the new Under-Secretary for Air, the Duke of Sutherland, recognized the need to stimulate aircraft building and flying. He then offered a £500 prize for a British lightplane contest, with the Royal Aero Club handling the details. The London Daily Mail threw in £1000 more, and reported the prize as "open to the whole world." The primary goal of the contest was fuel economy, with the £500 to go to the airplane flying the furthest on an imperial gallon of gasoline.

The newspaper gave the "lightplane motor-glider" competition national publicity, attracting more sponsors. é500 was posted by the Abdulla Tobacco Company for the fastest speed. Oil magnate Sir Charles Wakefield contributed £200 for the highest altitude. £100 was added for a landing contest. The greatest aggregate distance award was set at £300, equal donations being received from a motor trade association and a cycle makers union. The cash awards totaled £2600 ($11,500 in 1923 dollars). It was just enough to spur the efforts of several of England's largest airframe manufacturers.

The primary specifications for prospective entrants were: a single seater with an engine no larger than 750cc (just short of 46 cu in); the aircraft designed to be disassembled (or wings foldable) and handled by two people, and capable of being transported over the road and pass through a ten foot wide gate. Twelve entrants appeared — ten from England and one each from France and Belgium.

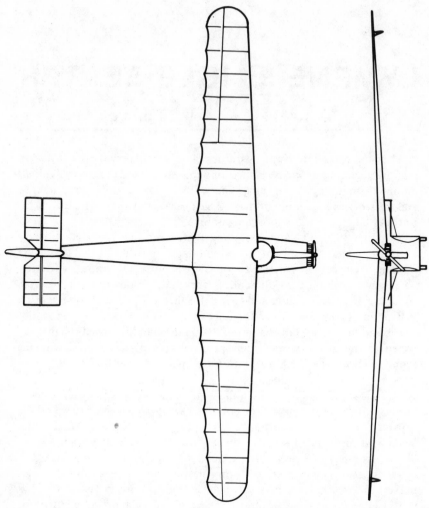

English Electric Wren

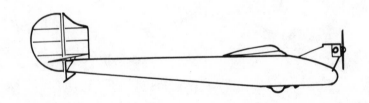

➂

ENGLISH ELECTRIC *WREN*

The following is a description of one of the top winners, the English Electric Company's "Wren." They entered two models to compete in the mileage per gallon contest. One tied with the A.N.E.C. (Air Navigation and Engineering Company) monoplane at 87.5 mpg, while the other finished second with 82.5 mpg. These airplanes were not entered in the competition for altitude or speed.

All parts of the Wren were designed to meet the standard safety factors of the British Air Ministry. In fact, it complies well with today's FAR103 for ultralights.

The fuselage was of orthodox wire-braced wooden frame construction, appropriately reinforced where the wing, landing gear, etc. were attached.

The main spars were of a substantial box section of spruce, with a special form of internal bracing for torsional stiffness. The upper surface of the leading edge was covered with three-ply. The entire structure was covered with a special light fabric, doped with titanine glider dope and finished in aluminum.

The stabilizer, elevator, fin and rudder were of substantial build, following the standard constructional methods of the day. The control system, which also followed the approved standard practice, was said to be very efficient.

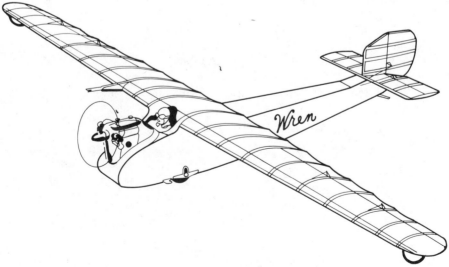

Fig. 1-5. Artist's conception of English Electric Wren. It was a top winner in the 1923 Lympne Lightplane Trials. Flew on 9 - 12 hp.

Power was supplied by a 398 cc A.B.C. horizontally opposed twin-cyclinder, direct drive to a laminated wooden propeller. This package produced top speed of 52 mph, sea level climb of 200 fpm, and a service ceiling of 3000 feet. At the time, this was considered adequate for cross-country flying, except in strong headwinds. It was also considered sufficient for a quick takeoff from reasonably level fields. The large diameter, rubber sprung wheels were more than half covered by the fuselage, not only to reduce drag, but also to allow landing on rough or plowed fields, without the risk of a nose over.

The forward portion of the fuselage bottom was protected by a three-ply covering. It served as a braking surface which, when preceded by the landing speed of 25 mpg, brought the airplane to a standstill within a few yards.

The controllability was said to be perfect, even at speeds probably near 20 mph, as shown in the splendid performance exhibited by the so-called "crazy flying." The engine was operated at a comparatively low speed, insuring reliability and durability.

Specifications

Wingspan	37 ft
Length	23 ft
Height	4 ft 9 in
Power	12 hp
Gross Weight	450 lbs
Empty Weight	232 lbs
Top Speed	52 mph
Cruising Speed	40 mph
Landing Speed	25 mph
Ceiling	3,000 ft
Climb	200 fpm

The Wren had a fully cantilevered wing. It was designed by N.S. Norway, better known as author-novelist Neville Shute.

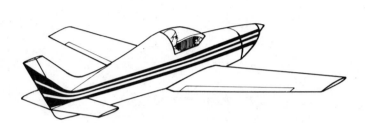

Parnall *Pixie*

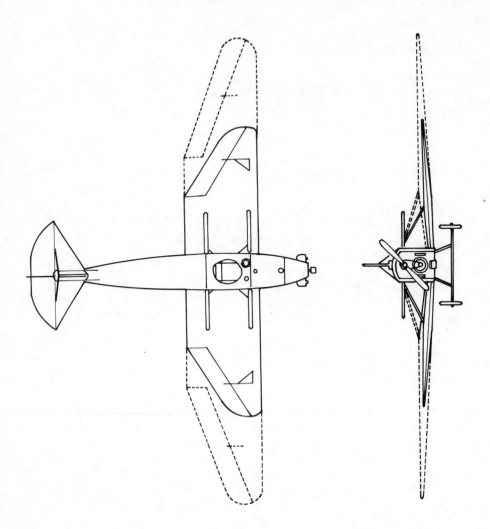

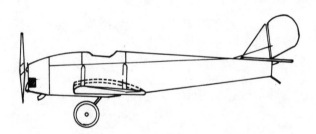

PARNALL *PIXIE*

Another of the winners at Lympne was the Parnall "Pixie" manufactured by George Parnall and Company. It attained the greatest speed, being clocked at 76.1 mph.

George Parnall, whose firm occupied a large building called the Coliseum Works on Park Row, was primarily engaged in woodworking. He had gotten into aviation during the WWI. Despite a devasting postwar slump, the industrialist was determined to stick it out, convinced a greater demand for his airplanes would soon be forthcoming.

Parnall's chief designer, Harold Bolas, had exhibited a rare aptitude for his work which bordered on genius. As a result the company had produced a number of outstanding navy planes, notably the Panther reconnaissance machine and the Plover fighter. Bolas was delighted by the Royal Aero Club's announcement. He sketched and calculated; finally there evolved a design which was nothing less than sheer brilliance. Fresh and original in concept, it was a low-wing, semi-cantilever monoplane employing an all-wood airframe, except for the steel tube tail group. An interesting feature was the ingeniously simple steel tube landing gear, an innovation popularized in principle years later by Steve Wittman.

At this stage Bolas was thinking mainly in terms of low fuel consumption. He, therefore, designed the wing with sufficient area to sustain flight on very reduced power. The Douglas motorcycle engine, also a Bristol product, had showed great promise on the test stand. Bolas decided to try the 500-cc model, which weighed approximately seventy pounds complete and developed 17-hp at 4000-rpm.

Captain Norman Macmillan (later Wing Cdr.), the Parnall company's test pilot, had been collaborating closely with Bolas from the start. One evening, when they were working late, Macmillan pointed out that it

Fig. 1-6. Artist's sketch of the Parnall Pixie II. This clipped wing version of the Pixie (long winged version was Pixie I) could attain 100 mph.

would be simple to make the little machine an all-round contender. It was going to have quickly detachable wings anyway, so why not an alternate set of short-span panels for speed? Furthermore, Macmillan continued, Douglas produced a 750-cc cycle engine which was identical externally to the 500-cc model. Why not try interchangeable combinations? The original configuration would be used only for the fuel consumption event, the big engine and short wings for speed and the big engine/long wing formula for the altitude test. There was a possibility of a clean sweep. Instantly seeing the logic in Macmillan's thinking, Bolas got busy designing another set of wings.

Careful attention was given to converting the engines and tuning. Due to the high crankshaft speeds, a gear reduction had to be devised in order to achieve optimum efficiency. Bolas designed an overhead propeller shaft driven by chain at 0.4 engine speed. This arrangement permitted the use of either engine without changing propeller shafts. Douglas technicians tuned both engines, installing small carburetor jets in the 500-cc unit, thereby improving fuel economy, and hopping up the larger one with high-lift cam and higher compression. On the test stand it delivered 36-hp at 6000-rpm. Bolas and Macmillan were delighted.

Aptly named the Pixie, flight testing commenced late in the afternoon of September 13th with the long wings and small engine. This combo was designated the Mark I configuration. Macmillan took the craft up to eight hundred feet, felt out the controls for about five minutes, then spiraled down for a landing. It had handled well enough, but quite glider-like. The next 3 hours in the air consisted of consumption and airspeed indicator calibration tests. Meanwhile, the shop crew was at work on a set of shortened panels for the Mark II.

Pixie II emerged from the assembly shop on October 4th. It was nearly six o'clock in the evening and the light was fading as a group of skeptical spectators from the nearby Bristol Aircraft Co. came to witness the occasion. It was thought by many that the Pixie would never get off the ground with a mere 60 square feet of wing surface and a puny cycle motor in its nose.

Macmillan lowered himself into the cockpit, adjusted the oil forcefeed control and primed the carburetor. "Contact!" called the pilot as he switched on the magneto. The mechanic grasped the tiny propeller and swung it. The Douglas came alive, buzzing merrily. After a short warm-up Mamillan waved his hand, indicating he was ready to go. The chocks were pulled and the Pixie rolled forward, rocking slightly as it accelerated quickly across the not quite level furrows of the once plowed field. The landing gear tubes flexed against Macmillan's back as the Pixie picked up speed. At 45-mph the wheels lifted from the turf and the tiny machine was soon 500 feet above the air field. Mamillan made a fast circuit and landed. Bolas' brainchild had behaved beautifully. The Parnall crew was jubilant.

There remained only time enough for two short flights the next morning, aggregating twenty minutes, before the machine had to be dismantled and trucked to Lympne Aerodrome, near Folkstone, on the Dover coast, which was the site of the now well publicized contest. The Pixie I combination was assembled first and test hopped at Lympne on October 7th; another practice lap was flown on the 8th, opening day morning. Two hours later, Macmillan got off again for the eighty minute flight, completing five laps of the 12½ mile course. Fuel consumption worked out to 49.5 miles per gallon. He tried it again in the afternoon, making an 85-minute flight at 500 feet. This time the consumption was down to 53.4-mpIg. However, it had become apparent that the performance of the English Electric Company's two Wrens, one of which had gone 87½ miles on one Imperial gallon, could not be equaled. In the process of converting to the Mark II configuration, the Pixie was tried out during a brief 5 minute hop with the 750-cc engine and long wings on October 9th.

Despite very rough and gusty air, Macmillan qualified for the Abdulla speed prize by making the required two laps at noon on the 11th. The flight lasted twenty minutes and a speed of 76.1-mph was recorded. During the night the Pixie went through a metamorphosis, emerging in the morning as the Mark I for a shot at the economy prize. However, a rising gale blew up a storm and all flying had to be canceled. That night the Pixie changed back to a clipped wing speedster, in which form it seemed likely to prove unbeatable.

On the final day of the meet, Saturday, the 13th, Macmillan took off and flew one lap at 81.2-mph. Unfortunately, the Douglas' intermediate timing gear loosened and began boring a hole in the gear case cover, necessitating immediate attention. Macmillan took off again at noon, but was down four minutes later with a defunct spark plug. In the meantime, another contestant had come into view after having made an attempt at the Wakefield altitude prize. It was Maneyrol, the Frenchman, in his Peyret monoplane. On opening day Bolas had done his best to have the Peyret disqualified for very good reasons. The machine was obviously woefully understressed. The wing struts were much too light. The officials listened politely, but declined to take any action which might create an unpleasant international situation. Maneyrol had won the celebrated Itford glider contest the year before. The Club would almost certainly be accused of unfair play if the Frenchman and his machine were excluded.

Macmillan was about to fly again when Maneyrol appeared to the southeast. He was coming in for a landing and the Peyret was descending at rather a steep angle. Leveling out at betwen 150 and 200 feet, the monoplane's nose dipped perceptibly. Suddenly both wings collapsed simultaneously and the machine plunged to the ground. Maneyrol, a flyer of exceptional ability, was fatally injured. Though the Peyret had made numerous flights, some in rough weather, it had been clear to Bolas that the wing struts, normally in tension, could not support a strong load in compression. A sudden, violent updraft had been the Frenchman's undoing.

Macmillan took off two hours after Maneyrol's crash and managed to do one lap at 81.5-mph. The second time around and several miles from the finish, the magneto loosened, causing the gears to disengage. Although he was flying at treetop level, Macmillan had enough reserve speed to swing a quarter turn into the wind and land in a meadow surrounded by tall elms. "She was so nippy on the controls and so light," wrote the Pixie's pilot years after ". . .she was a dream to handle in a forced landing."

It had begun to look as though one of the A.N.E.C. monoplanes might turn in a better speed than the Pixie's 76.1 of two days previous. Jimmy James, one of the A.N.E.C. pilots, had come within two-mph of Macmillan's score and he was going to try again after an altitude attempt. James' partner, Maurice Piercey, succeeded in reaching an altitude of 14,400 feet that afternoon, which took the Wakefield prize. Numbed by the cold, however, Piercey overshot his landing and headed straight for one of the de-Havilland entries. A quick-acting observer had the breath knocked out of him when he grabbed for the A.N.E.C.'s wingtip. Luckily, the machine swung away from the deHavilland enough to minimize the damage. The de-H's tail was clipped by the A.N.E.C. wingtip. It was bad news for the A.N.E.C. team, because they were not able to complete their repairs in time for another shot at the speed mark and Pixie skipped off with the Abdulla award.

After the Lympne meeting, Macmillan flew the Pixie II at the Hendon races on October 27th. During the handicap race, the engine refused to give full power owing to the carburetor being choked with flakes from the lining of the "fuel resistant" plumbing. Upon cleaning the carburetor and replacing the line, he won the Sir Charles Wakefield £50 scratch race with an average speed of 81-mph, beating the nearest competitor, a deH 53, by more than two laps. The five lap course was flown around pylons erected inside the airfield perimeter and covered a distance of about 7½ miles.

The Pixie showed up at Croydon Aerodrome on November 10th for a formal demonstration staged for the Dominion prime ministers. Shortly before Macmillan was scheduled to take off, a mechanic discovered that someone had trampled on the wing and cracked two ribs while peering into the cockpit. The culprit hadn't bothered to use the footrest. Bolas was not in attendance. Had he been there the Pixie almost certainly would have been grounded. The countenances of the two mechanics registered acute disappointment. Macmillan took another look at the damaged wing and decided to take a chance. Trusting that Bolas had made the ribs stronger than necessary for flight safety, he pulled on his helmet and slid into the cockpit.

Even before the Pixie was off the ground the Douglas began to run badly. Just off the runway one cylinder quit firing altogether. Unable to land straight ahead because of buildings, Macmillan eased around in a shallow 180 degree turn to the right. Crossing the Croydon boundary at little more than ten feet, he flew back past the spectators and made another one-eighty behind the hangars, came in very low over the fence and made a perfect landing. If the performance impressed the dignitaries as being a stunt staged for their amusement, the Pixie crew knew better. Macmillan heaved a sigh of relief as he stepped out of the small cockpit for the last time. The Pixie went back to the Coliseum Works on Park Row;

Macmillan took a new assignment as the Fairey Aviation Company's sole test pilot.

Reconditioned and fitted with a 696-cc Blackburne inverted Vee twin of 20-hp, the Pixie II next showed up for the Hendon RAF display on June 28, 1924. Frank T. Courtney, the noted test pilot, flew it in the Grosvenor Trophy Race at Lympne the following October.

On June 31, 1925, it was once again in the Lympne races lineup.

The next day, during the finals of the Light Aeroplane Holiday Handicap, a rainstorm developed and the Pixie's propeller started to come unglued, causing an alarming rpm loss. Courtney landed before any further problems arose. Later in the afternoon, he placed second in a threeplane-finish scratch race. The following day, Sunday, August 2nd, Courtney turned in a speed of 85.4-mph over a 50-km course. He raced again on the following day in the 100 mile International Handicap preliminary. It was described as the most exciting event of the entire meeting, being hotly contested and the flying low and close. Courtney flew brilliantly, taking the corners in near vertical turns. He did not manage to make the finals, however.

The Pixie II flew the Grosvenor Challenge Cup Handicap, also 100 miles, on the same date, but was out-classed by a new generation of lightweights, which included the two place Pixie III flown by Ft. Lt. R.A. de Haga Haig.

Specifications (Pixie II)

Wingspan	17 ft 10 in
Length	17 ft 10 in
Height	4 ft 2 in
Power	20 hp
Gross Weight	N.A.
Empty Weight	N.A.
Top Speed	105 mph
Cruising Speed	N.A.
Landing Speed	45 mph
Climb	N.A.
Ceiling	14,500

The 1925 Lympne races marked the Pixie's last public appearance. It went into storage soon afterward and did not reappear until 1936, when it was sold to a private owner. An Airworthiness ticket was issued in August 1937 and it flew around Cornwall for a while with the Mark II wings. It crashed in April 1939 and thus ended the saga of the Parnall Pixie.

5

LYMPNE TWO-SEATER COMPETITION

A year after the single-seaters flew, Lympne was the site of a two-seater competition. The object of the contest was to produce an airplane suitable for flight training purposes. Various prizes were awarded for the following qualifications, during that September 29 to October 4, 1924 event. Perhaps a similar competition would make good sense today.

Entry Qualifications

The airplane was first presented to the officials completely assembled. It was then disassembled or folded, and transported not more than 75 feet and placed in a shed 10 feet wide. The airplane was then removed from the shed and re-erected by two persons only, within two hours.

A demonstration of dual control was next. The pilot was required to make two flights, one from each seat. Each flight was to follow the course of a figure eight, flown within the boundaries of the airport.

Speed Range

The greater portion of the prizes were awarded for this qualification, which was determined by the following formula:

Speed Range % = (High Speed—Low Speed) x 100/Low Speed

High Speed was not to be less than 60 mph, and low speed not to exceed 45 mph.

Takeoff

This test required starting from a standstill and clearing a 25 foot high barrier in the shortest distance. One award was made for every yard below 450 yards.

Landing

In this test, the airplane was required to cross a barrier six feet high and come to rest in the shortest distance. One award was made for every yard less than 150 yards.

Reliability

Awards made in this test went to the airplane flying the greatest number of circuits during the period of the competitions, with total mileage not to be less than 400. A further stipulation required that an airplane fly at least 10 hours during that period.

High and Low Speed

The high speed test was conducted over a 12.5 mile triangular course in two separate flights of 75 miles each, or six laps. A break was allowed between the two flights for refueling only.

The low speed test was carried out over a straight course of about 500 yards long by 25 yards wide. Red flags were placed at intervals on both sides. The course was covered twice in each direction at a constant height of not more than 20 feet. The average of the four flights would represent the speed flown.

Comment

From an aerodynamic and structural point of view, a majority of the airplanes were reasonably successful, most failures owing to the engine. The requirements of the engine it developed, were rather severe. The Bristol "Cherub" horizontally opposed twin was the only one to pass the gruelling test with any degree of satisfaction. It was predicted however, that another year of development would produce an engine suited to the requirements of the two-seat light airplane.

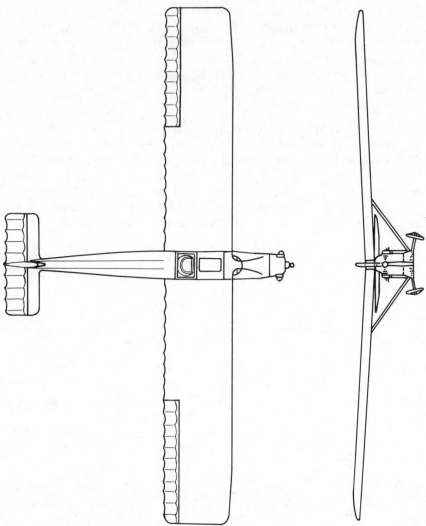

Beardmore Wee Bee

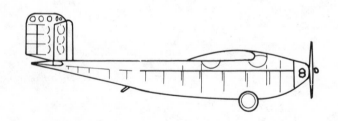

6

WEE BEE 1

The Wee Bee I was the first place winner at the Lympne two-seater competition. It was astonishingly efficient for a two-seater, with a Bristol "Cherub" engine of 1096 cc (67 cu in). Its construction was simple yet sturdy and comparatively inexpensive. Its performance was listed as follows:

High Speed - 70.11 mph, Low Speed - 39.66 mph

Speed Range - 76.77%. Take off Distance - 235 yards

Landing Distance - 124 yards, Miles Flown - 737.5

Hours Flown - 11

The Wee Bee was a wooden airplane. The fuselage was built with longerons and formers of spruce and three-ply, the frame being covered with 1/16 inch birch plywood. The wings were orthodox for the time, with two box spars of three-ply. The skin was plywood from the leading edge to the rear spar (out to the strut attachments) and, from the leading edge to the front spar all the way to the tip. This obviated the need for drag bracing either internally or externally. High aspect ratio aileron afford good roll control. The tail surfaces were wooden construction similar to the wing, with large control surfaces.

Specifications

Wingspan	38 ft
Length	22 ft 2 in
Height	5 ft 2 in
Power	32 hp
Gross Weight	N.A.
Empty Weight	N.A.
Top Speed	70 mph
Cruising Speed	64 mph
Landing Speed	N.A.
Climb	N.A.
Ceiling	N.A.

The Wee Bee won the two-seater event because it was an aerodynamically efficient example of the period's conventional construction practices. It broke no new ground otherwise.

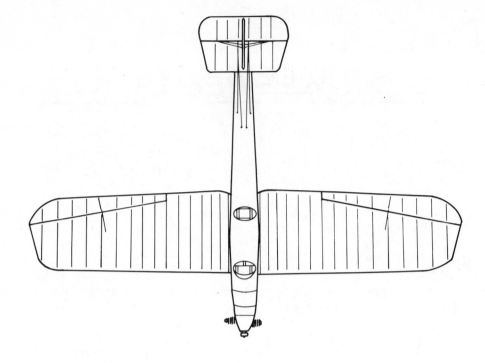

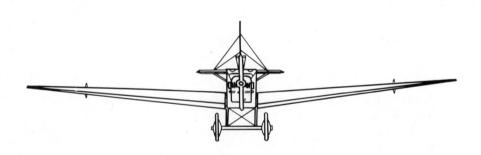

Bristol *Brownie*

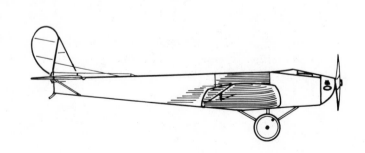

7

BRISTOL *BROWNIE*

The number two winner in the 1924 Lympne competition was significant in terms of its construction, while winning the Air Ministry Prize and the best take-off and climb event.

The Brownie was designed by Captain S.F. Barnwell, designer of WWI's best two-seater fighter, the Bristol "Brisfit." Two were built for the competition. Both featured steel tube fuselages with sweated joints braced by steel wire tierods. The tail group was also steel tube. One version had the then orthodox wooden spar wings with wooden truss ribs. The other featured steel spars and aluminum ribs. Both were fabric covered.

The Brownie's performance was quite good, especially considering its 870 pound gross weight and 32 hp Bristol Cherub engine. Top speed was 70 mph, cruise 58 mph, and landing was 36 mph. The takeoff run required but 150 yards and the ceiling was 8,000 feet. Other statistics include a wing spar of 36 ft 7 in, length of 26 ft 3 in, height of 6 ft 8 in, wing area of 204 sq ft, and an empty weight of 500 pounds. The landing run was only 50 yards.

Specifications

Wingspan	36 ft 7 in
Length	26 ft 3 in
Height	6 ft 8 in
Power	32 hp
Gross Weight	870 lbs
Empty Weight	500 lbs
Top Speed	70 mph
Cruising Speed	58 mph
Landing Speed	36 mph
Climb	N.A.
Ceiling	8,000 ft

Overall, the Brownie was quite significant and could even be called a trend setter, in light of its steel tubing fuselage and metal framed wings. It was certainly a sign of things to come.

Fig. 1-7. Artist's sketch of the innovative Bristol Brownie two-seater. Aircraft was far ahead of its time with all metal airframe.

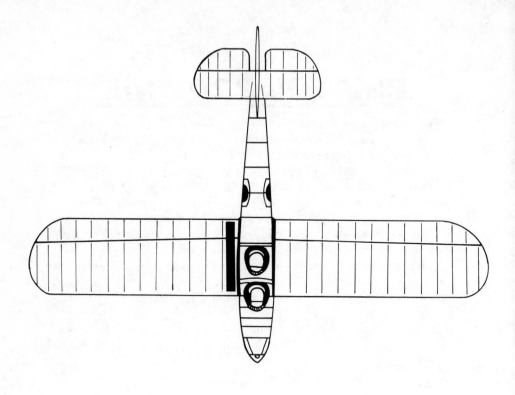

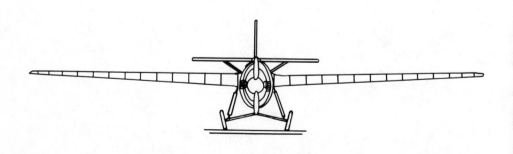

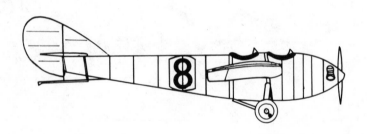

⑧

SHORT *SATELLITE*

The Satellite was an exceptionally aesthetically pleasing design, being a cantilevered mid-wing monoplane with oval cross section fuselage. While it only managed seventh place in the 100 mile handicap race, it was far ahead of its time in construction.

Lightly loaded, it flew and responded well to its controls, (it had full span ailerons) but was hopelessly underpowered. It pioneered the use of an all metal monocoque fuselage, hence its high empty weight. The wing spars were wooden, while the ribs were made of aluminum. The engine mount was unique, consisting of a neat, light-weight aluminum casting.

Specifications

Wingspan	34 ft
Length	23 ft 9 in
Height	4 ft 10 in
Power	32 hp
Gross Weight	N.A.
Empty Weight	N.A.
Top Speed	N.A.
Cruising Speed	N.A.
Landing Speed	N.A.
Climb	N.A.
Ceiling	N.A.

The two models entered in the competition made a very favorable impression, but did not take part in any event except the race. Unfortunately, one failed to arrive on time due to engine troubles, while the other was forced to withdraw because of damage sustained in a crash after its first flight. No performance figures were available due to the aircraft not doing any official flying at the meet.

Fig. 1-8. The Short Satellite was aesthetically pleasing, and far ahead of its time. It featured an all metal, oval-sectioned fuselage.

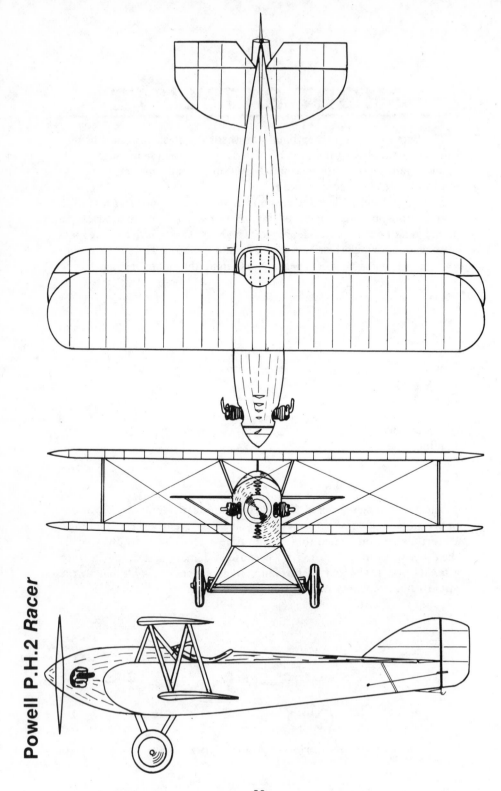

Powell P.H.2 Racer

9

POWELL *P.H.2 RACER*

At a time when the very-lightplane was most often thought of as a monoplane, many still believed in the biplane. Following the construction techniques proven at the end of WWI, this neat little ship was state of the art in 1923.

The aircraft was well engineered and featured a welded steel tubing fuselage and tail. Twenty guage tubing (.035 wall) was used throughout. The longerons were 5/8″ diameter, while most other members were of ½″ diameter except where specified otherwise. The turtle deck was 28 gauge sheet aluminum. The wings were well braced wooden, with routed spars, and 1/16″ plywood ribs with ¼″ square cap strips. The struts were 2″ x 17 gauge streamline steel tubing. Bracing was ¼″ streamline steel wire.

The P.H. 2 was considered an exceptionally clean and sturdy design for its day and had the advantage of being powered by the most reliable engine, as well. It would certainly make an interesting project today. Drawings were readily available in *Modern Mechanics and Inventions* and the annual *Flying Manual*.

Specifications

Wingspan	15 ft 9 in
Length	14 ft 6 in

Fig. 1-9. Powell P.H.2 Racer had a top speed of 85 mph on its 32 hp Bristol Cherub engine. Won 1925 Mitchell Field Air Races at an average 71.16 mph. C.H. Powell, builder, is shown measuring gas for the craft. Peter M. Bowers Collection.

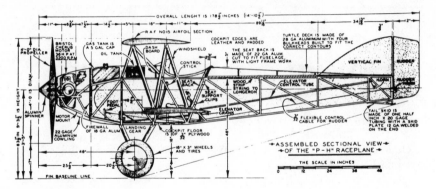

Fig. 1-10. Inboard profile of Powell Racer reveals structural details. Construction was welded steel tube and fabric fuselage and tail, with wire braced wooden wings.

Height	5 ft 3 in
Power	32 hp
Gross Weight	475 hp
Empty Weight	310 lbs
Top Speed	95 mph
Cruising Speed	80 mph
Landing Speed	32 mph
Ceiling	14,000 ft

The little racer was originally built by a class of aeronautical engineering students at the University of Detroit. It was designed by their professor, C.H. Powell, head of the Aeronautics Department. It placed first in the *Scientific American* Trophy Race at the 1925 National Air Races. Average lap speed was 76 mph.

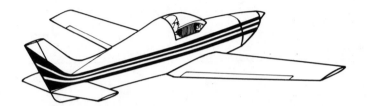

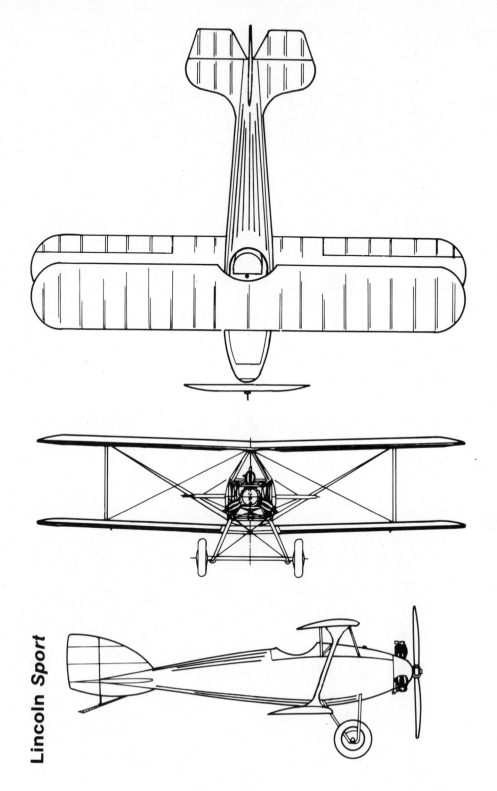

Lincoln Sport

🔟

LINCOLN *STANDARD* *SPORT PLANE*

This fascinating little biplane of 1924 was built by the Lincoln Standard Airplane Company of Lincoln, Nebraska. Hundreds of parts sets were sold, and planes were published in the *Modern Mechanics Flying Manual.* It featured all wooden construction, and was said to be one of the best planes of its day, according to the Flying Manual.

The airplane was said to be stressed to 11 g's. It   was similar to WWI types, with a fuselage of ⅞″ square longerons trussed with number 14 wire. Forward, the trussing was ⅛″ cable, with struts ⅞″ x 1/38″. The fuselage tapered in both plan and side view, with the tail post horizontal. This was claimed more streamlined and resisted the torsional loads of rough handling better than the vertical tail post types.

The wings were built up of two routed spruce spars, with a dihedral of 2°. The ribs featured solid wooden webs with lightening holes and cap strips. The bottom wing was actually mounted rear of the fuselage, like the Bristol Brisfit of WWI. The interplane struts were of the I-type, made of solid spruce. Wire bracing tied it all together.

The tail surfaces were cantilevered wooden frames, with ribs similar to the wing ribs. The main landing gear struts were steel tubing "V's" with bunges spring axle, ala WWI.

Fig. 1-11. Swen Swanson, a qualified aeronautical engineer, built his SS-3 and powered it with a 28 hp war-surplus ground trainer engine. The aircraft was put into limited production by Lincoln Aircraft, but was built in the greatest quantities by amateurs, from magazine plans. The all wood craft was stressed to 11-g's. Peter M. Bowers Collection.

Specifications

Wingspan	20 ft
Length	16 ft
Height	6 ft 6 in
Power	28-35 hp
Gross Weight	600 lbs
Empty Weight	370 lbs
Top Speed	90-100 mph
Cuising Speed	75 mph
Landing Speed	35 mph
Climb	800 fpm
Ceiling	8,000 ft

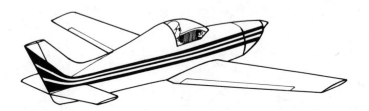

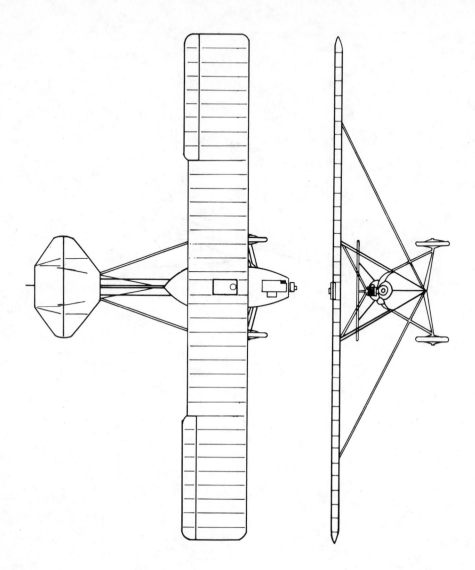

Dormoy Bathtub

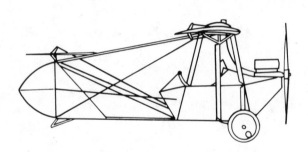

46

11

DORMOY *BATHTUB*

At the 1924 National Air Races held in Dayton, Ohio, this diminutive airplane captured the Richenbacker Trophy by flying to Columbus and back at an average speed of 70 mph. The 140 mile non-stop, two hour trip was won mainly because it was the only plane in its class of three, to finish the race without a forced landing. It was designed by Etienne Dormoy, a Frenchman who began an illustrious aeronautical career as a draftsman for Deperdussion, before coming to the US in 1913.

The original Bathtub was powered by a 20 hp Henderson motorcycle engine, one of the first aircraft conversions of this engine. The fuselage was a rather unique cable braced steel tubing affair, arranged in a series of triangles, resulting in a very light airframe. The total empty weight was well under 300 pounds. The wing was of built-up wooden construction, strut and wire braced to the fuselage.

The Dormoy could make an interesting project today and in part, its been done by Mile Kimbrel. He completed and successfully flew his replica in April of 1978, after seven years of on and off effort and about $800 worth of materials. If flew hands off on the first flight and proved to be a remarkably good airplane. Now, let's take a look at the Kimbrel replica and how it is built.

The Kimbrel Dormoy Replica

The Kimbrel Dormoy Bathtub is of fairly conventional construction, using 4130 steel tubing for the fuselage and tail surfaces, and wooden

Fig. 1-12. The original Dormoy Bathtub won the Rickenbacker Trophy Race at the 1924 National Air Races. Average speed was 70 mph. Picture shows modified version with full fuselage. Peter M. Bowers Collection.

47

wings. The airframe is covered with 1.702 Stits Polyfiber, Polydope through silver with a silver Bueatyrate finish.

Kimbrel built the fuselage structure mostly of ⅞" x .028 steel tubing, welded together. The nacelle sides were both welded to the bottom longerons and center section struts were assembled in a jig. After the sides were both welded to the bottom longeron forming two Vs, the assembly was set upright and the tailpost and upper tail booms were attached. Nacelle cross members are ½" x .028 tubes. Center section struts, gear legs, and wing lift struts are faired with balsa, wrapped in cotton, and painted with several coats of polyester boat resin. This proved to be very light, and added considerable rigidity.

The main wheels are heavy duty 20" bicycle rims and spokes, homemade steel hubs and "Olite" bronze bearings. The hubs are 1-5/16" x .090 tubes, from inches long, with 2" diameter .090 steel washers welded to both ends. They are then dressed in a lathe to accept the standard 1⅛" DD x ⅞" ID bushings. The bushings must be reamed slightly with fine energy paper to slip over the ⅞" x .058 axles (4130 aircraft tubing is about .003 over nominal size).

The axles have short pieces of ⅝" x .028 tubing slipped into their inner halves before welding, for reinforcement. The remainder of the gear legs are ⅝" x .028 tubes. They are quite flexible, but have proved to be strong enough so far. Doing it over, Kimbrel would use ¾" x .035 for more rigidity.

Shock struts are sprung with 48 inches of ½" shock cord. Since they are on top of the gear, they become shorter when the wheel moves upward. All gear attachments are made with ¼" aircraft bolts.

The tailwheel spring is two leavers from an International Harvester Model A Farmall tractor seat. Kimbrel fabricated a simple tailwheel with 2" caster, using 11/16" steel for the frame. The airplane does not have any brakes (it stops in about 300 feet in still air or grass), but the tailwheel does improve ground handling.

Tail surfaces are made of ⅝" x .028 and ½" x .028 welded steel tubing of conventional layout. The horizontal stabilizer is braced with two ½" diameter struts underneath. Trailing edges are ¼" x .028. Although the tail is short and the surfaces small (all have 30° travel both ways with stops installed), they are very effective at all speeds, and the airplane is stable in pitch and yaw.

The wing ribs are conventional ¼" square spruce trusses, with 1/32" plywood gussets. Kimbrel's airfoil is a 42" Clark Y, while the original used a Gottingen 385. In the aileron areas, the ribs are extended to 45" cord, by expanding the rib aft of the rear spar.

Wing spars are conventional "I" beams, using ⅛" door plywood for the web - and ½" x ⅝" (front spar) and ½" square (rear spar) spruce flanges. The spars are therefore 1-⅛" thick and located at the 15% and 65% chord positions.

Compression members are made of ½" square spruce, glued to both sides of the compression ribs. Drag and anti-drag braces are ⅛" 4130 rod threaded 6-32. The ⅛" is undersize for this thread size, but Kimbrel felt it adequate in this application.

The wing leading edge is .016 aluminum nailed on. The trailing edge is 1/16" aircraft cable, soldered to ¼" x 2" copper strips nailed to the ribs. The end ribs and ailerons must be well braced diagonally with a cable trailing edge, but it's light and looks good. The entire wing weighs but 58 pounds, including the 5.7 gallon center section aluminum wing tank.

Wing lift struts are nine feet long. They are made of ⅞" x .028 steel tubing, braced with ½" x .028 tubes at the outer ends. The struts are faired with balsa as previously described, and weigh three pounds each. The ⅜" x .035 jury struts were added to the design to stiffen the struts. The wing is also braced with 3/32" cable lift wires, for and aft. The left jury strut holds a homemade airspeed indicator, which is simply a sprung vane. Kimbrel says it is quite accurate.

Dormoy complained that the tail boom tubes vibrated excessively, due mainly to the rough running Henderson engine (especially when the rear cylinder would overheat and cut-out). Kimbrel successfully dampened the slightly excess vibrations with small wires between the tube centers.

Kimbrel's "Tub" has the CG at 33% M.A.C. with a 170 pound pilot and full fuel. He is well pleased with the airplane, as it provides him with usable, though slow, 1924-type flying at very low cost (two gallons per hour).

It is very stable in pitch and yaw, and neutrally stable in roll, because of no dihedral or sweeptback. All three controls are very effective down through the stall.

The stall occurs at 35 mph indicated and is very manageable and very 1924ish, i.e., it shudders, quits flying and drops. Recovery requires lowering the nose, but you know you have stalled. Kimbrel has not spun the airplane, but he feels it is very comfortable at the stall and claims you would have to fall asleep to enter a spin.

Performance is strictly 1924ish. It stalls at 35, climbs at 45, cruises at 55 at 3100 rpm, to speed is 65, and redline is 70. Kimbrel has gone up to 4000 feet, and says it will go higher. Initial climb rate is 300-400 fpm.

Specifications

Wingspan	24 ft
Length	13 ft 7 in
Height	6 ft 8 in
Power	VW, 40 hp
Gross Weight	540 lbs
Empty Weight	302 lbs
Top Speed	65 mph
Cruising Speed	55 mph
Landing Speed	35 mph
Ceiling	400+ ft

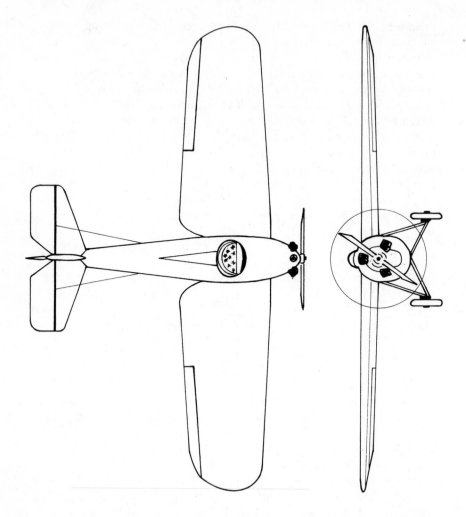

Pander Type D

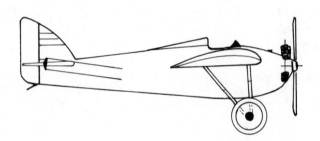

12

DUTCH *PANDER-D*

This neat looking, efficient very-light shoulder-wing cantilever monoplane was first shown at the 1924 Paris Air Salon. It's greatest recognition however, didn't come until 1928-29. It was well engineered and quite streamlined for its day. The manufacturer's main product was furniture, and the aircraft reflected this know-how.

The Pander was stressed to 7½ g's, in accordance with the Dutch Technical Air Service requirements. It was designed primarily for sport and aerobatics, with the Dutch Military Service using many for student training. Pilots of various nations flew it and liked its handling qualities.

The fuselage is a monocouque, with wooden formers, three longerons and two stringers. The fine streamlined form is covered in plywood, except the forward part which was metal. The fuselage was actually flat sided, but the bottom fairings and turtle deck blended in so gradually that it appeared elliptical.

The wing is built as a single piece resting on the top longerons, with each spar fastened via long U-bolts holding yokes above the spar. The spars are box sections, with three ply walls and spruce flanges. The frontspar also forms a box in conjunction with the leading edge plywood shin. The wing tip is thick, being built up of manination into a near semi-circular section.

The cockpit cutout resides between the two spars and it, along with the wing, is easily removed from the fuselage. A seven gallon fuel tank is located in each wing root, on either side of the cockpit opening.

The landing gear is a streamlined V-strut arrangement, anchored to the top longerons, at the same fittings that pick up the wing spars. A third

Fig. 1-13. The Dutch Pander "D" cantilever monoplane with 25 hp Anzani radial engine, was a masterpiece of aeronautical engineering. All wood structure. Peter M. Bowers Collection.

member runs to the bottom center of the fuselage. The tail skid is sprung and steers with the rudder.

The controls consist of a center mounted stick and tubular rudder pedals with toe guards and heel rests. In flight, the airplane was reported to handle well and lacked the vices then associated with small planes. During a demonstration flight in England in 1925, the factory pilot flew low, with tight turns, loops, rolls, etc. His flying was said to be impressive and the British concluded that the very light airplane was no longer a toy.

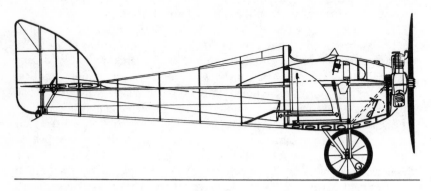

Fig. 1-14. Inboard profile of Pander "D" shows fuselage structure, controls, engine, etc., of the beautiful airplane.

Specifications

Wingspan	25 ft 3 in
Length	16 ft 3 in
Height	4 ft 4 in
Power	34/42 hp
Gross Weight	680 lbs
Empty Weight	420 lbs
Top Speed	83 mph
Cruising Speed	71.5 mph
Landing Speed	39 mph
Ceiling	12,500 ft
Climb	600 fpm

While the Pander D was originally fitted with the 25 hp Anzani three cylinder radial, its best performance was realized with the English ABC Mark II Scorpion of 34/42 hp. The specifications above are for the Scorpion.

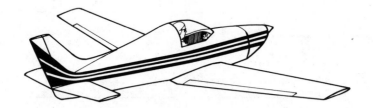

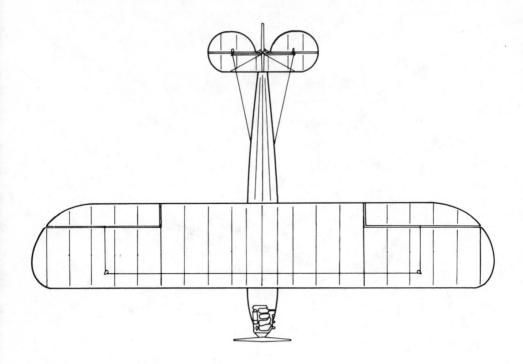

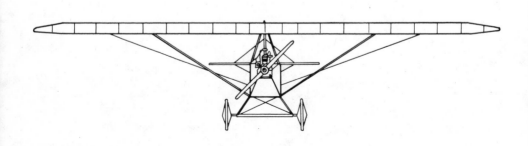

Heath *Parasol*

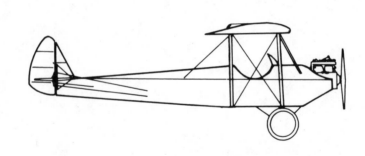

13

HEATH *PARASOLS*

So man learned to fly. And almost immediately the cry went up: "Give us an inexpensive sport plane!"

This problem isn't new; it's been around since 'way back when. Right at the heels of the Wright Brothers, there was a little guy who dreamed of solving it. He finally did, too! And for a few years the fly-happy pilot with the lean pocketbook knew heaven on earth.

This fellow's name was Edward Bayard Heath, and he was born in New York State in 1888. Small, about five feet, and weighing about 110 pounds, Ed had bright eyes, a sharp, inquiring nose and an abundance of determination. A true aero pioneer, he was a contemporary of the Wrights, Curtiss and Martin. Like them, he had no formal training in engineering. Heath flew for the first time on October 10, 1909, at Amsterdam, N.Y., in a plane of his own design powered by a 25 hp, 2-cylinder opposed engine. The trip was brief—one-half mile; and uneventful, until he landed—he washed out the landing gear. On November 2, he flew for close to a mile but again crushed the landing gear. On July 4, 1910, in the same plane, he appeared (for $500) at a county fair. The fence at the end of the field was a mite high—he went through it!

Heath had an abiding love for that plane, or perhaps he lacked the money to build a new one, because he repaired it once more and flew it, this time successfully, at a fair at Gloversville, N.Y. His aviation career was now launched. After a bit of wandering, he settled in Chicago and founded what was probably the most unusual aviation company in the country. Someone once referred to it as Heath's "Airplane Trading Post."

Though he specialized in the manufacture of propellers, he also sold wire, cables, fittings, "dope," rebuilt engines, radiators, wheels and fuel tanks. If someone wanted a special wing or fuselage, Heath designed and built one.

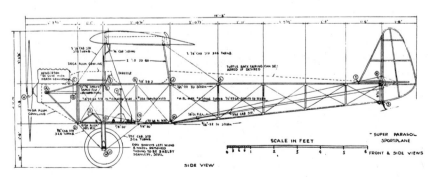

Fig. 1-15. Details for laying out the floor jig to construct the Heath Parasol's fuselage.

Fig. 1-16. The Heath Super Parasol of 1927 was probably the lightest (285 pounds) popular ARV between Santos Dumont's Demoiselle and today's Starlite. Was powered by 25 hp Henderson motorcycle engine. Peter M. Bowers Collection.

In 1913, he designed and flew a little flying boat powered by a 35 hp engine. When World War I broke out, his company turned out thousands of plane small parts. At the war's conclusion he focused attention on an idea that had been percolating in his mind for some time: *an airplane that the average man could afford to buy and fly.* He designed and built such a plane and named it the *Feather.* A single-seater, it had a 20-foot span, weighed, empty, 270 pounds, and was powered by a 7 hp Thor motorcycle engine that hauled it through the sky at 45 mph.

Heath was about to market this tiny number when the government released an avalanche of surplus warplanes. He couldn't compete with these cheap products, so he shelved promotion of the *Feather* and instead became a dealer in surplus planes and engines. He also founded a flying school. It was foolish, reasoned Heath, to sell a plane to a chap who would then spend his money elsewhere learning how to fly it.

During this period he instituted an apprentice plan—learn while you earn—which became a permanent fixture of his company. With this method he built a solid business and turned out finished pilots and A & E mechanics at the same time.

During the postwar years the lightplane bug never quite left Heath, though he did deviate slightly in 1923 when he built the *Favorite,* a 90 hp OX-5 biplane that he flew with four passengers to the National Air Races at St. Louis. The *Favorite* was entered in several events and won easily. In achieving these victories, Heath established a pattern that was to make his name famous in many succeeding National Air Races.

During 1924-25, he continued to do research on lightplanes and finally, with the aid of an associate, Clair Linsted, designed and produced the *Tomboy,* a beautifully streamlined tiny racer of cantilever monoplane design built around a 32 hp Bristol *Cherub.* The little single-seater had a top speed of 103 mph and won $2,500 in prize money for him at the 1926 National Air Races at Philadelphia.

While engaged in work on the *Tomboy,* Heath and Linsted continued to combine their talents and designed the first of the famous line of Heath *Parasols*. This prototype had a steel tubing fuselage, a wing (26-foot span) made from the lower wings of a Thomas Morse *Scout,* externally braced, and powered with a converted 27 hp Henderson motorcycle engine.

The little plane tested well and led Heath to produce a refined model of 24-foot span which he powered with a 32 hp Bristol *Cherub.* He named this one the *Spokane Super Parasol,* took it to the 1927 National Air Races at Spokane and collected the winnings in the light and sport plane events.

The Plane

This was the lightplane Heath had been searching for; this was the plane, he decided, that could be produced and sold cheaply; and this was the plane that thousands of enthusiasts either purchased fly-away or constructed at home during the succeeding years.

Heath at first produced the *Parasol* on a modest scale. He also continued his research and experiments in the small airplane field. In 1928, at the National Air Races at Los Angeles, he won several events, including the 50-mile free-for-all small engine race, in his *Baby Bullet,* a 2-cylinder powered racer with an 18-foot span. Top speed: 150 mph. In 1929, at Cleveland, a couple of his *Parasols* captured first and second place in their class. In 1930 he was back with a specially designed racer, the well-remembered Heath *Cannonball,* powered with a 110 hp, 4-cylinder Heath engine, which he flew to another win in the 275 cu. in. event with an average speed of 118 mph.

A canny businessman, Heath didn't hesitate to use the publicity he received at the National Air Races to push the sale of his *Parasols.* Around 1930, interest in gliding rose to unprecedented heights in this country and he quickly moved into this new market and offered a trim biplane glider to the public.

But his pet was the *Parasol.* Its initial success on the aviation market was gratifying and Heath decided to make the best selling lightplane in the country. He thoroughly analyzed the market and then, using just about every kind of bait possible, went out and practically cornered it.

You could buy a *Parasol,* fly-away, Chicago, for $975. If you couldn't afford that, you could buy it, less the engine, for $690. Still too much? Okay! You could buy it in kit form. The kit came in eleven groups. The first group cost $12.47. The total cost of the eleven groups, less the engine, was $199! Still too much? Well, you could buy the blueprints for five bucks and get your own materials. This was before the Department of Commerce dropped a restraining hand on homemade airplanes. Heath, naturally, was always ready to sell you finished parts or engines. You could buy a fuselage, for example, in kit form, and a factory-built wing. Or, if you desired, a kit wing and factory fuselage. The homebuilt *Parasol* differed from the manufactured one in that it used bolted tubing members instead of welded ones.

Pontoon Parasol

Suppose you wanted a *Parasol* seaplane? Heath had it, for $1,175, fly-away. Kit form, less engine: $228. It you wanted to convert your land *Parasol* into a seaplane (a simple operation), you could buy the pontoons for $250. You could make your own from a kit for $69. The blueprints were just two bucks. Skis? Heath had them. And you could have them for $25. Kit form: $10. Blueprints: 75 cents.

The Heath *Parasol,* or to be exact, *Super Parasol,* created an entirely new group of airplane owners. Guys who had never taken an active interest in flying because of the high cost flew into aviation sitting in a *Parasol* cockpit. Pilots who heretofore could not afford to own and maintain an airplane became *Parasol* owners. Thousands of these little planes were built in barns, garages and cellars. Some were assembled in rooming houses, others in deserted theatres, and one in a church.

The *Parasol* presented no storage problem for the rural owner; it could be parked in the barn or tied down outside. And it could safely be flown off the flat, north pasture. City owners were quick to appreciate its demountable wing; with wing panels strapped to its side it could be housed in the garage, and towed out to the flying field behind the family car.

Only tools necessary to assemble one of the kits were a pair of small pliers, screwdriver, hacksaw, hammer, small hand drill, chisel, center punch, file and drill. Some of the home-builders re-worked the original Heath blueprints and produced models of their own which bore a "family resemblance" to the *Parasol.* Others substituted wood longerons and wire bracing for the fuselage's steel tube construction. The home engineers also had a field day converting just about every type light engine for duty in the nose of a *Parasol.*

The little Heath craft was a well designed, compact monoplane with exceptionally clean lines. It was sturdy, stable and flew easily. The wing, which weighed only 68 pounds, was of the conventional spruce spars and spruce webbed ribs, Clark "Y" type. The tips were of thin steel tube. it consisted of two panels pinned together without a center section.

The Heath company supplied two engines, the Heath-Henderson and the heath B-4. The former was a conversion of the Henderson motorcycle engine; the latter a refinement of the H-H. Both were 4-cylinder engines and weighted, with prop, 115 pounds. The B-4 developed 30 hp at 3,000 rpm's; the H-H, 27 hp at the same revolutions. Though the company did not sell Anzani engines (popular lightplane engine of that day) it did offer a special Anzani-*Parasol* kit priced at $219, and a manufactured model, *sans* engine, for $750.

Here are the general specifications of the *Parasol* (1930 model) equipped with the Heath B-4 engine:

Specifications

Wingspan	25 ft
Chord	4 ft 6 in
Angle of Incidence	4 degrees
Wing Area	110 sq ft
Aileron Area	10 sq ft

Elevator Area	5.2 sq ft
Stabilizer Area	5.5 sq ft
Rudder Area	3.8 sq ft
Length Overall	17 ft
Height Overall	6 ft
Weight, Empty	285 lbs
Rate of Climb (first minute)	600 ft
Useful Load	300 lbs
Gas Capacity	5 gals
Oil Capacity	6 qts
High Speed	85 mph
Landing Speed	28 mph
Cruising Radius	200 miles

Fame and Fortune

Ed Heath had performed the impossible with his *Parasol:* successfully marketed a low cost airplane. His firm prospered and its product won an international reputation. Heath was wise enough to maintain his reputation by improving and refining *Parasol* design as the years passed. The little plane was a source of pleasure to the weekend pilot, and in the hands of professionals it won speed tests and set altitude records in its class.

In fact, it was so successful that by 1931 several competitors were in the field. With customary energy, Ed decided to offer two new models, the Center Wing and the Low Wing. One day in early February of that year, he warily studied one of the new models, a low-wing job. Although one of his test pilots had okayed one, he said, "I'm going to take it up and wring it out."

At 1,500 feet, he slipped the sleek little ship into a tight, perfectly executed wingover. For a few seconds the low-wing cut the sky cleanly, then, suddenly, the right wing wobbled violently, ripped loose and jackknifed against the fuselage. Moments later the remains of the plane were scattered over the field and Ed Heath, a great pioneer who has never really received the recognition due him was dead.

Heath's driving determination and genius had created and guided his company. His death was a severe loss. This, coupled with the Department of Commerce's ruling against home-constructed airplanes, staggered the firm. It existed for a few more years and in 1932 offered an improved *Parasol,* the Heath LN, *which could be assembled at home and which was eligible for a Federal NC license.* Fly-away, the LN sold for $1,074. In kit form, less engine, $499. Subsequently these prices were reduced to $925 and $399 respectively.

Blame the depression, or blame the absence of Ed Heath, but even with additional offerings of *Parasols* and centerwings of advanced design, the heath firm was unable to maintain itself in business and shortly thereafter passed from the aero scene. It and its famous product have been sorely missed ever since.

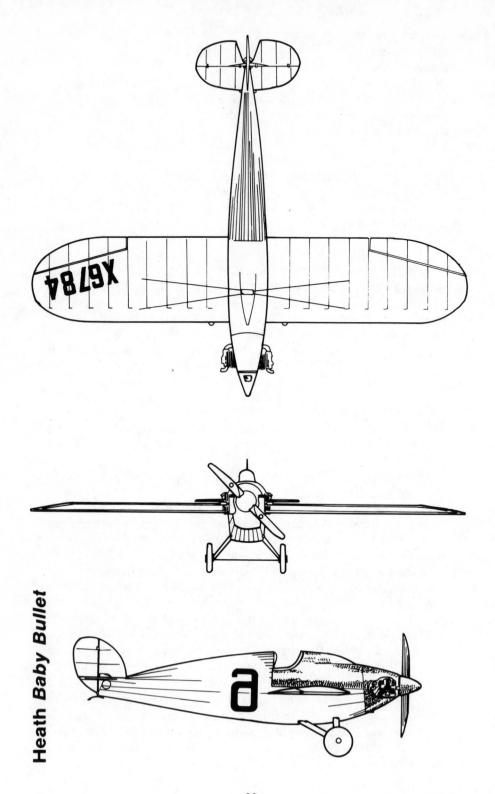

Heath *Baby Bullet*

60

14

HEATH *BABY BULLET*

The Heath "Baby Bullet" which won the 300 cubic inch race event at the National Air Races, Los Angeles, California, on September 14th was flown by Mr. E.B. Heath who for three consecutive years has carried away the titles for light planes at the National Air Races.

During the race the plane was equipped with a 4'4" diameter 3'6" pitch propeller turning 2,800 r.p.m. on the ground. On the steep climb the motor turned 2,700, and on flattening out the revolutions would increase to as much as 3,450. As the motor manufacturer recommended that the motor be run not higher than 3,200 for a period not to exceed five minutes it was deemed advisable to fly the ship in the race at half throttle. At this throttle setting the motor turned at 3,150 when the plane flattened out in horizontal flight, hence the speed was only 112 miles per hour around the course carrying a useful load of 200 pounds.

In the morning prior to the race this plane was unofficially timed once around the course in two minutes and six seconds wide open. This works out at approximately 142 miles per hour.

As a wooden propeller without tips was used it was found impractical to decrease the throttle setting sufficiently without killing the motor. This limited the possible top pitch for the propeller and therefore ran the revolutions up to such a high figure when flattening out.

It was found when increasing the pitch of the propeller above 3'6" it was not possible to set the plane on the ground without cutting the switch as the propeller pulled sufficiently with the minimum throttle allowed to keep the

Fig. 1-17. Heath Baby Bullet of 1928 attained speeds in excess of 150 mph on 32 hp Bristol Cherub engine. Peter M. Bowers Collection.

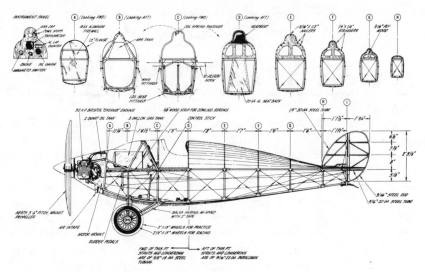

Fig. 1-18. Inboard profile and sectional views of Baby Bullet structure.

plane flying before the stall was reached.

The Heath Company is endeavoring to make an adjustable pitch metal propeller which will allow a further reduction of throttle whereby the pitch may be increased to 3'8" giving the plane added top speed and keeping the motor within mechanical limits.

The constructional details are more or less along conventional lines. The fuselage is of welded tubing from the pilot's cockpit forward, being further trussed with wire bracing.

Welded integral with the fuselage is an upright pylon which acts as an anchorage for the landing wires and at the same time eliminates all cross wires in the landing gear, as all side forces are transmitted through the wings to the upright pylon. This pylon streamlines into the general contour of the fuselage.

The longeron and pylon supports are constructed of $\frac{5}{8}$-inch 20 gauge 1025 S.A.E. tubing. The rear of the fuselage is constructed of dural 17 S.T. [Ed. Aluminum].

Welded steel fittings are shrunk and riveted to the rear longeron, and all cross struts in the rear are dural. Connecting wire bracing is then used throughout.

The tail surfaces are conventional welded tubing of very light gauges and diameter.

Tail skid is of the spring steel type mounted on the stern post.

There are two things that are unique in the construction of this ship in addition to its fine streamline form.

The first is the fact that all streamline wires terminate internally, either in the fuselage, landing gear, or wings. This required a departure from standard practice in the wing anchorage. Due to the amount of overhang or cantilever it was not considered advisable to have streamline wires pass through the center of the spar as was practiced in the curtiss Navy racers, but to have an anchorage straddle the spar would expose the terminals. It was therefore advisable to have anchorage at a place where it pulled from one side of the spar only. This would develop considerable eccentricity and torsion in the spar. This was eliminated by placing a steel bulkhead at the point of anchorage; on sand test it showed up to be as strong as was possible with the fittings straddling the spar.

The other unique feature was that no shock absorbers were used on the landing gear. The particular truss layout made it impractical to use shock absorbers and there was some little apprehension to landing without shock absorbers at such a high speed. Since the ship was very light, however, no difference was noticed, on account of lack of absorbers, even with the small tires.

Neither spreader bar or cross wires are used in the landing gear. A streamline tie-rod which takes all the wing load, as well as all four flying wires, terminates in the hub of the wheels thus covering the bulky terminals of the streamline wires. Two sets of wheels were built with the plane, one set 18 by 3 and a set 15 by 2½. Due to the fact that the plane had considerably more speed than was necessary, it was felt inadvisable to use the smaller wheels.

The following are the general specifications of the Heath "Baby Bullet":

Specifications

Span	18 ft
Chord	3 ft 6 in
Wing Section	St. Cyr 52
Angle of Incidence	0 degrees
Aileron Area	5 sq ft
Elevator Area	3 sq ft
Fin Area	1 sq ft
Rudder Area	2¼ sq ft
Length Overall	13 ft
Height	4 ft
Weight (empty)	235 lbs
Useful Load	300 lbs
Gasoline Capacity	4½ gals
Oil Capacity	3 qts
High Speed	150 mph
Landing Speed	55 mph
Cruising Radius	300 miles
Ceiling (estimated)	14,000 ft
Engine	Bristol Cherub 32 h p at 2,900

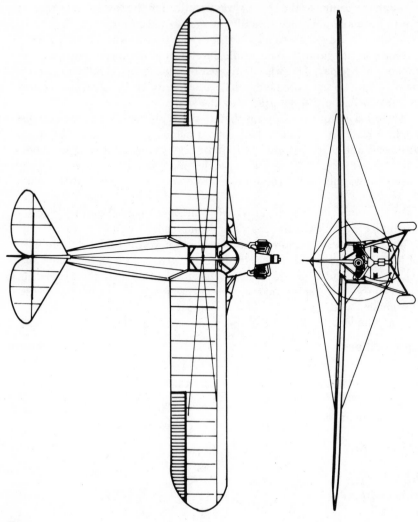

Aeronca C-3 Collegian

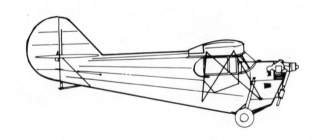

15

AERONCA C-3
AIR KNOCKER

Founded in 1928, the Aeronautical Corporation of America, based at Cincinnati, Ohio, made one of the most popular aircraft recreational vehicles of the early 1930's. They were dependable in performance and construction and got more people flying than any other airplane of the day.

Under the acronym trade name of Aeronca, the company began manufacturing the single seat C-2 in 1929 at the height of the depression. The design was based on the 1925 work of Jean A. Roche, then senior aeronautical engineer of the U.S. Army Air Corps. He had begun working on a glider for the Army. He took a wing from an old Curtis Jenny and positioned it atop his fuselage. But he felt this approach just wasn't right. What was needed was a better wing and an appropriate engine. Roche wanted his airplane to be a safe, reliable fair weather fun machine, with no thoughts of high performance in mind.

As luck would have it, a couple of years prior, a new airfoil had been developed - the since then famous Clark-Y. The new wing incorporated the new airfoil. It was constructed of two spruce spars, spruce ribs, solid spruce or bass construction ribs, aluminum leading and trailing edges, double wire drag bracing and fabric covered. It was cable braced to the fuselage and a kingpost.

Fig. 1-19. Aeronca C-3 "Collegian" was the most popular ARV of the early to mid-1930s. Proved flying was not just for the rich. Peter M. Bowers Collection.

The fuselage featured welded steel tubing in a curious looking three longeron arrangement aft the cockpit. This inspired the nickname "Razorback." To make room for the pilot, while allowing for propeller clearance with a short landing gear, the bottom of the nose was given a pudgy look, inspiring the name "Bathtub."

A couple of different engines were tried. The final one was actually the development of a blimp ballast air pump. Designed by another Army engineer at McCook field, Harold Morehouse, the final version weighed 89.5 pounds and put out 20 hp. The completed airplane now weighed in at a mere 339 pounds.

Rouche's building partner, John Dohse, was the test pilot. He had flown only as passenger once, so he was the most qualified of the three after feeling the ship out in crow hops, he got airborne and managed to land okay. No formal flight testing was actually done. However, a couple hundred flights were made.

In 1926 Morehouse left the duo with one engine, while taking his drawings and hiring on with Wright Aeronautical Corporation. Before too long, the C-2 was wrecked, ruining the engine. The engine was redesigned by two mechanical engineers, a bit heavier than before.

Then, in the fall of 1928, a group of Cincinnati investors got together and formed Aeronca, without an airplane to manufacture. Shortly, they heard about Dohse and his little plane and after a demonstration flight, the company bought it.

Official flight testing was done and proved the airplane to be docile and forgiving. If provoked to spin, it would recover simply by releasing the controls, and be out of it in one-and-a-half turns. The prototype now had an empty weight of a little under 400 pounds, enabling it to climb 500 fpm on its 30 hp engine. It burns only two gallons per hour. The pilot could carry a passenger in tandem.

Instrumentation and creature comforts were about like today's ARVs - minimal, but then, that's part of the charm of these aircraft and simple fun flying. Even the options list was similar to today's ARVs: floats, heater, electrical system and brakes. The base price was only $1495, ready-to-fly.

The stock market crashed on October 29, 1929, and a lot of ultra-light aircraft companies soon went out of business. (At that time, the aviation authorities, the CAA, considered aircraft under 600 pounds as ultra-light). But, Aeronca survived. The little C-2 proved its mark. A total of 164 were sold by 1931.

Specifications

Wingspan	36 ft.
Length	20 ft.
Height	7 ft. 6 in.
Power	30 hp
Gross Weight	672 lbs.
Empty Weight	398 lbs.
Top Speed	80 mph

Cruising Speed	62 mph
Landing Speed	31 mph
Ceiling	16,500 ft.
Climb	500 fpm

By now, a lot of people were getting exposed to flying, what with Lindbergh's success, the entire country was enamored with aviation. It soon became obvious that pilots wanted to share their flying experiences with the wife or a friend. So, in 1932, the Aeronca C-3 "Collegian" was introduced - a side-by-side seating version of the C-2. It featured side-by-side seating, the 40 hp Aeronca engine, tripod landing gear, and balloon tires. Creative comfort was also enhanced, with the options of doors and windows. The tailskid could be replaced with a non-steerable tailwheel, if desired.

A deluxe version of the Airknocker, called the Master, was introduced in 1935, with still more refinements - like single oleo landing gear struts, and standard right door and window. Cabin heater, brakes and a left door and window were options. By now, the empty weight had grown to 569 pounds and the cost to $1890. In all, 200 Collegians and 250 Masters were produced.

Specifications

Wingspan	36 ft
Length	20 ft
Height	7 ft 10 in
Power	40 hp
Gross Weight	875 lbs
Empty Weight	461 lbs
Top Speed	85 mph
Cruising Speed	70 mph
Landing Speed	35 mph
Ceiling	16,000 ft
Climb	450 fpm

The Aeronca C-3 was truly one of the first practical, mass produced ARVs on the market. Borne of the depression, it maneuvered the public's desire for inexpensive recreational flying. It's success proved people wanted to fly and would, if the costs were reasonable. Flying was no longer just for the rich.

It's interesting how the C-2/C-3's development and success are being repeated today, in much stronger numbers, for essentially the same reasons. People's urge to fly seems to be growing, as evidenced by the success of the ultralights and now the heavier ARVs. History is definitely repeating itself.

Aeronca, of course, went on to be successful in developing the lightplane. The Chief and the Champion come to mind. Thousands were produced, and thousands of people learned to fly in them in the forties and fifties. Many are still in service today.

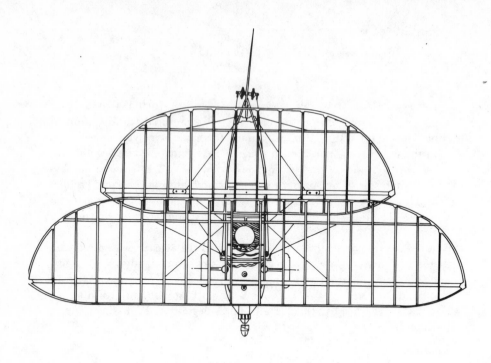

Mignet *Pou-du-Ciel (Flying Flea)*

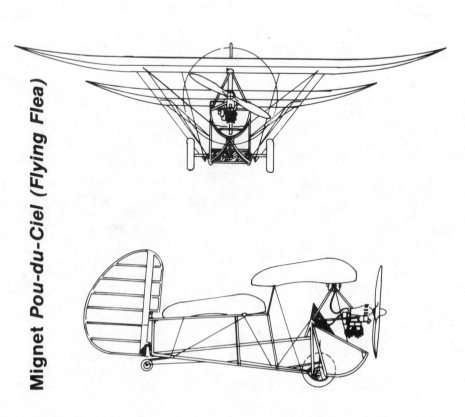

68

16

MIGNET *FLYING FLEA* *THE START OF* *A CRAZE IN EUROPE*

In the summer of 1935, Mr. Henry Mignet unveiled a most curious ultralight ARV, the infamous Pon-du-liel or Flying Flea. In an attempt to devise an aircraft for the man of average means and minimum flying ability, he created a sensation.

The Flea was of all wood construction. The fuselage was plywood covered, while the wings and rudder were fabric covered. The rear wing was fixed, as pitched was controlled by the variable incidence front wing. The rudder controlled yaw, and induced turns as well. Power was supplied by 22 hp two-stroke Aubier-Danne engine. Motor mount and cabane struts were steel.

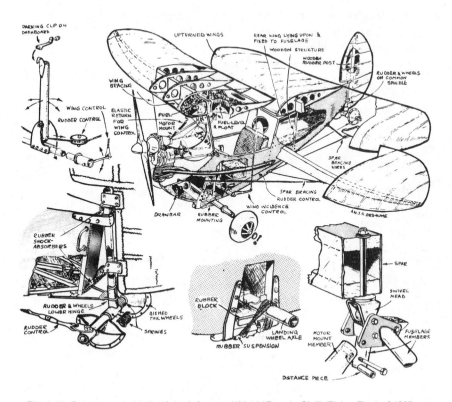

Fig. 1-20. Cutaway and details of the infamous HM-14 "Pou du Ciel" (Flying Flea) of 1935.

69

Fig. 1-21. The Mignet "Flying Flea" started a sport flying craze in Europe and England in the mid-1930s. Was powered by 22 to 32 hp engine. Peter M. Bowers Collection.

The Pon-du-liel craze spread like wildfire, beginning in France then world-wide. Mignet wrote a book, *Le Sport de'l'Air,* which became the bible of the sport flying movement. It wasn't long before the English version was published, and the British went wild. Hundreds were being built and, Mignet was in business.

Before too long however, people started getting killed. Regrettable as it was, the accidents were not at first alarming. But, they continued...something was wrong. As it turned out, Mignet had not thoroughly tested the Flea and, his trusting customers were becoming involuntary test pilots. It seems as though an uncontrollable nose down pitching moment could be established at certain angles of attack, cocking the little airplane into an irrecoverable dive. The French Air Ministry banned the Flea from flying.

Specifications

Wingspan	19 ft 8 in
Length	13 ft 5 in
Height	5 ft 2 in
Power	22 hp
Gross Weight	485 lbs
Empty Weight	275 lbs
Top Speed	70 mph
Cruising Speed	60 mph
Landing Speed	28 mph

Several years later, the airplane was redesigned and the diving problem cured. Today, plans are available for a modernized version, but none are ever seen in public.

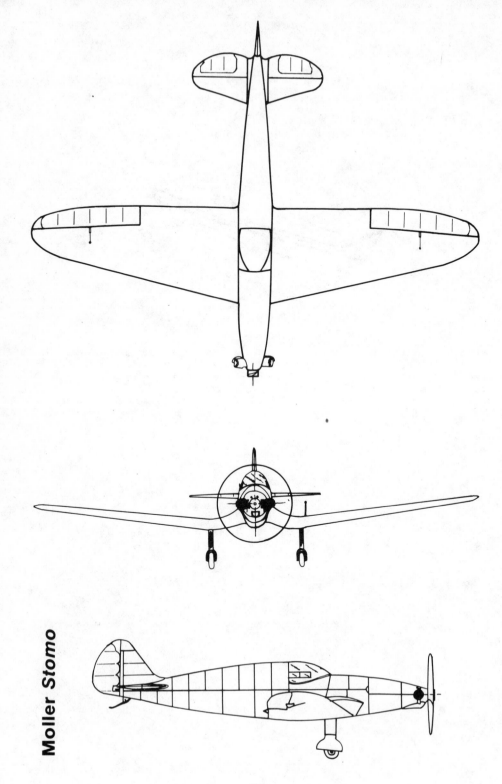

Moller Stomo

17

MOLLER *STOMO*

The Stomo was unquestionably, one of the sleekest, most aesthetically pleasing ARV class aircraft ever built. It was an aeronautical work of art, years ahead of its time, beautifully streamlined and quite efficient, with its inverted gull wing. Unfortunately, it was so complex in construction that, only two were ever built. It featured an all wood, built up structure with a plywood skin. The wings folded for towing behind a car.

Stomo number one made its first appearance at a lightplane fly-in held near Berlin in 1937, where it reached a speed of 91.8 mph on its 18 hp engine. After number one was crashed, the second version was built, with but minor modifications, particularly a redesigned canopy. Many pilots flew this machine among them Professor Kurt Tank of FW190 design fame. He reached a speed of 94.3 mph.

The aircraft then underwent some major developmental changes. A larger, heavier 42 hp Zundapp engine was installed in a shortened nose, the span was reduced, flaps added and the landing gear beefed up. This new model was designated the Stomo 3V11 Sturmer, which captured a couple of world records in its class at Bremen in 1939. It reached a speed of slightly more than 123 mph. One additional aircraft was made, the two seater Zandapp powered Stomer. The outbreak of war interfered with its continued development.

The Stomo was an incredibly beautiful machine. Perhaps someone will borrow its lines to make a modern ARV.

Fig. 1-22. Two seat version of the Stomo shared clean lines and efficiency of Stomo single seater. Both featured all wood monocoque construction. Stomo was powered by 18 hp, while two seat had 50 hp engine. Peter M. Bowers Collection.

Specifications

Wingspan	27 ft 11 in
Length	19 ft 8 in
Height	4 ft 3 in
Power	18 hp
Gross Weight	528 lbs
Empty Weight	323 lbs
Top Speed	96 mph
Cruising Speed	88 mph
Landing Speed	30 mph
Ceiling	9,500 ft
Climb	600 fpm

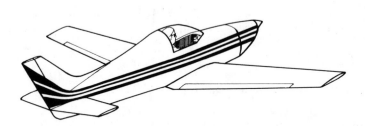

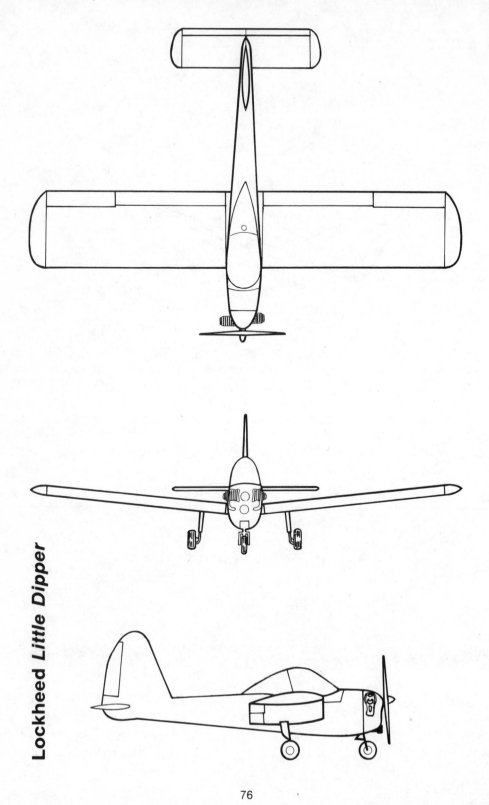

Lockheed Little Dipper

76

18

LOCKHEED 33
LITTLE DIPPER

The Little Dipper was without doubt one of the most interesting and inspired ultra-light airplanes ever built. It was also Lockheed's smallest and least publicized product. While it never got beyond the prototype stage and was doomed almost from the beginning, the Little Dipper was unique in many respects. The design concept was unparalleled in its simplicity, performance was remarkable and, above all, it was thoroughly safe and easy to fly.

During the middle part of 1944 the decisive phases of World War II were already history and the end of the conflict was in sight. It was only a question of months before civilian aircraft production could be resumed and Lockheed, like other large airframe manufacturers, was exploring other avenues in an effort to cushion the period of transition back to peacetime operations. Tens of thousands of service-trained pilots would soon be returning to civilian life, and it was only reasonable to assume that each one represented a potential customer to the small plane manufacturer. Postwar prosperity for the lightplane industry was unlimited...or so it seemed.

John W. Thorp, then assistant chief of preliminary design of the Vega Division, had been working on the design of a light two-seater (Thorp T-11

Fig. 1-23. Lockheed's "Little Dipper" was designed to meet an anticipated post-WWII demand for recreational aircraft. The airplane was well engineered and offered outstanding performance. Unfortunately, the demand never developed.

77

Sky Skooter) which he proposed to power with a 50 hp Franklin opposed-twin. His boss, Mac Short, was impressed with the design study, but he was skeptical of the low power. At about this time Lockheed's president, the late Robert Gross, became interested. Gross was intrigued with the idea of commuting to his office in a small single-seater capable of taking off and landing on his backyard tennis court (the Gross residence occupied grounds somewhat more expansive than average). An airplane possessing this kind of versatility would be in great demand, he reasoned.

Prospects for such an airplane did appear promising indeed, both from the military and civilian point of view. Gross gave Short his blessing and the Dipper project was formed in the Vega Division in June 1944, with Thorp in charge. The group, which included five designer-draftsmen and five experimental mechanics, immediately set up shop and began constructing the prototype Little Dipper Model 33 (Vega V-304) and a four-place pusher companion model called the Big Dipper. Progress moved at a rapid pace and in about three months' time the first machine, NX18935, was ready to fly.

Vega's chief test pilot, Bud Martin, flew the Little Dipper for the first time during the last week of September 1944. The event took place without incident at the old CAA emergency field near Newhall, California. A few days later the Little Dipper took to the air again, this time in the hands of the famous Milo Burcham, former Lockheed chief of flight testing. The tiny plane was a complete success, giving all that was expected of it and more.

While most of the test flying was conducted at Newhall, the Little Dipper made a number of appearances at Burbank for the benefit of official observers. In order to avoid the heavy traffic and remain out of public view, flights were usually made from the taxi strips on the northwest side of Burbank Air Terminal. Circuits were flown at low altitude, well inside the normal traffic pattern.

In spite of the fact that he was not an official test pilot, John Thorp did much of the initial flying. The Little Dipper, which was a direct development of his original two-place design, was his baby and he was anxious to prove the airplane's worth and versatility. Thorp never missed an opportunity to demonstrate its amazing maneuverability and short-field performance. He could and often did take off, fly around for fifteen minutes, or until he got dizzy, and land the airplane—all within a 300-ft circle! Its turning radius was so short that it could almost pivot on a wing tip.

Thorp was on the point of demonstrating the Little Dipper's maneuverability by flying it inside Lockheed's huge Constitution hangar, which happened to be temporarily unoccupied at the time. The scheme was abandoned, however, when management officials got wind of the plan. The hangar was soon so packed with airplanes that a gnat would have had difficulty getting airborne.

An aerial cavalry had been proposed and visionaries saw in the Little Dipper a possible mount for the airborne trooper of the future. Because of its docile handling characteristics and simple structure, the training program would have required only a short ground school flying and maintenance course and little or no dual instruction. In the summer of 1945, the Little Dipper was demonstrated to the Army at Fort Benning, Georgia, at which time the projected military version was designated the V-308 Airtrooper.

The feasibility of such an unorthodox training program was effectively demonstrated to military observers at Fort Benning. An army PFC, a youth with no previous flying experience, volunteered to be the guinea pig. Prior to the flight he was carefully briefed by Lockheed pilot Prentice Cleaves. A walkie-talkie receiver was then installed in the airplane and the soldier climbed in. The engine was started and Cleaves talked the fledgling airman into the air, around and back down again without mishap.

Delighted by his adventure, the soldier immediately started off on another hop around the strip on his own initiative. In his excitement, however, he failed to apply full throttle and nearly crashed before he was airborne. Cleaves had set aside his walkie-talkie and was unprepared to warn the embryo aviator during the critical period. Fortunately, by the time communications were re-established, the crisis was past. The soldier flew around for a few minutes and then came in for a landing. Again he was successful and the demonstrations were concluded with the airplane and PFC still intact.

During flight demonstrations at Andrews Air Force Base, the Little Dipper came to grief at the hands of an unfamiliar and perhaps overly confident Army colonel. While executing a steep turn at low speed and close to the ground, the officer, an experienced military pilot, chopped the throttle at the worst possible time. A wing tip struck the ground and the little plane cartwheeled. Fortunately for the dejected colonel, only his pride was injured, but damage to the Little Dipper was extensive, particularly to the wing. Crated and shipped back to Burbank for repairs it was flying again within two weeks.

Another rough landing nearly resulted in disaster when a female pilot, the aviation editor of a popular national publication, was flying the Little Dipper near New York City. Confused by poor visibility, she became lost and, unable to find an airport, proceeded to put the airplane down on a potato patch. This time the Little Dipper flipped ingloriously over on its back. The damage was not serious, however, and repairs were completed locally in several days.

In the hands of Prentice Cleaves the Little Dipper buzzed around Washington performing for any and all civilian and military officials who showed the slightest interest. Finally the Army ordered several pre-production Airtroopers for evaluation.

At about this time Cleaves hopped over to show the airplane to some War Department people, landing on the then unlandscaped inner grounds of the mighty Pentagon. It is said that Air Force General Hoyt S. Vandenberg witnessed the spectacular arrival from his office window. Apparently the General was not favorably inclined toward the idea of a flying cavalry and the Little Dipper's unceremonious arrival did nothing to improve his disposition in that regard. On the following day the purchase order was cancelled. Thus ended all hopes for further consideration by the military.

After failing to sell the Airtrooper to the Army, Lockheed carefully studied the prospects offered by the civilian market. Surveys were conducted and production cost established. There was a definite demand to be sure, but not for tens of thousands as authorities had predicted earlier. Based on a more realistic production run of a thousand units, Lockheed's sales people came to the unhappy conclusion that the Little Dipper could not be profitably manufactured and sold at a price within the range of the popular market.

Following the crash of the prototype Big Dipper in the spring of 1946, the entire project was written off the books. The Little Dipper was then placed in dead storage along with a second partially completed example. In spite of several sincere efforts to save the airplanes, the Little Dippers were subsequently broken up for tax purposes a few months later.

"We cried tears as big as billiard balls," said a Lockheed experimental mechanic, "when those two little airplanes were chopped up and sold for scrap."

CONSTRUCTION DETAILS: The Little Dipper's all-metal airframe was more or less conventional in concept, the fuselage being a semi-monocoque structure and the lifting surfaces fully cantilever. However, its small size permitted a high degree of simplification and the production version would have required a minimum of fabrication time, components and materials. Basically the fuselage consisted of ten stamped sectional formers and two pairs of longitudinal stringers running from the firewall to the fifth and sixth formers, or approximately half the length of the fuselage. The 2024-T3 .020 skins were formed in halves, the larger panels having external dorsal and ventral flanges which greatly facilitated the mating and riveting operations.

From the standpoint of advanced design the stab or "flying" elevator, with its anti-servo tab, was perhaps the most unusual feature. This was a Thorp innovation and provided the basis for U.S. patents still the exclusive property of the Lockheed Aircraft Corporation. Elevators of this type were later used on several transonic fighters and more recently in the lightplane field on the Fletcher FU-24, Piper Aztec, Cherokee, Comanche and Beech Mustketeer. Both elevator and vertical stabilizer employed sheet metal spars of channel section. The vertical stabilizer and elevator leading edge were skinned with .020 and the rudder and aft portion of the elevator were covered with .012.

The wing was constructed in two units, each panel consisting of four stamped ribs supported by a single truss-type spar of channel section with extruded angle caps. An NACA 4415 airfoil was used and reinforcement of the .020 skin was accomplished by riveting four internal stiffeners between each pair of ribs. The differentially operated ailerons and four-position (10 thru 40 degrees) slotted flaps were constructed of light Alclad sheet. Two

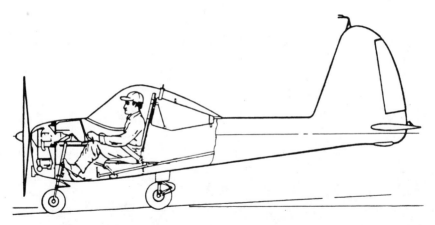

Fig. 1-24. Inboard profile of "Little Dipper" shows primary details.

sets of experimental wing panels were also built. One featured internal modifications and was very light due to extensive use of magnesium. The other was similar to the original wing but employed a beaded skin instead of internal stiffeners.

Specifications

Wingspan	25 ft
Length	17 ft 6 in
Height	7 ft 6 in
Power	50 hp
Gross Weight	725 lbs
Empty Weight	425 lbs
Top Speed	100 mph
Cruising Speed	90 mph
Landing Speed	30 mph
Ceiling	16,000 ft
Climb	900 fpm

Long before the Little Dipper was conceived Thorp began developing a 50 hp opposed-twin composed of 90 hp Franklin 4AC-199 parts. The crankcase was shortened by cutting out the section between cylinder port centers and joining the case ends by heliarc welding. The crankshaft was shortened by cutting off the last two throws and machining the end of the rear journal for the timing gear boss. After correcting vibration by installing balancing weights on the front and rear propeller flanges, the engine ran smoothly and gave completely satisfactory service. This engine was known as the Franklin 2AL-112 and it powered the Little Dipper during initial flight testing. Aircooled Motors continued its development as the Franklin 2A4-45 and 2A4-49, producing a small batch of preproduction units under ATC E-240.

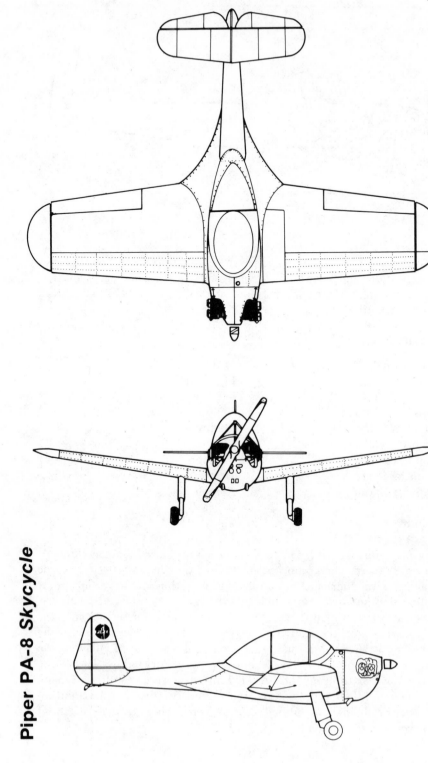

Piper PA-8 Skycycle

19

PIPER PA-8 *SKYCYCLE*

Like Lockheed and countless other airplane manufacturers after WWII, Piper wanted to produce an airplane that would fill the need created by returning servicemen. Little did the industry know that most men would be interested in women and making babies. The simple, inexpensive flying time had not yet come.

At any rate, Piper's entry in the ARV race was the Skycycle. To keep costs down, the main part of the fuselage was designed to use a jettisonable fuel tank from a Navy F4U Corsair fighter. In front of this was the engine mount and cowling, the aft part of the fuselage was simply a tapered boom made of sheet aluminum.

The wing structure was an aluminum spars and ribs cantilever, with metal ailerons and fabric covering. Tail surfaces were fabric covered welded steel tubing, including fin, rudder, stabilizer and ailerons.

Power was provided by the Lycoming O-145A four cylinder opposed engine of 55 hp. Performance was quite good, with a cruising speed of 95 mph and a range of 400 miles. The Skycycle was stressed for 7g's and capable of aerobatics. It was said to be stable, responsive and easy to fly. Instrumentation was minimal, in keeping with the ARV concept. The plexiglass bubble canopy provided the pilot with excellent visibility, as

Fig. 1-25. PA-8 "Skycycle" was Piper's entry into the hoped-for postwar recreational flying boom.

well. A steel rollover structure was located behind the pilot's head. The project was abandoned in favor of continuing production of Cubs, Super Cubs and Cruisers.

Specifications

Wingspan	20 ft
Length	15 ft 8 in
Height	4 ft 10 in
Power	55 hp
Top Speed	120 mph
Cruising Speed	95 mph
Landing Speed	55 mph

"The October 1945 issue of *Model Airplane News* had this to say about the Skycycle and the anticipated postwar boom in recreational flying. How true it still is today.

"Sensational new single seat sport plane may be the answer to your future flying plans.

"Three years and ten months ago the Japs struck Pearl Harbor and our nation went to war. Simultaneously *Model Airplane News* covers went to war, and the ensuing months and years saw a glittering and dramatic array of fighting planes parade across our covers. Fighters and bombers, American, Allied and enemy, *all* the famous combat planes of World War II were caught in the striking colors of our cover and fully described inside. That was *one* of the war jobs of M.A.N.

"Last month, with the peace, we turned our attention again to commercial planes and presented the Douglas DC-4 transport. This month we present the Piper *Skycycle,* a lightplane type. Just as the nation's aircraft manufacturers, pilots and air enthusiasts have turned their thoughts from military to civil aircraft, so have we.

"It is not alone the *Skycycle* on which we focus attention this month, but private flying and personal aircraft of all types. With 500,000 potential airplane owners champing at the bit the lightplane manufacturers are speeding new models to completion as rapidly as possible, and as you read this the first production models will be coming off the assembly lines. The Air Age, more than anything else, means a flying America and the lightplane is the instrument to bring this long-visioned dream to reality.

"But the transition from 30,000 private airplanes to 500,000 will not be an easy one, nor a swift one. Private flying cannot and will not "return" in the pre-war meaning of the term. Widely scattered, poorly operated and wholly inadequate airports must never again loom a major obstacle to flying progress as it has in the past. Restrictive legislation, high costs and the demand for skilled piloting technique must forever disappear in this new Air Age. Many moves are pointing the way towards this brighter future and plans are already past the blueprint stage to bring flying into every home that desires it.

"First must come the airport, for it alone can give the utility to the lightplane that it must possess for wide, popular appeal. Out of a total of 16,000 communities in the United States only some 3,000 have airports. More than 10,000 of these have no landing facilities whatever. *Every* community in the nation must have an airpark lest progress pass it by. In addition to its utility as a landing place for airplanes, an airpark can provide beauty, services, jobs, entertainment and recreational facilities to the community. It can become an integral part of the community life, instead of a distant, ostracized area on the outskirts of town regarded only as "that dusty, greasy, noisy section out there, where the airplanes fly." The modern airpark will be none of these things if proper planning and operation are achieved. The National Airport Plan is gaining new members every day and the United States can soon look forward to a national system of airports that will bring every community into the Air Map and give the lightplane a genuine, utilitarian meaning that it long has lacked.

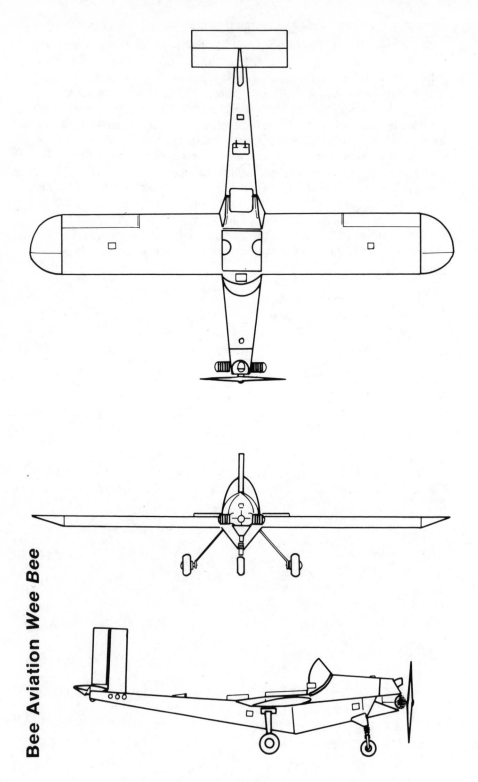

Bee Aviation Wee Bee

20

WEE BEE

Back in 1946, a small group of aeronautical engineers at the Boeing Company began discussing the question: "How small could you build an airplane that would still carry a man?"

Ken Coward was one of those imaginative engineers. In 1947, he left Boeing to work for what is now Convair, in San Diego. While there, he met up with Bill Chana and Karl Montijo. After some discussions, the challenge was undertaken. Nine months and $250 later, the Wee Bee made its debut.

On two occasions, the Wee Bee was flown by Chana for the Newsreels. *Life* and *Time* magazines accredited the Wee Bee as, "The World's Smallest Airplane." The Guiness Book of World Records even recorded it as "The Lightest Airplane ever flown," as late as 1967. It checked in at a scant 210 pounds long before the modern ultralight took its title away. Newspapers and magazines throughout the world gave extensive coverage to this littlest airplane with its unique prone pilot position.

Following its retirement from flying, the Wee Bee was put on static

Fig. 1-27. The "Guiness Book of World Records" recorded the "Wee Bee" as "the lightest airplane ever flown," as late as 1967, until the modern ARV's started to appear.

display at various air shows and functions promoting the San Diego Aero-Space Museum. At the invitation of Harold Keen, TV newscaster, the Wee Bee even made an appearance in the KFMB-TV studio. It was then put on permanent static display at the San Diego Air Museum.

Then, on February 22, 1978, tragedy struck — the museum was burned to the ground by arsonists, destroying the Wee Bee, as well as many other fine aircraft. But, practically before the ashes had a chance to cool, the three original Wee Bee builders got together and decided to build a replica. Unfortunately the designers hadn't made detail drawings of the original, so they had to start over from scratch. Luckily however, they had photos and Ken Coward's original design book to go by. Bill Chana had enough information to make drawings. An original engine was located. Construction commenced in April of 1978 and the airplane rolled out in December, just in time for the dedication of the rebuilt museum.

Specifications

Wingspan	18 ft
Length	14 ft 6 in
Height	5 ft
Power	30 hp
Gross Weight	410 lbs
Empty Weight	210 lbs
Top Speed	82 mph
Cruising Speed	78 mph
Landing Speed	48 mph
Climb	300 fpm

The airplane was of all metal, cantilever construction, and featured three-axis controls. Originally conceived as a taildragger it was reconfigured to a tri-gear because the nose was too high in takeoff. It also had a hydraulic brake and the nosewheel steered.

The most peculiar feature of the Wee Bee though, was the fact that the pilot had to lie prone to fly it. To facilitate this arrangement, three foam cushions were fastened to the top of the fuselage. The pilot was restrained by seat and shoulder harnesses that held him tight against the pads. He had support at his chest, thighs and shins, and was about as comfortable as could be expected. The toes were inserted into recesses half way along the tail boom for operation of the rudder pedals. The pilot's hands were inserted into cutouts in the upper fuselage shin, so he could grip the stick and throttle buried inside.

Power was supplied by a two-cycle, horizontally opposed Kiekhaefer target drone engine developing up to 30 hp to 4600 rpm. It was quite noisy, but could propel the airplane as fast as 82 mph, and produce a 300 fpm climb. Only shallow turns were made. Landing speed was 48 mph, which must have made landings a bit touchy considering pilot positions and the aircraft's small size.

The Wee Bee was certainly an interesting engineering exercise, and proved how small a man-carrying airplane could be. It never caught on though. The ARV movement was still a generation away.

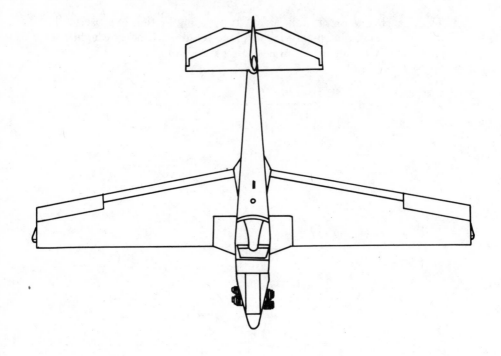

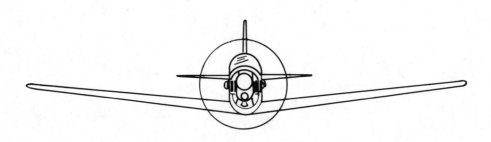

21

MOONEY M-18 *MITE*

The Mite was another attempt at cashing in on the anticipated post WWII aviation boom. The prototype featured a 25 hp liquid-cooled Crosley auto engine. It was priced at $2,000 and earned the distinction of being the smallest, least expensive, type certified aircraft ever produced. A total of 284 were sold over a six-year period. The public just wasn't quite ready for the ARV — but, the situation was improving.

The wing is fully cantilevered wood and fabric construction, employing a modified laminar flow airfoil. It features a single spar with D-section leading edge. Ailerons and 70% span flaps grace the trailing edge.

The tail is laminated wood construction with variable incidence for trim. The wood skins are fabric covered. The control surfaces are constructed of welded steel tubing, fabric covered, and gap sealed. The entire empennage moves up and down with flap actuation to maintain trim automatically.

The fuselage aft the cockpit is all wood, monocoque construction. From the rear cabin former forward however, the airplane features a welded steel tubing frame covered with aluminum. A compartment behind the seat will hold 40 pounds of baggage.

The production version Mites had the engine cyclinders out in the breeze, because the lines had been previously established by the Crosley. The first production units, the M-18L, featured 65 hp Lycomings. The factory turned out 81 of these before the gross weight was upped from 780

Fig. 1-26. Mooney's M-18 "Mite" of 1948 was a mostly wooden structured single-seater offering excellent cross-country performance. Unfortunately, only a couple hundred were sold, because the recreational flying boom just didn't want to happen.

to 850 pounds. This also gave buyers a choice between the Lycoming (M-18LA) and the similar 65 hp Continental (M-18c). The final production model was designated M-18C-55, and was available only with the Continental. It supported a larger cockpit and canopy. By now, the price was up to $3,695.

During the Korean War (1951) Mooney attempted to sell the Army an anti-liaison version of the Mite. They fitted a 90 hp Continental into a fully cooled nose and installed two .30-cal. light machine guns in the wing. Provisions were also made for HVAR rockets under the wings, for close-in ground supports.

The military version, designated the M-19 "lub killer," had a gross of 1450 pounds, and a top speed of 150 mph. The aircraft was impressively demonstrated to the Army brass in both strafing and rocket firing. Unfortunately, no orders were placed. At that time, the Army wasn't allowed to use armed, fixed-winged aircraft—that was the Air Force's job.

Flyingwise, the Mite offers no surprises. However, it cannot be slipped due to limited rudder action. This in turn, makes it virtually impossible to stall the aircraft in a cross-controlled turn. Descents are steepened by "S" turns, which are quite practical due to the Mite's rapid roll rate. Of course, flaps may be used as well to steepen descents.

The controls are sensitive to the new Mite pilot, many being over-controlled at first. The gear comes up by a hand lever and locks into place. A windshield type warning system waves a red disk back and forth to indicate the gear is not down and locked, when throttle is retarded.

A 1950 issue of *Flying* reported that FBO's renting Mites found that, "folks who used to fly together were renting two or three single-seaters for breakfast flying and Sunday sport. The demand has exceeded expectations, and it seems to prove there's a good market for lightplanes that have the correct combination."

Specifications

Wingspan	26 ft 10½ in
Length	17 ft 7¼ in
Height	6 ft 2½ in
Power	65 hp
Gross Weight	780 lbs
Empty Weight	500 lbs
Top Speed	138 mph
Cruising Speed	125 mph
Landing Speed	43 mph
Ceiling	19,400 ft
Climb	1090 fpm

Back in the mid-1960's, the Mooney Mite Owners Association was formed to help owners maintain and enjoy their airplanes. It provided a headquarters for exchanging experiences and information. Then, in the mid-1970's, Fred Quarles of Charlottesville, Virginia, introduced a kit program to amateur builders. It featured a computerized parts system, but just didn't catch on. Perhaps it would work with today's growing popularity in ARV's.

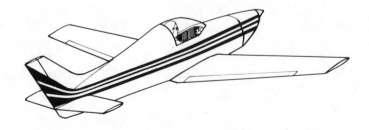

Section II

The Formation Of The EAA And VW-Powered Homebuilt Airplanes

The development of the modern ARV is a logical expression of the times—certain key elements were present in the economy and marketplace that weren't there before. The stage was being set for more and more folks to fly.

One of the most significant events in the history of recreational flying, was the organization of the Experimental Aircraft Associaton. This happened in the Milwaukee garage of its founder and current president, Paul H. Poberezny. "In late 1953, I was building an airplane and some of my friends I had watched build planes in the 1930's would come over and give me advice," Poberezny recalls. "We decided to form an organization of members with like interest."

Later that year, forty airplanes appeared at EAA's first convention at Milwaukee's Timmerman Field. Most of them were antiques with a few warbirds and homebuilts on hand.

While the EAA was still a local organization, an article on building the "Baby Ace" was published in Mechanics Illustrated in 1955. It caused a flood of inquiries from airplane enthusiasts from all over the world asking to join. (Excerpts from that historic article appear as the first entry in this section of the book). In a few short years, the EAA blossomed from a membership of eight to a roster numbering in the thousands. The EAA had the answer to the average man's desire to fly. If he couldn't afford to buy an airplane, he'd just build his own.

EAA's growth during the 60's was so substantial that early fly-in sites at Timmerman and Rockford, Illinois, would no longer accommodate the more than 10,000 aircraft and 300,000 people attending the annual celebration of flight. In 1970, Oshkosh, Wisconsin, was selected as the permanent site for the world's largest aviation events.

In subsequent years, EAA became a strong international organization, issuing over 125,000 membership cards to people in 91 countries. At the heart of the organization is a system of over 600 local chapters conducting meetings, and scheduling their own local fly-ins. The chapters provide an active cohesive force where anyone can really learn about aviation by building and flying airplanes. You are urged to join your local chapter if you decide to build your own ARV. See the Appendix for details.

While most homebuilt aircraft of the 1950's and 1960's were powered by conventional aircraft engines, many were designed around the converted VW engine. While they might not be classified today as true ARVs they were nonetheless, low powered aircraft that weighed under 500 pounds— substantially less than the typical homebuilts of the day. In fact, the primary reason they were heavier than today's ARVs is due to the heavy VW engine, and the necessary higher airframe weight to support it.

At any rate, the lighter VW-powered homebuilts are included herein, because they demonstrate the thinking of visionaries of a couple decades ago. And, in fact, all the designs presented have plans, and even some kits are available today. One of them just might be the answer to your needs in an ARV.

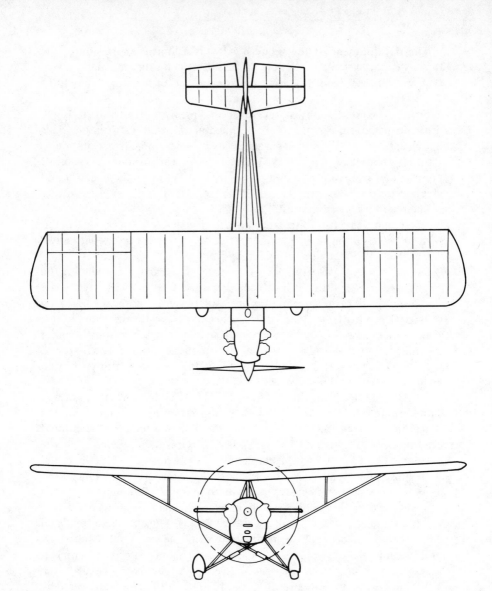

Corben Baby Ace

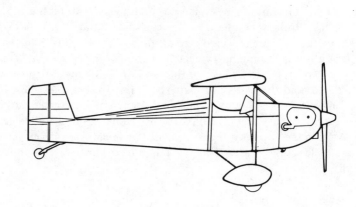

22

CORBEN *BABY ACE*

Originally designed and built in 1931 by Ace Corben, the Baby Ace was destined for great things twenty-four years later. In 1955, a Paul Poberezny built modification, graced the pages of *Mechanics Illustrated* magazine from May through July that year. It created a sensation and helped the newly formed EAA (Experimental Aircraft Association) get off the ground.

Construction of this open cockpit parasol wing monoplane was strictly conventional, incorporating parts from the venerable Piper J-3 Cub. The fuselage consisted of welded steel tubing, typical of lightplanes of the day. The tail surfaces were also of steel tubing, cable braced to each other and the fuselage. The wing featured your basic twin solid spruce spars with truss type ribs, and a sheet aluminum leading edge. Drag and anti-drag wires were anchored between the spars and three bays within the wing. Ailerons were hinged from the rear spars. The entire airframe was fabric covered and doped.

The wing panels were attached to the fuselage via cabane and twin parallel wing struts. The rear struts could be modified from the rear struts of a Cub, using the adjustable end fittings to set the wing's washout or washin. The front strut could be modified from a Cub, Aeronca or Taylorcraft.

Fig. 2-1. The original "Baby Ace" was atually a modification of the Heath "Parasol." The Paul Poberezny built version was featured on the May, June, and July issues of *Mechanix Illustrated*. It helped launch the EAA.

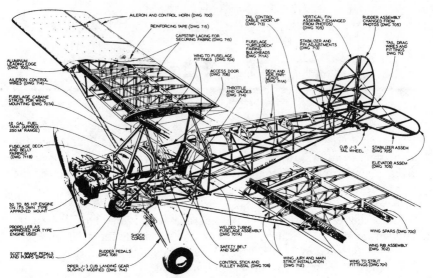

Fig. 2-2. Cutaway reveals structure and inner workings of *Mechanix Illustrated* "Baby Ace."

The stabilizer was designed to be ground adjustable to trim the ship by eliminating any nose or tail heaviness. The vertical fin was also ground adjustable to compensate for torque induced yaw. After a few flights, the airplane would be flying properly trimmed for maximum pilot comfort.

The fuel system was borrowed from the Piper Cub, including its 12 gallon tank. If a Cub engine was used as well, its carburetor heat system could be installed with few alterations.

Instrumentation was, of course, minimal, consisting of primary flight and engine gauges. The airplane will be powered by any Lycoming, Franklin or Continental ranging from 55 to 90 hp. The forward section of the fuselage was modified to accept the various engine mounts for these engines.

Specifications

Wingspan	25 ft 4 in
Length	17 ft 5 in
Height	6 ft
Power	65 hp
Gross Weight	800 lbs
Empty Weight	500 lbs
Top Speed	110 mph
Cruising Speed	95 mph
Landing Speed	30 mph
Ceiling	15,000 ft

At the end of the series, *Mechanics Illustrated* had this to say about flying the Baby Ace.

"Since the Baby Ace is a single seater, it must be assumed that you already are a licensed aircraft pilot or you would not be able to fly it at all. Therefore, we are simply going to give you a few words of advice regarding the flight operation of the aircraft. If you have ever flown a Piper Cub, Taylorcraft, Aeronca or any other popular lightplane, you will not have the slightest difficulty in handling the Baby Ace."

The Baby Ace was not designed as an aerobatic airplane. All normal maneuvers are permitted, including spins. The recommendations of air speeds are: stall - 30 mph, cruising speed - 95-100 mph. Maximum diving speed is 125 mph. If you operate the aircraft within this speed range you will have no need to worry about structural failure.

Again make certain that your first flight in the Baby Ace is made under the supervision of your local CAA Agent. He will discuss your flight path and propose maneuvers before allowing you to "take her up." He will also make suggestions that will result in safe and sane flying for you and those who may fly the plane after it is certified. HAPPY LANDINGS!

Druine Turbulent

23

DRUINE *TURBULENT*

The trim little French Turbulent of the mid-1950's was quite popular in Europe. This neat, all wood airplane weighed in at a scant 342 pounds, even though it was powered by a relatively heavy VW engine.

The aircraft is an excellent example of masterful aeronautical engineering in wood, and Mr. Druine is to be congratulated. A true expression of form follows function, in which every part was designed to do its job with minimal weight, and maximum aesthetics. The lines were extremely well conceived and lead to a ship with a pleasing appearance and good performance on low power.

The accompanying cutaway tells more than words ever could about this classic ARV. Every price is where it belongs. The cantilever wing features a main box spruce spar and built-up truss type ribs. The fuselage is a wood frame covered with plywood. The tail surfaces are also cantilevers, but they have solid ribs. The landing gear is a tripod arrangement with steel legs hinged to the spar-fuselage intersections, with a shock strut to the front spar. The tail wheel steers with the rudder.

Normally, if an airplane looks right, it'll fly right, and as gently as the Turbulent looks, so it flies. It is quite responsive to the pilot's smallest control inputs, yet can be flown hands off for long periods of time. Trim is via either an elevator trim tab or cockpit adjustable stabilizer. With just the 30 hp VW, the Turbulent will reach a top speed of 88 mph and a climb rate of 500 fpm. Calm conditions let you break ground in 500 feet, while landings require only 300 or so to stop. Slotted wings assume aileron effectiveness down through the stall.

Fig. 2-3. Druine "Turbulent" was popular in Europe during the mid-50s to mid-60s. Was of all wooden construction. Peter M. Bowers Collection.

Fig. 2-4. Cutaway of "Turbulent" reveals an extremely well engineered, all wood aircraft.

Specifications

Wingspan	21 ft 7 in
Length	16 ft 11 in
Height	5 ft
Power	30 hp
Gross Weight	620 lbs
Empty Weight	342 lbs
Top Speed	88 mph
Cruising Speed	75 mph
Landing Speed	40 mph
Ceiling	10,000 ft
Climb	500 fpm

As cute as the Turbulent is, it is difficult to build. Perhaps some modern materials and engineering could be applied to the design to bring it up to date and ease construction.

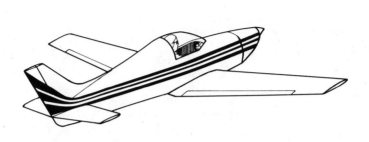

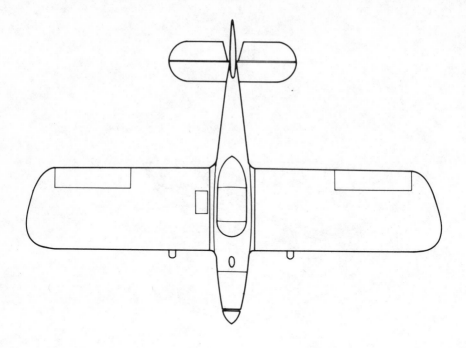

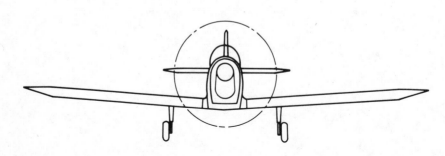

Taylor Monoplane

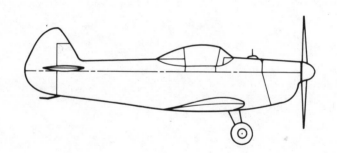

24

TAYLOR *MONOPLANE*

The Monoplane is a single place low wing monoplane of all wooden construction. It was designed specifically for the amateur builder who does not have an extensive workshop, and one who is also interested in a low budget project.

The wing features two spruce spars, and is covered in plywood. The left and right panels are bolted to the center section, which is integral with the fuselage, at a dihedral angle. The trailing edge is fitted with split trailing edge flaps and differential ailerons, which are covered in plywood and fabric. One rib bag may be deleted per panel for a 19 foot span version, for enhanced roll rate.

The fuselage features four main longerons carrying curved formers, covered entirely with plywood. The single seat is covered by a bubble plexiglass canopy, and is fitted with a fully acrobatic harness. The Monoplane is stressed for 9 g's. An eight gallon fuel tank is mounted behind the firewall.

The empennage is of conventional two spar construction. The stabilizer and fin are plywood covered, while the rudder and elevator are covered with fabric.

The main landing gear is the split type, including single spring compression legs fitting into a bracket bolted to the front spar. Twelve to fourteen inch diameter wheels are recommended. The tailwheel is suspended by a leaf spring and is steerable.

The metal fittings are to be made from 4130 steel. They are as simple and as few in number as is possible for the design.

Fig. 2-5. The Taylor "Monoplane" is an English all wood cantilever low wing, powered by a 30 hp, two cylinder engine.

The prototype was fitted with the 38 hp, two cylinder J.A.P., engine turning a two bladed wooden prop. However, the airplane can accommodate anything from 30 to 65 hp. The various VW conversions are a good choice, in view of the fact that (a) they simply bolt straight onto the bulkhead without the usual "plumbing," (b) availability is good, and (c) Ray Hegy of Texas produces a similar prop that allows excellent power extraction from the engine.

The airfoil section was carefully chosen for its high lift and gentle stall characteristics, with a neutral pitching moment. This allows for a smaller lighter structure, plus a relatively short fuselage.

Every pilot, without exception, who has flown a Monoplane, commented on its excellent yet docile handling qualities under all conditions. The prototype was flown by a great variety of pilots ranging in experience from several hours solo, airline and R.A.F. (Royal Air Force) types, even the Duke of Edinburgh's personal pilot took a flight in this English airplane.

The design provides for split trailing edge flaps, which some builders have left off. It is a matter of choice whether or not to install them. The designer preferred flaps however, for getting into and out of small fields. When full flap is used; the "Mono" greatly increases its angle of descent without an increase in airspeed. The designer further believes they should be installed if for no other reason than to increase the fun of flying, never mind an emergency situation.

Contact Mrs. Taylor for further details or plans.

Specifications

Wingspan	21 ft 0 in
Length	15 ft 0 in
Height	4 ft 10 in
Wing Area	76 sq ft
Engine Make, Model, HP	J.A.P., 38 hp
Prop Diameter/Pitch	N.A.
Reduction Ratio	1-to-1
Fuel Capacity/Consumption	8 gal/2½ gph
Gross Weight	620 lbs
Empty Weight	410 lbs
Useful Load	210 lbs
Wing Loading	8.16 psf
Power Loading	16.32 lb/hp
Design Load Factors	+9, -9
Construction Time	N.A.
Field Assembly Time	N.A.
Pricing	$55 (plans only)

Flight Performance

Velocity Never Exceed	N.A.

Top Level Speed	105 mph
Cruise Speed	90 mph
Stall Speed (in free air)	38 mph
Sea Level Climb Rate	950 fpm
Takeoff Run	200 ft
Dist. Req'd. to clear 50 ft	N.A.
Landing Roll	150 ft
Service Ceiling (100 fpm climb)	N.A.
Range at Cruise	230 mi

Monoplane
Mrs. J.F. Taylor
25 Chesterfield Crescent
Leigh-on-Sea
Essex, England
Mrs. Taylor

Stewart Headwind

25

STEWART *HEADWIND*

The Headwind is a strut braced, high wing cabin monoplane of steel tubing and wooden construction. It was the first airplane designed, built and flown in the U.S. with a VW engine. It received the EAA's "Best Auto-Powered Design" in 1962.

The airframe was designed to meet FAR 23 utility specifications. The fuselage is a triangular cross section of welded steel tubing, much like the old Aeronca C-3 "razorback." The tail group is also welded steel tube, wire braced together. The horizontal stabilizer is ground adjustable for trim. Sheet metal trim tabs on the rudder and elevator enable you to trim the aircraft for hands-off, straight and level flight.

The wing is primarily of wood, with two spruce spars, and sawn truss type ribs. The leading edge is covered with sheet aluminum back to the front spar. Drag and anti-drag cables run between the two spars and compression members, forming three bags per panel. Stuts, complete with jury struts, brace each panel to the lower fuselage longeron. The wing mounts fuse type ailerons, which are actuated via cables.

The landing gear consists of a steel tubing tripod supporting each wheel. Shock absorption is not needed, provided large, soft, 8.00 x 4 inch cub-type wheels and tires are used. Smaller wheels can be used provided a rubber shock strut is installed. No brakes are fitted, and are considered unnecessary. The tailwheel steers with the rudder.

Designer Stewart describes the Headwind's flight characteristics: "It's not quick and skittish like a lot of homebuilts of 1962 and, in fact, flies a lot

Fig. 2-6. Stewart Headwind was a mid-60's ARV-type based on the VW engine, with belt reduction drive.

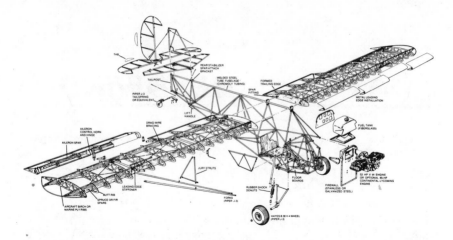

Fig. 2-7. Exploded drawing of "Headwind" shows old conventional style construction of welded steel tube fuselage, and wooden wings. Heavier engines of the day dictated heavier airframes than are necessary for today's ARVs.

like a J-3 or a Champ, with a very docile stall. The angle at which it stalls is quite high and I can't explain it. It probably stalls at 30 to 35 mph, though the airspeed indicator reads zero because of the relative wind over the pitot tube at that high angle."

In landing, Stewart says: "You just watch the wheels and fly the airplane onto the ground. It's fun to watch the wheels touch, although doing this almost always causes a one-wheel landing. It's a very stable airplane on the ground, due to its low CG."

The Headwind represents ARV technology of the mid-60's. It weighs more than today's ARV's primarily due to the heavy engine's available for the low hp needed for the design. The engine's weight required more structure, ad infinitum. Construction time was also quite high, at a thousand hours, which was actually low for the period. The Headwind nonetheless, represents the trend toward ARV's. A key element to the Headwind's success, was its reduction drive, a multi-belt unit that preceded ultralight units by 15 years. It was the only way to get adequate thrust from the higher revving VW engine.

Specifications

Wingspan	28 ft 3 in
Length	17 ft 0 in
Height	5 ft 6 in
Wing Area	111 sq ft
Engine Make, Model, HP	VW Conversion, 53 hp
Prop Diameter/Pitch	66 in
Reduction Ratio	1.6-to-1
Fuel Capacity/Consumption	6 gal/3 gph
Gross Weight	700 lbs
Empty Weight	433 lbs

Useful Load	267 lbs
Wing Loading	6.3 psf
Power Loading	13.2 lb/hp
Design Load Factors	N.A.
Construction Time	1000 man-hrs
Field Assembly Time	20 min
Pricing	Inquire at Stewart Aircraft Corp.

Flight Performance

Velocity Never Exceed	110 mph
Top Level Speed	85 mph
Cruise Speed	75 mph
Stall Speed (in free air)	35 mph
Sea Level Climb Rate	650 fpm
Takeoff Run	300 ft
Dist. Req'd. to clear 50 ft	N.A.
Landing Roll	400 ft
Service Ceiling (100 fpm climb)	10,300 ft
Range at Cruise	195 mi

Headwind
Stewart Aircraft Corp.
11420 State Route 165
Salem, OH 44460
(216) 332-4400
Don Stewart

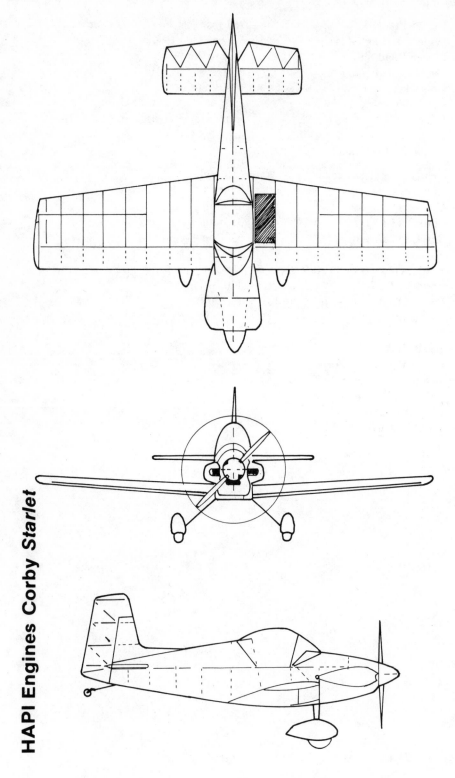

HAPI Engines Corby *Starlet*

26

HAPI ENGINES
CORBY *STARLET*

The Starlet is an all wood, ply and fabric covered, single seat, low wing cantilever monoplane.

The layout of the Starlet's designed to allow maximum detail variation with little or no change to the basic structure. For example, most existing VW powerplants up to 75 hp, 160 lb maximum, may be fitted without basic structural change. The design was drawn around the prototype Rollason Ardem VW 1600 conversion. Production aircraft engines are not recommended for Starlet due to size and weight limitations.

Basic hardware and materials are to U.S. specifications, with alternate British material specs given where appropriate.

The wing, which can be built in either one or two pieces, is a single "D" section nose type. The main spar is solid spruce built-up with ½" limitations, and varying in both depth and total width from root to tip. Provision is made for center section spar joint fittings which allow the wing to be dismantled into two 9 ft 3 in semispan halves.

Wing torsion, drag and anti-drag loads are reacted by the plywood covered "D" section leading edge, and transferred at the root through the main spar and leading edge attach points.

Wing and aileron fabric spars are also solid spruce of constant width and tapering depth. Ribs are the conventional built-up turns type. The wing is

Fig. 2-8. The Corby "Starlet" was originally designed in Australia in 1966. It's now marketed by HAPI Engines and powered by one of their acclaimed VW derived engines.

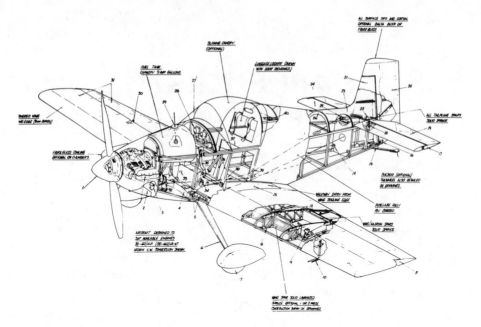

Fig. 2-9. Cutaway of the "Starlet" reveals a classic wooden structure, designed for limited aerobatics.

fabric covered aft of the main spar, with fabric doped on to caps stripped ribs. No rib stitching is used.

The tail surfaces are similar to the wing in that they are of single solid spar design, with a ply covered horizontal stabilizer and fin. The rudder and elevator are fabric covered.

The fuselage structure consists of a built-up frame of spruce, completely covered with ply. The fuel tank is mounted between the firewall and instrument panel, and beneath the forward fuselage decking. Provision is made for a shoulder harness installation, and a luggage locker is built into the bulkhead behind the pilot.

The main landing gear is the spring steel leaf type, attaching directly to the fuselage via a solid spruce ash beam, which also serves as the wing leading edge attach member. Wheels and brakes are of optional type and size, within limits specified. A similar steel leaf is also used for the tail skid with or without optional tailwheel.

The control surfaces are actuated via cables. The designer claims several features of this type system: (a) elimination of belcranks, push-pull rods and mount brackets with resultant simplicity and weight savings; (b) complete freedom from control circuit slack due to accumulation of fitting tolerances and/or wear.

In general, the Starlet has light, responsive controls with no apparent hesitation between control input and aircraft response. Light and precise, pilot feel is probably more significant than outright experience. The two fingered approach to flying will ensure the quickest transition to Starlet proficiency. As in all taildraggers, high speed ground handling should never be taken for granted. Care and respect should ensure no problems as ample directional control is available. In flight stability is good and all controls have a positive and progressive feel.

An important point to be emphasized is that the aircraft is stressed in the Australian "semi-aerobatic" (4.5g design, 6.75g ultimate) category. Any loading over 4.5g must be considered likely to damage the airframe (depending on actual material strengths above minimum specification figures, loading combinations, etc.) A "g" meter is strongly recommended if aerobatics are intended.

Spins are not approved. Recovery from inadvertent spin entry, however, is conventional and should occur readily in 1/4 to 1/3 turn, while losing about 200 feet of altitude.

Comprehensive testing has indicated all approved maneuvers can be flown comfortably under 3g's maximum loading. Stick force ranges from 2.7 lb/g to 4.5 lb/g over the typical CG range (the further aft the CG, the lower the stick force). The stick force provides good feel for aerobatics but certainly calls for intelligent respect and restraint to insure the airframe limits are not exceeded.

The current drawing set consists of 17 sheets and 30 pages of builder's notes. It has been steadily expanded and updated since the prototype's first flight in 1966. All significant developments in design, engines, equipment, materials and methods are included.

Specifications

Wingspan	18 ft 6 in
Length	14 ft 9 in
Height	4 ft 10 in
Wing Area	68.5 sq ft
Engine Make, Model, HP	HAPI "S" (VW based), 60 hp
Prop Diameter/Pitch	
Reduction Ratio	
Fuel Capacity/Consumption	8 gal
Gross Weight	650 lbs (630 lbs aerobatic)
Empty Weight	405 lbs
Useful Load	245 lbs
Wing Loding	9.5 psf
Power Loading	10.83 lb/hp
Design Load Factors	+4.5, -4.5
Construction Time	
Field Assembly Time	
Pricing	

Flight Performance

Velocity Never Exceed	N.A.
Top Level Speed	130 mph
Cruise Speed	112 mph

Stall Speed (in free air)	47 mph
Sea Level Climb Rate	850 fpm @ 58 mph
Takeoff Run	N.A.
Dist. Req'd. to clear 50 ft	N.A.
Landing Roll	N.A.
Service Ceiling (100 fpm climb)	N.A.
Range at Cruise	N.A.

Corby Starlet
HAPI Engines, Inc.
Eloy Municipal Airport
R.R. 1, Box 1000
Eloy, AZ 85231
(602) 466-9244
Rex Taylor

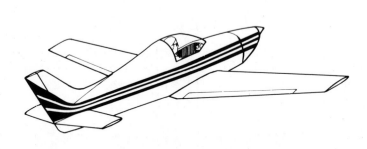

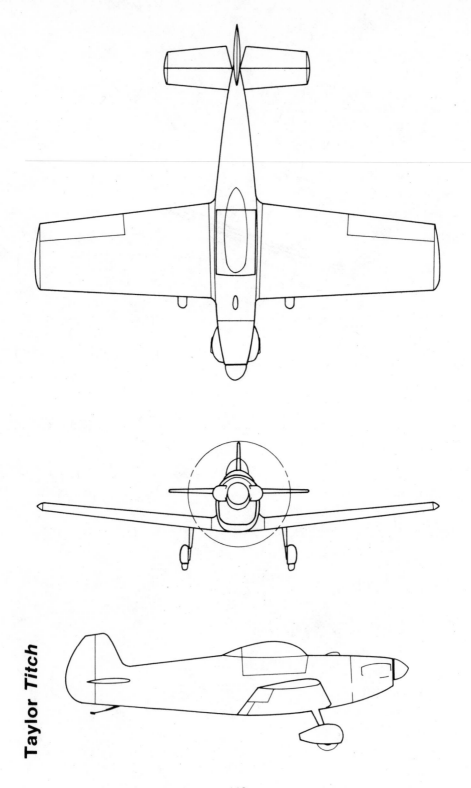

Taylor Titch

27

TAYLOR *TITCH*

The Titch is an all wood, single seat low wing tractor monoplane with taildragger gear. It is more or less a higher performance version of the Taylor Monoplane (described earlier) and is fully aerobatic.

The wings are made up of two panels, joined at the center with simple plates and bolt fittings. The main spar attaches to the main fuselage frame with four bolts. No metal fittings are required.

The wings are built-up on two spars, the front one being a box with two flanges and ply shear webs on either side. The flanges are straight tapered with no lamination. The spar tapers in only one directon, even though the wing is also tapered in plan form. To simplify the manufacture of this important component even more, the airfoil has been carefully modified in the spar region. No shaping is required for the spar flanges to conform to the airfoil shape. This modification also serves the dual purpose of rounding off the stall, while increasing the maximum lift coefficient.

The rear spar is a simple plank, tapering in one direction. It is located to carry the half span differential ailerons. The flaps mechanism consists of a lever connected directly to a torque tube, within easy reach of the pilot's right hand. Both surfaces are hinged by piano hinges.

The wing ribs require no jigs or steaming of flanges. Each rib is drawn full size and needs only to be cut out and pasted directly on the plywood. Rib flanges are glued and tacked to one side of the web only. The plywood nose covering is attached into operation. This is done by building up the leading edge top and bottom to provide increased glueing area. The top is skinned

Fig. 2-10. The Taylor "Titch" is a fully aerobatic, all wood airplane designed for the VW engine. It is basically a development of the Taylor "Monoplane."

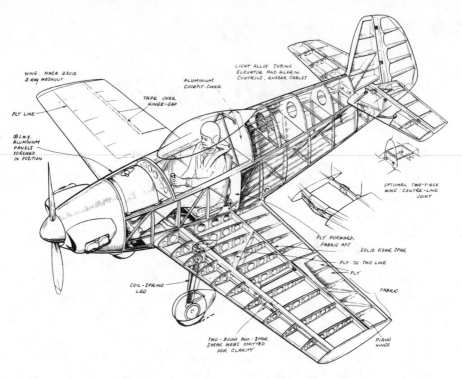

WING: NACA 23012
2 deg WASHOUT

ALUMINIUM
COCKPIT-COVER

LIGHT ALLOY TUBING
ELEVATOR AND AILERON
CONTROLS, RUDDER CABLES

TAPE OVER
HINGE-GAP

PLY LINE

18 S.W.G.
ALUMINIUM
PANELS
SCREWED
IN POSITION

OPTIONAL TWO-PIECE
WING: CENTRE-LINE
JOINT

PLY FORWARD,
FABRIC AFT

SOLID REAR SPAR

PLY TO THIS LINE
PLY

COIL-SPRING
LEG

FABRIC

TWO-BOOM BOX-SPAR
SHEAR WEBS OMITTED
FOR CLARITY

PIANO
HINGE

Fig. 2-11. Cutaway of the Taylor "Titch" shows well thought out wooden structure for VW powered, fully aerobatic low wing monoplane.

first, scarfed-down on the outside of the leading edge, and then the underside is attached and again scarfed to a feather edge from the outside.

The fuselage is built up of four main longerons, and four secondary longerons carrying curved formers on all sides. It can be either totally covered in plywood, or partially in ply over the forward fuselage, with fabric covered stringers over the rear half. Both methods are shown on the plans.

A 9.7 gallon fuel tank is mounted between the instrument panel and engine bulkhead. It is covered by an aluminum decking which is screwed into position and can be removed for tank inspection or replacement.

The cockpit has a folding seat for access to the controls and floor, and a fully aerobatic harness. The simplest and most streamlined cockpit cover is an aluminum frame of ⅝ inch angle, supporting the aluminum cover. To this is fitted a plexiglass bubble canopy which is hinged on the right side with a checkcable to limit opening to about 100 degrees. A suggested instrument panel layout is included. The forward cockpit area carries the main fuselage frame which the main spar is bolted to. The rear cockpit area carries the seat bulkhead which is attached to the rear spar and the flap operating gear. The rear fuselage tapers down to the stern post with integrally built fin and tailplane box. A small compartment can be built into the top decking behind the cockpit.

The tail group is conventional, with solid spars carrying plywood and spruce ribs. The fin and tailplane are plywood covered, with a fabric covered elevator and rudder. There is a choice of three hinge arrangements. The tailplane is attached to the fuselage by four bolts without the need for any metal fittings.

The controls are push-pull tubes running from the base of the control column, direct to the aileron quadrants, and to a pick-up lever mounted centrally on the flap torsion tube. From there, another tube connects to the elevator. The rudder is operated directly from the pedals via cables.

The builder has a choice of two landing gear systems. The first is a spring leg attached to the fuselage main frame. The second is a telescopier spring leg attached to the main spar by two steel plates clamped over the spar depth. The first is usually the heavier of the two, but has advantages. It leaves the fuselage on wheels after wing removal, and doesn't stress the wing on a hard landing. The second is more reliable in operations, but requires the additional fabrication of blade type scrap iron legs in order to keep the fuselage mobile after wing removal. Either type may, of course, be fitted with fiberglass wheel pants and brakes.

The tail skid is two blade spring steel, and a steerable tailwheel is recommended.

The aircraft is stressed for any engine from 40 to 90 hp, the only provision being a reposition if firewall for 65 hp and above. The two firewall positions are indicated on the plans. Less than 40 hp is not recommended for this aircraft.

Builder Jim Miller, of Kansas City has this to say about his C-85 powered Titch, according to an article in *Homebuilt Aircraft*. "It gets off the ground in 300-400 feet, climbs 1800 to 2000 fpm, and stalls at 60 IAS at altitude with no flaps. Control pressures are well balanced, and all aerobatic maneuvers compatible with the standard fuel and oil systems are easily accomplished." Wood construction is in no way old-fashioned. In his work, "For a personal airplane, the Titch is the ultimate."

Specifications

Wingspan	18 ft 9 in
Length	16 ft 2 in
Height	4 ft 8 in
Wing Area	71 sq ft
Engine Make, Model, HP	40 to 90 hp
Prop Diameter/Pitch	varies
Reduction Ratio	1-to-1
Fuel Capacity/Consumption	9.7 gal
Gross Weight	745 lbs
Empty Weight	500 lbs
Useful Load	245 lbs
Wing Loading	10.5 psf
Power Loading	8.3-18.7 lb/hp

Design Load Factors	+9, -9
Construction Time	N.A.
Field Assembly Time	N.A.
Pricing	$55 (plans)

Flight Performance	**(Continental C-85)**
Velocity Never Exceed	257 mph
Top Level Speed	190 mph
Cruise Speed	175 mph
Stall Speed (in free air)	60 mph
Sea Level Climb Rate	1800 fpm
Takeoff Run	400 ft
Dist. Req'd. to clear 50 ft	N.A.
Landing Roll	500 ft
Service Ceiling (100 fpm climb)	N.A.
Range at Cruise	380 mi

Titch
Mrs. John F. Taylor
25 Chesterfield Crescent
Leigh-On-Sea
Essex, England
Mrs. J.F. Taylor

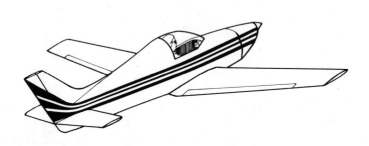

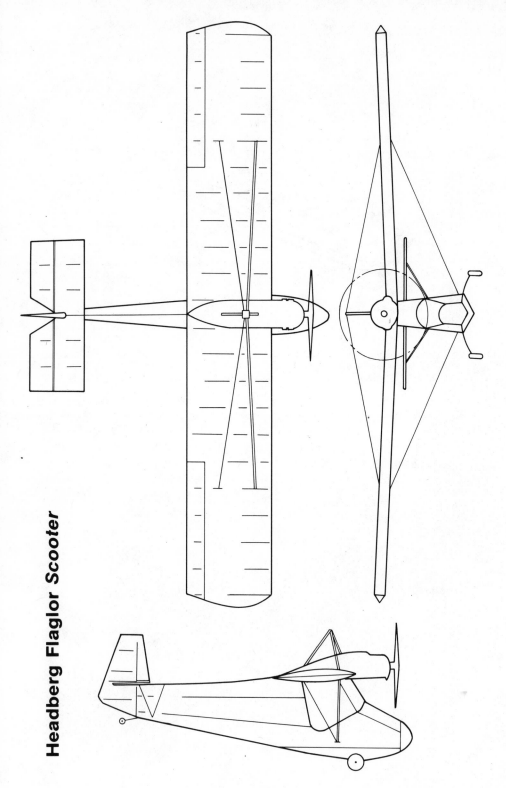

Headberg Flaglor Scooter

124

28

HEADBERG FLAGLOR
SCOOTER

The Scooter is an all wood, open cockpit high wing monoplane with tractor engine and taildragger landing gear. Originally flown in 1967, it won the "Outstanding Ultra-Light" and "Outstanding Volkswagen—Powered Airplane" awards at the EAA convention, which was then held at Rockford, Illinois. It was very well received by other pilots, and plans were made available. But, it was still ahead of its time by nearly 20 years.

The Scooter was the result of a great deal of effort to design and build a simple, low cost, easy to fly, low powered, economical airplane. It was conceived purely as a fun recreational machine to be flown for the joy of flight itself. Its performance and handling characteristics are good. Maneuverability is said to be excellent and it will turn on the proverbial "dime." No sluggish or sloppy control is evident. The airplane possesses real response with every control input, yet has good solid stability.

The designer used the proven and reliable traditional methods of construction, except where he felt building time could be saved for only a small weight penalty. Basically the Scooter is constructed of marine spruce and plywood, for a considerable savings and availability. However, aircraft quality materials may be used and, are recommended for the wing spars. All fittings are of 4130 sheet steel, while the motor mount is of 4130

Fig. 2-12. The Headberg Flaglor "Scooter" was one of the lightest ARVs of the 60's, although still powered by a converted VW engine.

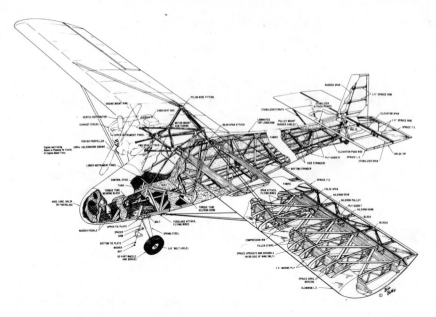

Fig. 2-13. Cutaway of the "Scooter" shows an airframe of conventional wooden construction, except for unique triangular cross section fuselage — somewhat reminiscent of the Santos Dumont Demoiselle.

tubing. The metal fairing and wing leading edge can actually be made of "hardware store variety" aluminum, as on the prototype.

The fuselage is constructed on a plywood workbench and is not difficult to build. The structure is composed of spruce longerons with plywood gussets aft and plywood sides in the cockpit area.

The landing gear is made of steel or alternately of aluminum. Go-kart wheels and tires work well, with brakes optional. The landing gear may be built or purchased.

The wings are easily made and are said to go together quickly. All ribs are contour sawed from ¼" marine plywood. Main spars are spruce, as are the false and aileron spars. The wing uses a wood cross hatching in the form of an "X" between each rib and the spars, serving the drag anti-drag load carrying duties. Plywood wing tips and wooden trailing edges complete the structure, with an aluminum leading edge shim. The wings are braced with 1 x 19 stainless steel aircraft cable to the fuselage on the bottom and a kingpost on top. The wires, of course, save weight over struts.

The controls are actuated via cables running on ballbearing pulleys, resulting in a smooth, low drag system. The entire airframe is covered with lightweight glider dacron. This is cemented to the ribs, eliminating rib stitching, producing a smooth wing. The usual primary flight instruments are on the panel, while the prototype used automotive engine gauges consistent with its VW engine.

The original prototype Scooter was underpowered with its first engine, the 18 hp Cushman. The minimum recommended power is a 25 hp VW,

126

but the aircraft can handle up to 40 hp. Today, there are a couple of VW-based engines available, as well as some new engines as developed for ultralights and ARV's.

Highly detailed, professionally drawn plans are available. All fittings are detailed full-size, as are the wing ribs. In addition, assorted photos are used to show key assemblies and construction details. Contact Headberg Aviation for further details and kit prices.

Specifications

Wingspan	27 ft 10 in
Length	15 ft 6 in
Height	7 ft 0 in
Wing Area	115 sq ft
Engine Make, Model, HP	VW, 25-40 hp
Prop Diameter/Pitch	54 in/27in
Reduction Ratio	1-to-1
Fuel Capacity/Consumption	7 gal/2 gph
Gross Weight	625 lbs
Empty Weight	390 lbs
Useful Load	235 lbs
Wing Loading	5.4 psf
Power Loading	16 lb/hp
Design Load Factors	N.A.
Construction Time	450 man-hrs
Field Assembly Time	N.A.
Pricing	$45.00 for plans

Flight Performance

(VW 1500, 36 hp)

Velocity Never Exceed	N.A.
Top Level Speed	88 mph
Cruise Speed	75 mph
Stall Speed (in free air)	34 mph
Sea Level Climb Rate	600 fpm
Takeoff Run	250 ft
Dist. Req'd. to clear 50 ft	N.A.
Landing Roll	350 ft
Service Ceiling (100 fpm climb)	12,000 ft
Range at Cruise	175 mi (no reserve)

Scooter
Headberg Aviation, Inc.
265 Needles Trail
Longwood, FL 32750
(305) 788-0471
Dennis Headberg

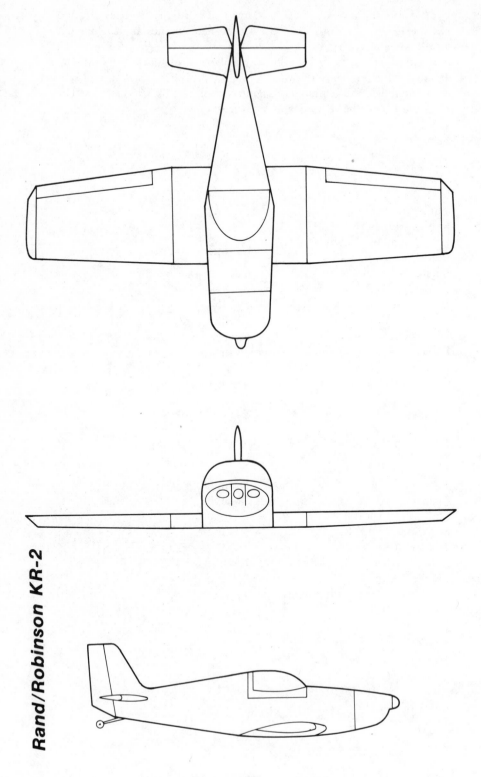

Rand/Robinson KR-2

29

RAND/ROBINSON
KR-1 AND KR-2

The KR-1 and -2 are low wing monoplanes with retractable landing gear and removeable wings. Both aircraft feature simple foam over structure airframes. The KR-1 is a single placer, while the KR-2 carries two.

The design goal for these aircraft was to provide the cleanest lines and the best performance possible with the available and reliable VW engine. The cost and construction time for achieving this goal is minimized by using a combination of wood structure, polyurethane foam, fiberglass and epoxy-resin. The result is a structurally strong, clean, hard surfaced and exceptionally fast airplane for the power used.

To achieve construction simplicity, the airplane is designed so that no machining or welding is necessary to build the airframe. All parts can be made and assembled with ordinary hand tools and small power tools.

If there are any wooden homebuilt airplanes in your area, visit with the owners and get a good look at the airplane and the quality of the workmanship. Construction of the KR's is not unlike that used in making flying model airplanes, but scaled up, of course. The gluing technique is very similar, even to the use of waxed paper to prevent parts from sticking to the jig board. Rigid foam is very easy to work with. It can be sawed, carved, cut and sanded easily and rapidly into straight, curved or

Fig. 2-14. The KR-2 (foreground), and the KR-1 feature foam over structure construction, and offer excellent performance on VW power. Both feature retractable gear.

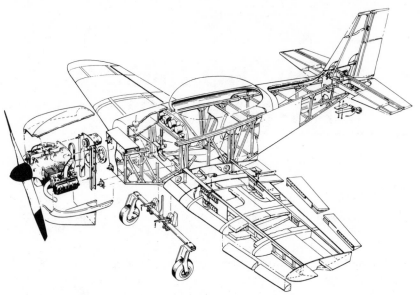

Fig. 2-15. The Rand/Robinson "KR-1" in cutaway.

complicated shapes, such as: leading edges, wing tips, fillets and cowlings. If you go below contour, just glue on some more foam. When the glue is dry, sand to the desired contour. The fiberglass weave is open enough to adjust to almost any contour and resin penetration is rapid. Air pockets are easily seen and worked out before the resin hardens.

No elaborate jigs or holding fixtures are needed. However, a study and properly sized work table, adjusted to a working height that best accommodates the builder, is helpful. While applying glue or epoxy resin, care should be taken to observe precautionary instructions provided by the manufacturer. Tolerance to these materials varies with the individual. Adequate ventilation and skin protection are strongly suggested.

The desire to create or be different is very human. There are many opportunities in this design for the individual builder to express his own ideas, especially in: the cowling, forward and rear decks, the cockpit and instrument arrangement.

The Rand techniques of combining density controlled polyurethane sheet foams, fabric and epoxy resin into structural material for aircraft, is unique. Anyone who saw Rand walk on his KR-1 wing needs little additional convincing of the viability of the foam over structure method. The plans make every effort to transmit to you, by word and pictures, the "knowhow" acquired from the actual foam and fiberglass work performed in constructing the KR airplanes.

Most folks who elect to build these aircraft will probably already have the required tools. If not, the following are suggested: cross cut and rip hand saws, tablesaw, wood plane, sanding discs, belt sander, carpenter square, protractor/square set, hacksaw, files, ¼ inch drill motor, drill bits,

130

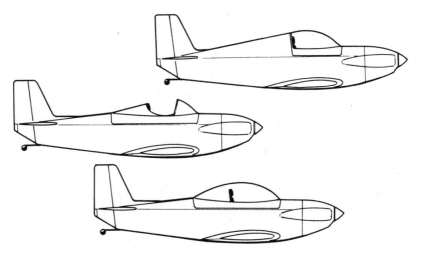

Fig. 2-16. The "KR-1" can take on different "personalities," depending on the owner's preferences.

screwdrivers, wrench set, staple gear, plumb bob, steel tape, or 2-inch circle saw on ¼ inch mandrel, glue brushes and squeeges, hammer, pair of pliers, and a bench vice. For outer wing attachment, a level is useful.

Make a level, well balanced table. For the top, use two sheets of 2 ft. x 8 ft-9 in. particle board, lengthwise, butt-end together and cut off to length of table desired. This material has a finished surface and is not susceptible to splintering or distortions during use. It makes a fine jig board. If particle board can't be obtained, use ¾ inch plywood. Expensive holding fixtures or assembly jigs would be required if interchangeability of assemblies or parts was required. However, in as much as each homebuilt aircraft is a "one-of-a-kind," much of the fit and drill becomes a progressive matter, with the airplane itself being used as the jig.

Both aircraft are easy to fly and possess predictable flight handling qualities. They have gentle stall characteristics and provide a comfortable spread between cruise and landing speeds. Performance can be enhanced by installing a turbocharger, upping the cruise to over 200 mph above 14,000 ft.

Contact Rand/Robinson Engineering for plans, parts and complete kits.

Specifications

Wingspan	17 ft 0 in
Length	12 ft 9 in
Height	3 ft 8 in
Wing Area	62 sq ft
Engine Make, Model, HP	VW 1835
Prop Diameter/Pitch	52 in 46 in
Reduction Ratio	1-to-1
Fuel Capacity/Consumption	8 gal/3.8 gph
Gross Weight	750 lbs

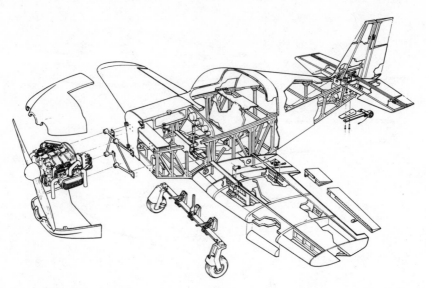

Fig. 2-17. The "KR-2" is essentially a scaled-up "KR-1," for two.

Empty Weight	375 lbs
Useful Load	325 lbs
Wing Loading	12.1 psf
Power Loading	12.5 lb/hp
Design Load Factors	9+,-
Construction Time	750 man-hrs
Field Assembly Time	20 min
Pricing	$3000

Flight Performance

Velocity Never Exceed	200 mph
Top Level Speed	200 mph
Cruise Speed	180 mph @ 80% power
Stall Speed (in free air)	52 mph
Sea Level Climb Rate	800 fpm
Takeoff Run	350 ft
Dist. Req'd to clear 50 ft	650 ft
Landing Roll	900 ft
Service Ceiling (100 fpm climb)	15,000 ft
Range at Cruise	1400 mi
L/D (Glide Ratio)	12-to-1 @ 85 mph
Minimum Sink Rate	550 fpm @ 85 mph

KR-1
Rand Robinson Engineering, Inc.
5842 "K" McFadden Ave.
Huntington Beach, CA 92649
(714) 898-3811
Jeanette Rand

Specifications

Wingspan	20 ft 8 in
Length	14 ft 6 in
Height	4 ft 0 in
Wing Area	80 sq ft
Engine Make, Model, HP	VW 2100
Prop Diameter/Pitch	52 in/48 in
Reduction Ratio	1-to-1
Fuel Capacity/Consumption	12-35 gal/3.8 gph
Gross Weight	900 lbs
Empty Weight	480 lbs
Useful Load	420 lbs
Wing Loading	11.25 psf
Power Loading	12 lb/hp
Design Load Factors	+ - 7+, -
Construction Time	750 man-hrs
Field Assembly Time	20 min
Pricing	under $3500

Flight Performance

Velocity Never Exceed	NA
Top Level Speed	200 mph
Cruise Speed	180 mph @ 90% power
Stall Speed (in free air)	52 mph
Sea Level Climb Rate	1200 fpm
Takeoff Run	400 ft
Dist. Req'd to clear 50 ft	650 ft
Landing Roll	1000 ft
Service Ceiling (100 fpm climb)	15,000 ft
Range at Cruise	1600 mi
L/D (Glide Ratio)	15-to-1 @ 85 mph
Minimum Sink Rate	550 fpm @ 85 mph

KR-2
Rand Robinson Engineering, Inc.
5842 "K" McFadden Ave.
Huntingdon Beach, CA 92649
(714) 898-3811
Jeanette Rand

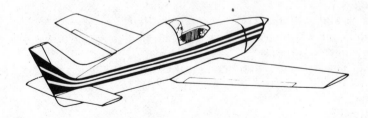

Section III

The 1983 ARV Competition And Today's ARVs

In the summer of 1981, the *Western Flyer/Ultralight Flyer* ARV Design Competition was announced—one of the most significant events in the history of sport aviation. The deadline for entries was July 4, 1982, and all were kept confidential until then. All entrants were asked to submit design specifications, engineering data, three-view drawings, photos of models (optional), and photos of prototype (also optional). After that, the material was released to the public. Two divisions were set up: Light Aircraft (less than 350 pounds) and Ultralight Aircraft (less than 254 pounds).

The following rules were to be observed:

1. The purpose of the contest is to stimulate new ARV designs that will be available to the people. The prototype must not have made its first flight prior to Labor Day, September 7, 1981. Contest winners must be willing to make plans and/or kits or finished aircraft available to the public (for appropriate fees, of course).

2. Light aircraft must have all restrictions flown off prior to June 1, 1983. Ultralight designs must have logged a minimum of 25 hours. Any design deemed unsafe by the performance judges will be disqualified.

3. Each airplane starts out with 100 points on each of judging categories. Judges will deduct points according to their objections (this is similar to the scoring techniques used in figure skating). Deductions can be appealed to the full body of judges if grounds for an appeal can be shown to the contest director or chairman. The plane with the most points left after judging will be the winner.

Paul H. Poberezny was honorary chairman, while Dave Sclair was the director.

The primary sponsor for the contest was the E.I. DuPont Company's Kevlar Aramid Fiber Division. Associate sponsors included: Aircraft Owners and Pilots Association, AOPA Air Safety Foundation, Cuyuna Engine Company, Experimental Aircraft Association and, Wicks Aircraft Supply.

A team of five internationally known judges inspected and judged the aircraft. They included: Antonio Bengelis; longtime EAA designer, columnist and author; Jack Cox, editor of *Sport Aviation,* and *Sportsman Pilot;* Peter Lert, associate editor of *Air Progress* and accomplished airplane pilot report writer; Ed Lesher, professor of aeronautics; and, Ed Tripp, editor of *AOPA Pilot.*

As reported in *ARV Designs '83,* Bengelis judged the construction and economics phase of the contest, while Cox looked at the entrant aircraft for their physical appearance and portability. Lesher, of the University of Michigan, handled the engineering and test data of the entries. Lert and Tripp judged the flying of the top finishers by observations from the ground.

All told, 44 ultralight and 82 lightplane entries were received by the entry deadline. All three-views were published on *ARV Designs '83.*

The judging criteria each with 20 points, was established as follows:

1. Performance, including: safety features, takeoff, cruise, landing, roll

rate, climb/sink rate, visibility, range, cross wind response and, pilot comfort.

2. Construction and Economics, including: safety features, simplicity, aircraft grade materials, ease of handling, costs, availability of materials and powerplants and, compliance with FARs.

3. Engineering including: safety and crash survivability, structural testing results (required), aircraft grade materials - strength, structural analysis and, design specifications.

4. Appearance, including: originality, style, finish, craftsmanship and, cleverness.

5. Portability and Assembly, including: method of transport, method of assembly/disassembly and, time of assembly/disassembly.

After it was all over, the final standings looked like this:

LIGHT AIRCRAFT DIVISION WINNERS

Rank/Aircraft	Flight	Construction & Economics	Engi-neering	Appear-ance	Porta-bility	Total
1. Starlite	19	20	20	19	17	95
2. XTC	20	18	18	18	18	92
3. Zippy Sport	17	19	19	17	17	89
4. LM-1	15	16	17	14	17	79
5. Twinstar	16	11	16	15	17	75
6. Shrike	14	9	15	14	15	67

ULTRALIGHT AIRCRAFT DIVISION WINNERS

Rank/Aircraft	Flight	Construction & Economics	Engi-neering	Appear-ance	Porta-bility	Total
1. Hawk	20	20	20	19	17	96
2. Ultrastar	17	17	19	19	19	91
3. Vampire	11	19	20	18	19	87
4. Falcon	18	14	17	19	17	85
5. Ultra Aire	15	15	18	16	18	82
6. B1-RD	15	20	16	16	15	82
7. Cloud Dancer	12	14	17	17	19	79
8. Cobra	16	13	15	17	17	76
9. Butterfly	15	15	14	15	17	76
10. P-Craft	15	8	15	18	16	72

Description of Contest

The Aircraft Recreation Vehicle Design Competition has been developed to encourage new homebuilt designs that are easy to assemble, economical, efficient and which incorporate modern materials and construction techniques.

The object is to encourage designers to create new aircraft in two categories: Light Aircraft and Ultralight Aircraft.

Light Aircraft:

The vehicle should be 350 pounds or less. It should be capable of being towed, trailered or transported on a cartop and setup by one person. The vehicle should qualify in the amateur-built, experimental category and comply with all applicable Federal Aviation Regulations.

Ultralight Aircraft:

This vehicle must meet with the Federal Aviation Administration's final determination of the Ultralight Aircraft. Should this FAA final determination by unavailable at the July 4, 1982 contest deadline, the Contest Director will establish criteria for the Ultralight Aircraft. For planning and design purposes, these criteria will closely follow the major recommendations of the Experimental Aircraft Association, Aircraft Owners & Pilots Association and Professional Ultralight Manufacturers Association to the FAA.

In addition to these criteria for the Ultralight Contest, the vehicle should also be towable, trailerable or car-toppable. One person set-up is also a prime consideration.

Prizes and Awards:

Winner of each division will receive a $5,000 cash prize and the Kevlar Trophy from E.I. DuPont.

Second place winners will each receive $1,500 and third place finishers will get $500 each.

A 50 percent bonus on prize money will be awarded by Cuyuna Development Company to any winner using a Cuyuna engine.

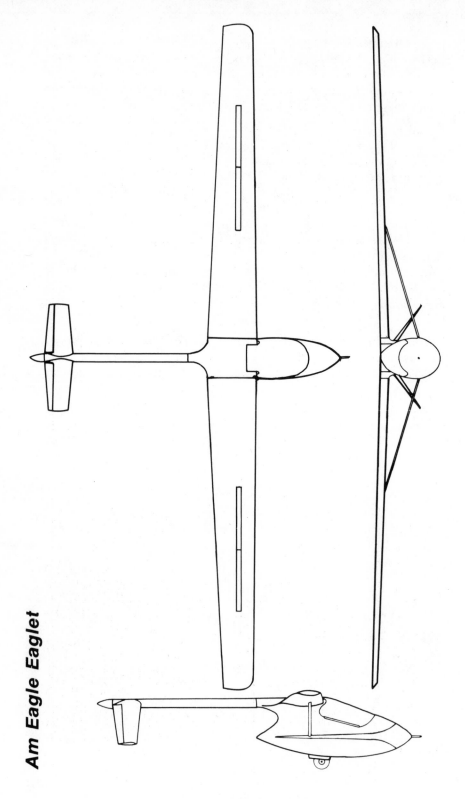

Am Eagle Eaglet

30

AMERICAN *EAGLET*

The Eaglet is a strut braced, high wing, pod and boom motorized sailplane. It provides true soaring performance while eliminating many of the encumberances normally associated with soaring.

All flying surfaces are nearly identical in construction, being comprised of spruce load bearing spars surrounded by urethane foam and covered with precured fiberglass skins. The skin material is supplied ready to use (much like sheet aluminum, only stronger and lighter) and is simply bonded to the shaped core using epoxy and a vacuum bag. An ordinary household vacuum cleaner supplies the required vacuum, the bag being nothing more than 6 mil. polye sheet taped closed with masking tape. When a surface has cured and been removed from the bag, it is nearly ready to finish, requiring minimal sanding.

The urethane cores are shaped with a sanding board that ultimately rides on two template ribs, one at the tip and one at the root, providing the final airfoil configurations. Prior to sanding, the cores are rough shaped with a carving knife and Surform plane. This is a rapid process which takes about 30 minutes for a stabilizer and 1½ hours for a wing.

Both wing and stabilizer kits are supplied with assembled and shaped aircraft grade certified spruce spars which the builder need only trim to length and mount attaching hardware. The wing leading edges and tips are also supplied premolded and ready for assembly. The lift struts are an extruded airfoil shape, anodized and ready to assemble.

The fuselage is comprised of two preformed fiberglass shells pop riveted to a load bearing aluminum tube framework and tail boom. The fuselage's

Fig. 3-1. The American "Eaglet" is actually a small sailplane with a 12 hp kart engine for self-launching capability. It features composite construction with wooden spars.

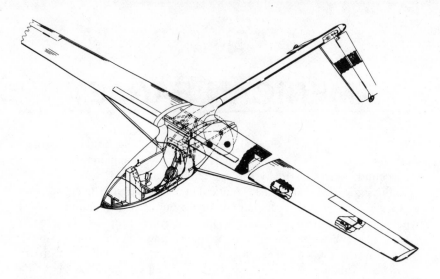

Fig. 3-2. Cutaway of American "Eaglet" shows main components, including engine and folding prop.

main load bearing element is an aluminum skinned urethane foam composite, incorporating special integral square aluminum extrusions that carry virtually all loads imposed on the aircraft. This bulkhead separates the pilot and engine compartments. The pilot's sling seat hangs on the front face, the engine on the rear face, the landing gear on the bottom edge, the tail boom at the top rear, the spar carry-through at the top, and lift strut carry-through at the middle. All longerons and tail boom support struts are also tied to it so it is, in fact, the backbone of the aircraft. Interestingly, it weighs only seven pounds.

The fuselage kit features several prefabricated components including the shells, tailboom, longeron, side braces, wheel and tire, canopy, control cables, spinner and tail cone. The skilled builder is urged to start construction with the fuselage, it being the most difficult assembly of the aircraft.

The motor mount and drive system is supplied as an optional kit. It is, nonetheless, recommended that the builder make provision for it even if not ordered with the kit, as operational experience will likely convince the sailplane purest to invest in the powerplant at some point in time.

The power package kit parts including drive shaft, clutch, prop hub, folding nylon prop blades and retracting mechanism are supplied fully machined, assembled, balanced and ready to use. The exhaust system, fuel system, control cables and vibration isolation are also supplied ready to use. The only parts the builder need fabricate are the engine mount proper and exhaust duct.

The only items not included in the Eaglet kit are the engine, instruments sling seat fabric, paint and a small amount of wood products. Some optional items also include such things as molded stabilizer tips, prefabricated metal components and trailer plans.

The kit is accompanied by five construction manuals, 42 sheets of drawings and a bi-monthly newsletter. The drawings include all necessary detail drawings, developed full-sized templates, sub assembly, assembly and, where necessary, exploded views to facilitate the builder's understanding of the task at hand. The manuals are written subjectively in ever increasing levels of detail so that each builder need read only as deeply as he must to understand. They are interjected with humor to make the building process more enjoyable!

The Eaglet has been thoroughly factory flight tested to all corners of the flight envelope, including flutter tests to 132 mph. (5% over the design red line). Normal slow speed entry does not produce a normal straight forward mild break with no tendency to drop a wing. Spins are not possible (due to the inverted V-tail), attempted spin entry resulting in an immediate return to a straight ahead high sink rate mush.

Controls are effective in all three axes with more roll and yaw control, but slightly less pitch control than the Schweitzer 1-26. Glide path control is positive but, unlike many other sailplanes, a high sink rate develops without a corresponding change in pitch attitude. Due to the dual function spoilerons (roll and glide path control) and linkage design, the roll rate in the glide path mode of spoilers deployed is approximately double the normal roll rate.

Control authority in pitch and yaw is enhanced under power as the prop wash impinges on the tail surfaces. Otherwise, the Eaglet handles like any other tail dragger sailplane during takeoff and climb. It should be mentioned that the Eaglet's powerplant is not intended for sustained power flight and the factory states that it cannot be operated as a powered airplane. The engine (and folding prop) are provided for takeoff, and inflight restarts and climbs only.

Specifications

Power	Mc101 (12 hp)
Span	36 ft
Length	16 ft
Height	3 ft
Wing Area	72 sq ft
Gross Weight	370 lbs
Empty Weight	170 lbs
Useful Load	200 lbs
Wing Loading	5 psf
Fuel Capacity	½ gal
Fuel Consumption	1 gph
Load Factor	+4.4, -2.2
Time to Build	500 man-hrs

Flight Performance

Top Speed	115 mph
Cruise Speed	60 mph
Stall Speed	39 mph
Sea-level Climb	375 fpm @ 72 mph
Takeoff Run	750 - 1,000 ft
Landing Roll	300 ft
Ceiling	N.A.
Range	N.A.
L/D	24 to 1 @ 60 mph
Sink Rate	3.3 fps @ 45 mph
Set-up Time	N.A.

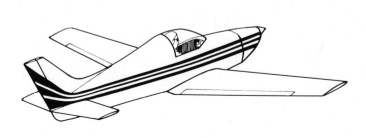

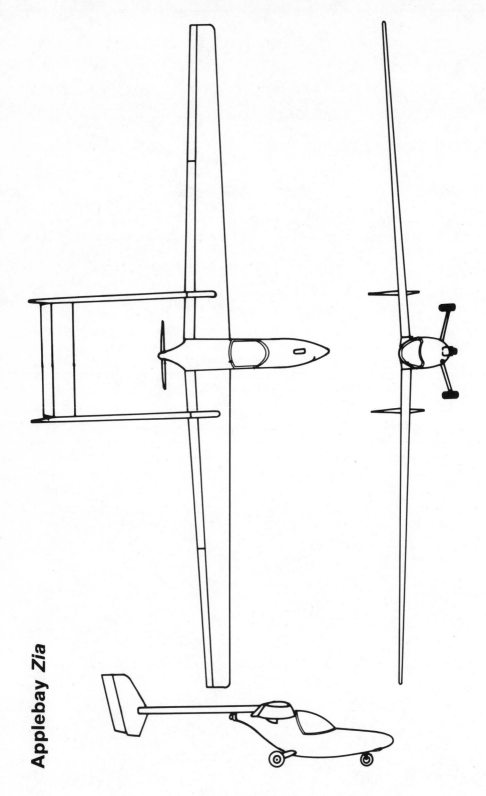

Applebay Zia

144

31

APPLEBAY *ZIA*

What's the difference between an ultralight airplane and a motorglider? Your point of view, mainly, or the FAA's point of view. Applebay sees FAA regulation of ultralights as inevitable and made no attempt to sneak past licensing requirements when designing the Zia.

Looking at the aircraft that Applebay has been producing for years—the exotic Zuni, Mescalero and Chiricahua sailplanes— you will see the heritage of the Zia. If it isn't an ultralight in the present sense of the word, at least is is the shape of things to come in the ultralight ARV world.

The Zia motorglider, unlike the Applebay sailplanes, was not designed with an elite clientele in mind. Those sailplanes cost upwards of $25,000. It was, while refining his sailplane designs out in the field, that he noticed the odd creations of cable and cloth buzzing around in the sky—ultralight aircraft. The idea of low cost powered flight was born in his mind. If he applied sailplane aerodynamics and modern composite construction, what form would it take?

Visitors to Oshkosh '81 were the first to see Applebay's Zia: a tailless canard airplane of smooth composite construction with a small pusher engine. The main wings were the high aspect ratio sailplane type, a 43 foot long cantilever with small vertical rudders on the tips, which also acted as ailerons ("ailerudders").

Fig. 3-2a. The final Zia canard prototype as discussed in the text.

The canard configuration was chosen because Applebay decided that it was the safest setup for tight spiral turns ("thermalling") at low speed. He estimates the Zia's turning radius to be 150 feet. Further flight testing back home showed the wingtip control system to be imperfect: as the aircraft rotated on takeoff the nose tended to yaw to the right.

Reluctantly, Applebay added twin rudders mounted on independent booms which plug into sockets on the trailing edges of the wings near the fuselage. The control system is now quite conventional, with the elevator (on the canard wing) and ailerons operated by a control stick, and the rudders by pedals. The free castoring nosewheel showed a tendency to be a little too free at times, so it was linked to the rudder pedals also. Now the pilot has both the independent brakes on the main wheels and the nosewheel for steering.

The Zia, with its little 18 hp engine can get into the air far more cheaply and fuel efficiently than any sailplane/towplane combination. The airplane's empty weight is 300 pounds, 550 gross, and the wing loading at gross weight is only 4.4 pounds per sq. ft. Its lift over drag ratio is 27 to 1, meaning that it will move forward 27 feet for every one that it sinks. Of course, without the stopped propeller and tricycle landing gear dragging in the slipstream it might get better than 30 to 1, but the Zia trades off some aerodynamic efficiency in order to achieve simplicity of construction and a lower cost to the buyer. It is intended for the man who wants something less primitive than the present crop of ultralights but who doesn't want, or can't afford, a full-sized airplane.

The whole idea of the Zia, says George Applebay, is to get its owner into the air with the least expense, both initially and in operation. Although the Zia will be available from the factory fully assembled and ready to fly for about $12,000, he believes that most buyers will purchase the airplane as a kit which will only cost half as much. The kit will be complete, including engine and propeller, and all parts will be pre-formed The "builder" will thus not have to build anything, only assemble what he is given, following the directions in his owner's manual.

To best understand how the Zia is constructed, let us assume the role of kit buyer and construct the airplane ourselves, right here and now, on paper. That way, instead of the 200 hours that Applebay estimates, it will only take a few minutes, and as any homebuilder can tell you, the airplane you build in your head always comes out better than the one in the garage.

As we pry open the crates containing the various pieces of the Zia, we are struck by the model-airplane-like appearance of the parts. They are all smooth composite shapes made at the factory in negative master molds with molded-in mating flanges so that all we basically have to do is glue them together with epoxy. The fuselage pod is in halves, as are the rudder booms and the wings.

All three wings (right, left, canard) consist of a top and bottom skin 5/16-inch thick, a sandwich made up of a ¼-inch layer of foam between layers of fiberglass. We build a wing by supporting it on three sawhorses (with the profile of the wing cut into the crosspiece of each sawhorse, using the templates provided), so that it is held level, inside-up, while we work on it. Into this half we install the aileron hardware, the hinges, push-pull tubes and the Teflon rollers that guide them, and glue in the long wing star.

The spar is a composite I-beam with carbon fibers embedded in it, giving it great strength. It is dozens of times stronger than a spruce spar of the same size, and incomparably stronger in bending than the aluminum tubes most ultralights use. The other half of the wing skin is then glued on.

The canard wing, which does not have to bear as much stress as the main wings, is even simpler because it has no spar, as such. What it has is a shear web, and that is already built into one half, so that all you have to do here is install the elevator hardware before gluing on the other half. Now hinge the elevator to the canard and the ailerons to the main wings, and that does it for wings.

Next, glue the fuselage halves together at the overlapping flanges. Fill the outside seam (with a slurry made of talcum powder in a polyester paint provided) and sand invisibly smooth. Bolt the engine mounting plate into the rear of the pod (against molded-in fiberglass L-angles, one on each side). Then put in the rudder pedals and toe brakes, nosewheel steering, the push-pull tubes forward to the elevator and rearward to the aileron linkages, the throttle on the left side of the cockpit, control stick in the center of the molded instrument panel, and the pitch-trim lever and its linkages on the right side.

After considering a number of makes of engine, Applebay chose the single cylinder 250cc Fuji Robin with a 28mm Mikuni carburetor. It is a well-proven powerplant in similar applications, and it has a built-in cooling fan and fuel pump. To insure that it stays cool inside the fuselage, he placed some air inlets on the sides of the pod. Air enters there and exists behind the cylinder head.

We install the engine now, with four bolts through the mounting plate. After hooking up the throttle linkage to the carb, you screw in the seat back which also serves as the firewall and seals the engine off from the cockpit. Fit the plexiglass canopy to the fuselage. The nosewheel simply bolts to the underside of the pod (linked to the rudder pedals on the inside), but we have to assemble the legs, or struts, of the other two. These are also supplied in halves which, after putting in the axles and brake cable hardware, are glued together.

For the "shear web" here we pour activated urethane foam into a hole in the base of each strut and allow it to expand and fill the entire interior cavity. After it cures, we have a strong, solid foam core.

Put the wheels on the axles, and hook up the cables to the brakes, which are the normal caliper type using pucks to squeeze a disc. You may now insert and pin the gear legs into the fuselage, hooking the brake cables to the toe brakes inside. Put the prop on the engine hub, and the fuselage is done too. Finally, put the push-pull tubes to each rudder into one half of each tail boom, glue on the other half, hinge on the rudders, and assembly is complete.

Since this is no sailcloth and aluminum pole ultralight, you can't carry it on top of a car. You have to have a trailer. A regular enclosed sailplane trailer is nice, if you can afford one, but a stretched boat trailer with wing cradles on it would do. Or you can get an axle, some wheels and some steel tubing and weld up a custom one.

Having trailered the Zia to the field and unloaded it, in pieces, we must now put it together. We have one fuselage on the gear (unless you took that off again for trailering; if so, put it back on), two main wings, one canard wing and two rudders on their booms.

Two people make the job easiest, but one can do it in a little more time. In that case you should have a sawhorse to support the outer end of each main wing as you plug it into the fuselage, and the horse should be padded or have a roller on it so the wing can slide across without getting scuffed. As you insert the wings into the fuselage, you see why the spars protrude 28 inches from the wing roots. It lets them stab clear through the 24-inch wide fuselage and four inches into the root of the wing on the opposite side (they are staggered so that they pass each other).

When the wings are in place, all you have to do to lock them is to insert a big T-handled lock pin through the spar where they overlap on the centerline of the fuselage (inside the cockpit, above and behind the seat). It seats itself with a snap, automatically safetied by a spring loaded latch. Reach in behind the seat and hook up the aileron linkage. The main wings go on in something less than two minutes.

Next, set the canard wing in place on the front of the fuselage, up under and against the molded flange shaped to receive it, and crank four bolts through the flange into the wing. That's how it was done on the prototype; on production Zias you'll just have to push a lever and the canard wing will be locked on and safetied. On top of the fuselage, just behind the front wing, a small opening lets you reach in and make the connection between the elevator and the control stick. Plug in the two rudder booms, held in place with one bolt each, and connect rudder linkages to the pedals.

The gas tanks are the spaces in the leading edges of each main wing's root and were formed when you glued the two halves together. The cavities are lined with PVC foam which is impervious to fuel, and thus makes a "wet" wing possible. Each wing tank holds four gallons. The Fuji engine will burn one gallon per hour at 55 mph. Since you're only supposed to use the engine when you need it, which may not be often on a good soaring day, you have a lot of range.

George Applebay is happy with the proven and reliable Fuji, but suspects that some customers who buy his sailplanes would demand an electric starter. He has his eye on some other engines which provide this. Of course, push-button starting is nice, but besides the extra expense it requires the addition of a six or seven pound battery to the airplane as well as the starter itself (he would use a ground-rechargeable battery, however, instead of adding a generator). That battery would make a full electrical system possible, which the same people would probably also want. But with a fuel pump, electronic ignition and possibly a wing-milling prop helping you in flight (after the first pull), starting should be easy without all that.

We will now climb into the Zia and take to the air. The seat puts you into a semi-reclining position. Strap into the fancy Hooker harness that all Applebay aircraft have, pull the bubble canopy down into place and latch it, crack the throttle, and depress the toe brakes. Flip the ignition switch to "on" and reach back over your left shoulder for the handle of the starter rope. Pull it downward across your chest (not upward, or you'll bang your knuckles on the inside of the canopy) hard, as many times as it takes to fire up the engine.

After it's warmed up, taxi out to the end of the strip (the small wheels should make it tough to operate out of an unimproved field), steering with the rudder pedals. Check to be sure that the pitch-trim lever is in the takeoff (high lift) position, and go.

As the Zia accelerates to flying speed (about 30 mph at sea level), the nose lifts off and you are airborne in less than 300 feet. You are climbing like mad, because this is such an aerodynamically clean aircraft with a high lift airfoil on its 42-foot main wing, and you quickly reach 200 feet. At that altitude you begin turning toward a suspected thermal, watching the variometer on the instrument panel as you go.

The controls feel smooth and positive, since all the control surfaces are

Fig. 3-2b. The Zia re-configured as a conventionally tailed aircraft.

operated by push-pull tubes instead of cables, and all linkages have ball, roller or needle bearings. When the variometer indicates that you are in the area of lift (for example, it was showing maybe a 400 fpm climb under power, and now it shows 500 or 600), you roll the Zia into a tight turn and hold it there, going around and around until the variometer indicates that you are centered in the rising column of air.

At this point you throttle back the engine, and seeing that the lift continues, you shut if off completely. The buzz trails off into silence, or maybe only the barely audible hiss of air over the Zia's sleek body outside. Falling away and expanding below you as you spiral quietly up into the sky, are the magnificent green fields and mountains of (insert your state here). This, you tell yourself, is what it's all about.

Topping out of the thermal thousands of feet high, you begin scanning your surroundings for signs of another one (since they are invisible); or maybe you spot something interesting on the ground off in the distance and decide to investigate. Need you fire up the engine again to get up a little cruising speed? No. Here is where that mysterious pitch-trim lever comes into play.

When you push it forward, the full span ailerons simultaneously move upward in proportion to how far you moved it. It's sort of like taking off flaps: you lose some lift but gain speed. The normal function of the ailerons is not affected by the pitch-trim setting. But now you can dash along cross country toward another thermal or whatever, and when you get there haul back on the pitch-trim control to resume your slow, high lift soaring. In practice the lever works like a silent throttle on the opposite side of the cockpit: push forward for more speed, pull back for less.

This is nothing new, really. Sailplanes have had it for years, but pilots of ultralights have never had such exotic things on their simpler craft. This is the kind of thing we will be seeing on the new generation of ultralights.

When you're ready to scoot along directly back to base, you can start up the engine again. Do it the same way as before, pulling forward and downward on the rope until it's running. Under power, pitch-trim in the fast cruise position gives an easy cruise of about 60 mph, at which you are using less than half of engine's 18 hp. The Zia is smooth, slippery and easy to push. As you begin to slant down now toward your landing area, throttling back, you'd better set the wings back up in their slow/high lift configuration.

Floating down into contact with the ground, the canard wing is held up in ground effect until the main gear touches down. A little forward stick eases the nosewheel down, and the rollout is a couple hundred feet. A half hour after landing you're on your way home with the disassembled Zia following along behind the car, safely tucked away in its trailer.

Getting back to reality—always painful after such a high—I must tell you that you can't buy a Zia, yet. You can put down money on a kit, but there is already a waiting list for them, and the wait will be quite awhile.

"Because of the complexity of the technology necessary to build a safe product, it will be January, 1983 at the earliest before we can start delivering kits," George Applebay says. That's engineer talk for it takes time to get all the bugs out and get tooled up for mass production, especially since the Zia project takes a back seat to Applebay's sailplane business. George and his new test pilot, Bill Wyatt, are out at the field with the Zia every chance they get, though, and it will be no half-baked flying machine when it is finally offered to the public. And it may well set the trend in ultralights for years to come.

Will the Zia, in fact, be the ultimate ultralight? Is it even an ultralight? George Applebay calls it a motorglider. The FAA calls it an airplane. We'll just call it a fine, fun, inexpensive way to fly—another formula for a comtemporary ARV.

Specifications

Wingspan	46 ft
Length	18 ft 6 in
Height	3 ft 10 in
Wing Area	100 sq ft
Engine Make, Model, HP	Rotax 277, 28 hp
Prop Diameter/Pitch	50 in
Reduction Ratio	N.A.
Fuel Capacity/Consumption	4 gal./1 mph
Gross Weight	600 lbs
Empty Weight	300 lbs
Usefull Load	300 lbs
Wing Loading	6 psf
Power Loading	21.43 lb/hp
Design Load Factors	N.A.
Construction Time	200 man-hrs
Field Assembly Time	15 min
Pricing	$11,800 (kit), $16,500 (factory built)

Flight Performance

Velocity Never Exceed	100 mph
Top Level Speed	90 mph
Cruise Speed	70 mph
Stall Speed (in free air)	26 mph
Sea Level Climb Rate	500 fpm @ 40 mph
Takeoff Run	300 ft
Dist. Req'd. to clear 50 ft	N.A.
Landing Roll	N.A.
Service Ceiling (100 fpm climb)	N.A.
Range at Cruise	300 mi
L/D (Glide Ratio)	30-to-1
Minimum Sink Rate	150 fpm @ 35 mph

Zia
Applebay Sailplanes, Inc.
15,000 Central S.E.
Albuquerque, NM 87123   (505) 298-3042   George Applebay

Bensen B-8M Gyrocopter

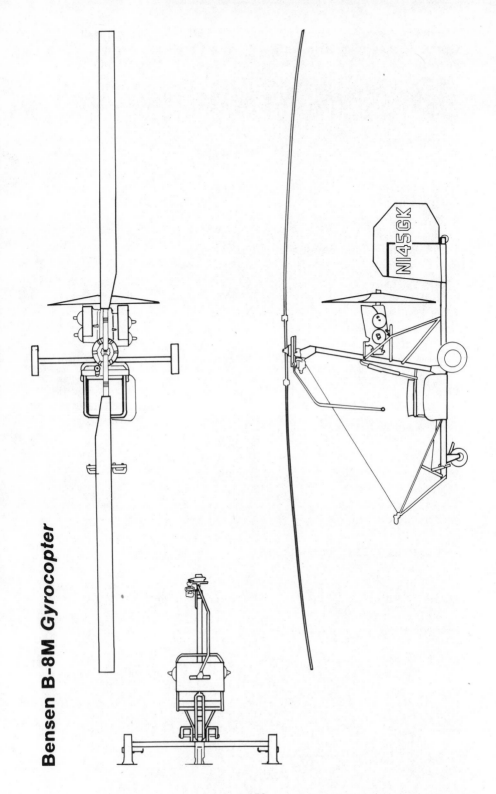

32

BENSEN *GYROCOPTER*

The Benson Gyrocopter is neither an airplane or a helicopter. It is a single occupant autogyro with a pusher engine. It generates lift by having the rotor disk tilted at a positive angle of attack. Air is forced through the rotor disk by forward and/or vertical motion causing it to rotate in a state of autorotation. It is an open air machine, but a pilot fairing may be added for pilot comfort.

The airframe is built primarily of square aluminum tubing, and features a tricycle landing gear. Aircraft quality materials and hardware are specified where appropriate, and the drawings and instructions are well presented. Assembly is bolt-together, and requires no welding, bonding or brazing in its fabrication. It will fit in the average garage without being dismantled. But, it can also be disassembled in about 20 minutes with a pair of wrenches when necessary to transport it via car top, trailer or station wagon.

The overhead, free-wheeling rotor always turns in "autorotation" independently of the engine, providing lift but no torque. This eliminates the need for a tail rotor, shafting, gear boxes, dutches, and other helicopter type components. The rotor blades consist primarily of laminated wood with a reinforcing steel spar running through the entire length of the blade.

Fig. 3-3. The Bensen Gyrocopter offers characteristics of both airplanes and helicopters. It's a different type of ARV, requiring different skills.

Fig. 3-4. Artist's sketch of Bensen Gyrocopter shows major details. Open air seating proceeded modern ultralights by fifteen years.

The rotor head uses a high strength aircraft quality aluminum alloy housing and special heavy duty FAA approved main bearing. All vital parts are said to be designed with a high safety factor, and substitutions are forbidden.

The engine is a lightweight air-cooled, four cylinder two-stroke built by McCulloch to Air Force specifications. They were used on radio controlled target drones and must be modified for man-carrying operations, but are relatively inexpensive. They develop 72 horsepower.

Although the gyrocopter, like the airplane, depends on forward motion to stay airborne, its forward speed may be reduced to zero without a stall, or loss of control. While it will not hover in calm air like a helicopter, it can descend vertically under full control and maintain altitude at a speed as low as 15 mph. In the right breeze, it can take off and land vertically, however. Because of its small size and light weight, it can turn in a small radius of only fifty feet.

Traveling in a straight line in calm air, requires a ground run of about 500 feet to takeoff—most of the run being used to accelerate the rotor from zero to flying rpm. (A one horsepower pre-rotation motor is available as an option, for shorter takeoffs.) Actual takeoff space needed, once the rotor is up to speed, is less than 100 feet. Landing in a calm is done by flaring out the glide from 40 to 7 mph, attesting the descent and rolling to a stop within 20 feet.

Apart from the "stall-less" characteristics of the rotor and the gyro's capacity for very slow flights, the craft is said to handle much like a high wing monoplane, with none of the extreme control sensitivities of pure helicopters. Power failure in a gyro does not require a reduction of collective pitch (there is none to adjust) as in a helicopter—the rotor always operates in autorotation. Power off, the craft glides twice as far as a helicopter because of the lightly loaded rotor disk, acording to the manufacturer. Dual instruction is recommended before solo, even for licensed airplane and helicopter pilots.

The Benson Gyrocopter is not sold in ready-to-fly form. It must be constructed by the buyer from kits and registered as an amateur-built aircraft. The aircraft may be purchased piecemeal in either materials or finished kits, allowing you to purchase it at your own financial pace.

Specifications

Rotor Diameter	20 ft
Length	11 ft 3 in
Height	6 ft 9 in
Disk Area	314 sq ft
Engine Make, Model, HP	McCulloch 4318E, 72 hp two-stroke
Prop Diameter/Pitch	48 in/ 20 in
Reduction Ratio	1-to-1
Fuel Capacity/Consumption	6 gal/4.5 gph
Gross Weight	500 lbs
Empty Weight	247 lbs
Useful Load	253 lbs
Disk Loading	1.59 psf
Power Loading	
Design Load Factors	+9
Construction Time	200 man-hrs
Field Assembly Time	20 min
Pricing	N.A.

Flight Performance

Top Level Speed	85 mph
Cruise Speed	60 mph
Min. Level Speed (in free air)	15 mph
Landing Speed	7 mph
Sea Level Climb Rate	1000 fpm
Takeoff Run	300 ft
Dist. Req'd. to clear 50 ft	N.A.
Landing Roll	20 ft
Service Ceiling	12,500 ft
Range at Cruise	90 mi

Bensen B-8M Gyrocopter
Bensen Aircraft Corp.
P.O. Box 31047
Raleigh, NC 27612
(919) 787-4224
Igor Bensen

"The good thing about early aviation was that in those days, designers flight tested their own machines." These words were spoken by Igor Sikorsky when Bensen first met him in the summer of 1939. Then he added with a twinkle in his eye: "That way poor designs and designers eliminated themselves."

Sikorsky was Bensen's high school idol long before I met him and his team of co-workers who developed the first successful helicopter, the VS-300. Although Bensen's family knew the Sikorskys in Kiev before the Russian revolution and he had studied in his physics class in school about Sikorsky's pioneering the first multi-engine airplane, it was a small miracle that he met him face-to-face that fateful day in 1939. The course of his life was decided right then and there.

Igor Sikorsky is the recognized "father" of the modern helicopter. What is not generally known is that in 1939 Sikorksy was finding that his third career in aviation (he had previously built large landplanes, then large flying-boats) was not being taken seriously by the industrial community, a state of affairs which dismayed and discouraged him. It is a matter of record that the first Sikorsky helicopters were ordered not by American commercial or military interests but by Britain's Royal Navy.

Meeting Sikorsky was an unforgettable experience in itself, for the young Bensen. Like Orville Wright, who was met later, he was a mild-mannered and soft-spoken man. Yet, in 1939, behind this gentle appearance, there was an intense man with the willpower of steel. The obduracy of his own parent company (United Aircraft) in not supporting his decision to cast his lot with the helicopter, and the rest of the industrial community treating him as a misguided maverick, had fired this man's willpower with a consuming determination to transform his vision into reality. His team of co-workers was possessed by the same enthusiasm. History proved them right.

Having been exposed to Sikorksy's inspiring and contagious enthusiasm, Bensen decided to follow in his footsteps. He was unable to accept Sikorsky's invitation to join him at Sikorsky Aircraft, as World War II intervened and Bensen had to set his own course. This turned out to be both a setback and a blessing. Having joined the General Electric Company as a research engineer, Bensen originated and supervised independent rotary-wing developments from autogyros to jet-propelled helicopters. His 11-year stint with the giant electro-mechanical company which led America into the age of jet propulsion would make an interesting chapter in itself. Suffice it to say, Bensen became a licensed airplane, autogyro and helicopter test pilot and pioneered such developments as the first ramjet helicopter, automatic rotor stabilization, rotary-wing glider (later named the "gyroglider"), pressure-jet helicopter (the giant Hughes-GE XH-17 "Sky Crane"), Rotochute air brake and other projects. His contacts with Sikorsky continued throughout the years at both profesional and personal levels. He remained Bensen's teacher, mentor and inspiring guide to the end of his life.

Bensen Aircraft Formed

Bensen left G.E. in 1951 for a two-year engagement with the Kaman Helicopter Company as their chief research engineer. Then in 1953, he formed Bensen Aircraft Corporation in Raleigh, North Carolina. His five basic goals were:

1. Aim at the development of a mass-producible "People's Flying Machine" capable of door-to-door transportation.
2. Make it inherently stable, easy to control and forgiving of small errors.
3. Conduct all developments on the smallest practical scale to cut down research time and costs. (This is why all Bensen prototypes are single-seaters.)
4. Test fly his own designs. The designer is the best man to spot functional deficiencies in his design and to correct them long before they become disasters.
5. Strive for simplicity and resort to complexity only when simplicity fails.

The amount of exploratory development work done within these guidelines is little short of amazing, as the photographs on these pages illustrate. The Bensen Aircraft Corporation is now on its eighteenth basic prototype model and has acquired a host of experimental data that would fill the engineering files of a major aerospace company. Another precious element comes into play when a great wealth of experimental data is collected—discovery. In aviation it happens so rarely nowadays (like the discovery of the laminar airfoil and coke-bottle "area rule" for instance) that it is assumed to be almost extinct. In the course of over 30 years of experimentation, Bensen Aircraft has run across a number of such discoveries which have not yet been made public. Nevertheless, they form the basis and explanation of some of the "impossible" performance characteristics of Bensen flying machines.

How It Started

When Bensen Aircraft was launched, it relied heavily on the promise of research contracts from the US Armed Forces. One of them was the ramjet-powered Model B-5 helicopter, another was the HEPARS project (High Efficiency Propulsion and Rotor System), later designated the Model B-4 "Sky Scooter" helicopter. It was a stroke of bad luck, or perhaps a blessing in disguise, that late in 1953 the US-Korean war ended and military research funds were abruptly cut off. Bensen Aircraft looked for other means of survival.

At about that time the widely-read American boy scout's magazine *"Boy's Life"* published an old General Electric publicity photo of the first "Gyro-glider" in flight with Bensen at the controls. The caption said that the machine was "so simple to build and fly, any high-school boy could master it." G.E. was swamped with inquiries which they could not answer, so they forwarded them to Bensen. Overnight they found themselves flooded with requests for rotorcraft building plans and kits. So they removed the ramjets from our B-5 helicopter and converted it into the Gyro-glider. Building plans were at first sold for $10 a set and the first kits for $100. Several large hobby magazines, such as *"Popular Science"* and *"Mechanix Illustrated,"* praised the new "$100 flying machine" in their August, 1954, issues, and were later followed by the multi-million-copy *"Life"* magazine. This massive publicity made Bensen Aircraft a major and permanent supplier to the "build-it-yourself" hobby market.

The Most Popular Homebuilt

All the models of rotorcraft which Bensen Aircraft has developed in the intervening 23 years cannot be described here. The most we can do is to review the major highlights and some milestones.

Aircraft home-building was officially born in 1953, at about the same time as Bensen Aircraft, when the FAA passed an airworthiness regulation licensing home-built aircraft in a new "amateur-built, experimental" category. Until recently, the aviation community treated these "home-builts" as poor country cousins; now, however, the FAA acknowledges that there are over 12,000 home-built aircraft in existence, some of which far outperform commercially-built models. Many new technologies have been developed by home-build enthusiasts, and their annual convention in Oshkosh is the largest event on the aviation calendar.

Some 2,000 Bensen Model B-8M Gyrocopters are currently flying, a figure that makes it the world's most popular home-built aircraft. Altogether, more than 4,000 have been built throughout the world, but many have fallen victim to natural attrition and inactivity.

World Records Set

For many years Bensen felt the burden of a stigma, as Sikorsky did in 1939. The aviation community was not taking his efforts seriously. To gain status and to get international recognition he did what Sikorsky did with his VS-300—set several official world records. It was not difficult, because the B-8M Gyrocopter was classified by the FAI (Fédération Aéronautique Internationale) as an "autogyro" and there were not records for autogyros (gyroplanes) at that time. In May and June, 1967 six world records for distance, speed and altitude were set for this type of aircraft. Four still stand. Two, the 3 km and 15 km record speed runs, were set along the beach at Kitty Hawk, the birthplace of aviation, using the Wright brother's monument as the starting point.

Popular Rotorcraft Association Formed

In 1962, in company with eight rotorcraft pioneers, Bensen founded the Popular Rotorcraft Association which within 10 years grew to a membership of 13,000. The PRA has some 50 Chapters throughout the world. Czechoslovakia alone, has 400 members. Builders of Bensen gyrocopters have been recorded in all 50 states and in 110 other countries. In 1972, Bensen retired as its founder-president and passed the reins to younger and abler hands.

The PRA's annual conventions were held alternately in North Carolina and California for 15 years, but in more recent times in Rockford, Illinois. As many as 110 Bensen gyrocopters have attended these meetings and the movement is growing.

Military Orders

At first, Bensen Aircraft sought military sponsorship for its research projects, but as time went on it became discouraged by the vast amount of unproductive paperwork that went with them. Highly-skilled personnel with priceless creative talent spent too much time writing reports and preparing proposals which went no further than filing cabinets. So it was decided to do all research independently and sell the finished products to the military services. Many Bensen gyrocopters and associated hardware have been sold to the US Army, Navy, Air Force and Marine Corps. In addition, Bensen products were supplied to NASA, the FAA, many universities and several major aerospace companies. The Bensen B-8M Gyrocopter has received the US Air Force designation of X-25, and one is currently exhibited in the Air Force Museum at Wright Field AFB in Dayton, Ohio. The famous "Spirit of Kitty Hawk" Gyrocopter which set world records is exhibited in the Smithsonian National Air and Space Museum in Washington.

Bensen gyrocopters have also been used in several interesting research projects conducted by other agencies. One of them was Kaman Aircraft's "Saver" project, a flying ejection seat. In other military projects the gyrocopter was remotely controlled by radio while carrying aloft electronic surveillance equipment, television cameras, etc. In all such cases Bensen supplied finished test-flown gyrocopters and trained the pilots and mechanics needed for their operation. So far, there has not been a single fatal accident with such Bensen-built aircraft. A number of military pilots and mechanics subsequently built their own private gyrocopters.

Why "Gyrocopter"?

The name "Gyrocopter" was coined to reflect in one word the dual nature of the basic Bensen design. It combines flight characteristics of the GYROplane and heliCOPTER. Its rotor blades are set in autorotative pitch, yet the rotor is powered in flight. In its present configuration it cannot hover, but it is capable of vertical takeoffs and landings, and represents a major advance over the old-style autogyro "jump takeoff" technique. The aircraft is always ready for power-off glide without any

159

changes to its controls. This is especially significant when the pilot experiences partial power failure. Many helicopters and pilots have been lost in the past when a power failure was not immediately followed by pilot-initiated autorotating procedure. This hazard is entirely absent from Bensen machines. The pilot does not even have the collective control stick to manipulate.

Landings are normally made with power off or partial power. Cyclic flare alone arrests all forward motion when the rotor is tilted aft to its full travel. Actually, the recommended technique is to land with a slight forward roll to eliminate any chance of a side drift at the moment of touchdown. Unlike helicopters, which normally use full power to land, gyrocopters land power off. This requires much less pilot skill and does not expose the occupants to risk in the event of engine malfunction during the landing approach. Because of the absence of tail rotors, gyrocopters use relatively larger rotor diameters and tilt them further back, both of which contribute to greater "floatability" and time reserve during the landing.

All of this spells increased safety for the occupants and simpler pilot techniques than are built into today's helicopters. This is proved by the fact that about 50 percent of today's gyrocopter pilots had not received instruction in any other type of aircraft or flown solo in either airplanes or helicopters. Bensen gyrocopters are also roadable; they are capable of travelling on streets and roads like motor scooters. In many states in the US they need not even be licensed as ground vehicles. This capability not only provides "door-to-door" transportation, but extends a pilot's ability to travel on the ground whenever he deems it unsafe to fly.

Hovering Gyrocopter At Least

Although Bensen Aircraft had built many models of flying machines capable of hovering, it was not until 1976 that they arrived at a truly practical hovering machine. It was named the Model B-18 "Hover-Gyro" and retained its generic name "gyrocopter." It can be described as a gyrocopter with two coaxial counter-rotating rotors. The upper rotor is larger in diameter, and its blades are set in autorotative pitch. The lower rotor has automatic collective pitch control which responds to engine power. Both are power driven. A pusher engine and propeller provide forward thrust and yaw control.

One is tempted to classify the "Hover-Gyro" as a helicopter because it does everything a conventional helicopter does: hovers, flies sideways and backwards. But, better judgment tells us not to classify it as a "helicopter," because it is so different from conventional helicopters. It is normally landed power off and has no manual collective pitch control; in forward flight it assumes a level attitude, not nose-down; it has no tail rotor and no torque compensation problems. The FAA correctly classified the prototype as a "gyrocopter," which is the name for the new category of powered-rotor autogyros. Aviation authorities in other countries may follow the FAA's lead. It is hoped they do, because pilot skill requirements for helicopters would be useless for flying gyrocopters and vice-versa.

160

Ironically, it wasn't until after man had acquired the technology to land on the moon that aircraft designers succeeded in making flight affordable for all. Light aircraft, gliders, hang gliders, and ultralights were steps in the right direction. The gyrocopter is yet another approach to flying for the average working man. . .another ARV.

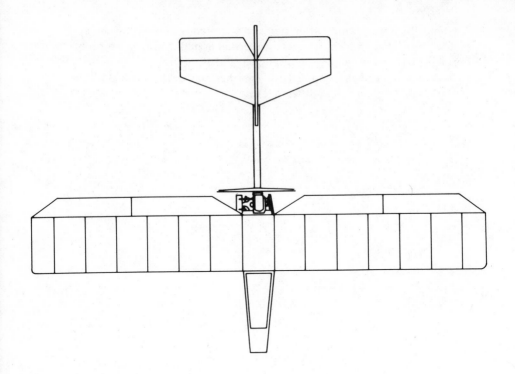

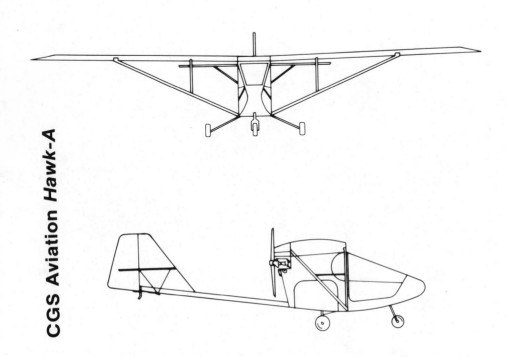

CGS Aviation _Hawk-A_

33
CGS AVIATION *HAWK*

The Hawk is a single engine pusher, high wing monoplane with a totally enclosed cabin. It features three-axis controls, plus four position flaps.

The airplane is contructed primarily of aluminum tubing with a truss type of fuselage and ladder frame wing. Two struts tie each wing panel to the fuselage, which has removeable side panels. Landing gear can be either taildragger, tricycle or pontoons, depending on personal requirements.

The wing frame is constructed of a 2¼ inch diameter aluminum leading edge and a 1¾ inch diameter rear spar. Flaps and ailerons are hinged to the rear spar. Preformed aluminum ribs are placed in the dacron covering, shapes the airfoil. The compression ribs are strengthened by gussets. Drag and anti-drag bracing runs between the bays formed by the compression ribs.

A unique curved tailboom extends from the bottom of the fuselage, supporting the empennage. The tail group forms a standard cruciform with separate fin, rudder, stabilizer and elevator. The moveable surfaces are large and provide ample control at low speeds, especially since they are immersed in the propwash. Structurally, the horizontal stabilizer is mounted a third of the way up the fin and strut braced to the tailboom.

The powerplant is the popular Cuyuna 430R with reduction drive. It features a quiet efficient muffler and turns a large diameter laminated wooden propeller, pusher fashion.

The Hawk's airfoil is the University of Illinois developed U1-1720, providing good lift-to-drag ratios. It does not have a sharp breaking stall—the Hawk would rather mush. Upon release of the back pressure on the

Fig. 3-5. CGS "Hawk" Model A is similar to the Model B ultralight version, which took first place in the 1983 ARV fly-off ultralight division. Model A is heavier and faster than Model B, and requires a license to fly.

stick, the Hawk's nose falls through slightly and the airplane starts flying again.

The Hawk's standard controls feature a joy stick controlled elevator and ailerons, rudder pedals, flap handle and throttle quadrant. Differential ailerons minimize adverse yaw. In general, the Hawk handles much like a J-3 Cub with gentle, predictable characteristics.

The kit comes complete with engine. Components are already cut, bent, sewn and machined. The wing, tail and control surfaces are factory built and ready for covering. The fuselage is pre-bent and the bulkhead mounted. No welding or machinery is required.

Optional accessories include: dual CHT, dual EGT, tachometer, airspeed indicator, compass, wheel pants, strobe and position lights, cabin heater, electric starter, dope and fabric surfaces, and the Spitfire liquid cooled engine. The aircraft can be flown with the side curtains on or off and is available from CGS Aviation, Inc.

Specifications

Wingspan	28 ft 10 in
Length	20 ft 8 in
Height	6 ft 10½ in
Wing Area	135 sq ft
Engine Make, Model, HP	Cuyuna 430R, 35 hp
Prop Diameter/Pitch	60 in/30 in
Reduction Ratio	2.37-to-1
Fuel Capacity/Consumption	5 gal/2.45 gph
Gross Weight	550 lbs
Empty Weight	270 lbs
Useful Load	280 lbs
Wing Loading	4.07 psf
Power Loading	15.71 lb/hp
Design Load Factors	+4, -3
Construction Time	100 man-hrs
Field Assembly Time	20 min
Pricing	$16,900

Flight Performance

Velocity Never Exceed	80 mph
Top Level Speed	63 mph
Cruise Speed	55-60 mph @ 75% power
Stall Speed (in free air)	26 mph (with full flaps)
Sea Level Climb Rate	600 fpm @ 45 mph
Takeoff Run	150 ft
Dist. Req'd. to clear 50 ft	N.A.
Landing Roll	95 ft (with full flaps)
Service Ceiling (100 fpm climb)	N.A.
Range at Cruise	100 mi

| L/D (Glide Ratio) | 8.85-to-1 @ 42 mph |
| Minimum Sink Rate | 250 fpm @ 30 mph |

Hawk Model A
CGS Aviation, Inc.
1305 Lloyd Road
Wickliffe, OH 44092
(216) 943-3064
Gary Grissinger

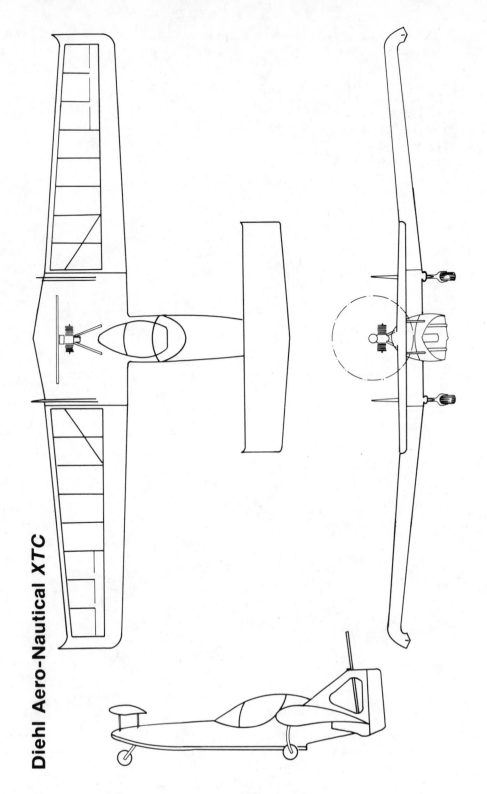

Diehl Aero-Nautical *XTC*

34

DIEHL AERO-NAUTICAL
XTC

The XTC is an amphibious, shoulder wing canard pusher with retractable landing gear and a steerable nosewheel. It features three-axis aerodynamic controls and is constructed of composite materials. It took second place in the lightplane division of the 1983 ARV Fly Off Competition.

The design of the aircraft is the result of the cooperative effort of two men, Dan Diehl and Ernest Koppe. They had met back in 1975 through a common interest in KR's (featured elsewhere in this volume). Diehl had built and flown a KR-2, while Koppe was publisher of the KR newsletter. For two years they had discussed various design concepts via long distance telephone, until they both lived in Oklahoma by Fall 1981.

At that point, Diehl, Koppe and Ken Winter, a friend and aeronautical engineer with canard experience, decided on the following design parameters for the XTC:

• Meet the proposed requirements for an ultralight aircraft—at that time, foot launching was still practiced, but considered out of the question.

• Canard configuration—recent acceptance of canards by the general flying populace, plus their proven safety features made this choice easy.

• Amphibious capability—Diehl and Koppe both enjoyed flying and water sports. They felt the amphibian offered them the most fun/utility for their efforts.

Fig. 3-6. Diehl Aero-Nautical "XTC" is amphibious canard of composite construction. It placed second in the 1983 ARV fly-off, lightplane division.

167

- Retractable gear—this was necessary because of the amphibious intent of the design. They wanted an ultralight that could be assembled on land, taxi down a boat ramp, retract the gear and become a flying boat. The XTC would fly off water and land in a cleared field and vice-versa.
- A stall speed of 20 mph or less—this, of course, was a tall order. The designers knew they would need a lot of wing area to achieve this, but what airfoil? They considered modifying one they were familiar with but realized the results would be unpredictable. They then contacted NASA who suggested the Eppler 748—a new computer generated laminar flow airfoil. It was nearly 20% thick and definitely required the smooth finish of composites in order to reach its potential.
- Composite construction—the designers believed that composites were the wave of the future in aircraft construction. Besides, they had both accumulated a lot of composite experience over the years—being involved in KR's and felt quite comfortable with the techniques.
- Three-axis control system—no explanation necessary. This is the only way to control an airplane.

As time went on and the prototype was developed, the XTC gained weight, putting it out of the originally intended ultralight category. It is now considered a lightplane, and that's the category it competed in as an ARV.

Kits are manufactured using aircraft materials and specifications, according to the factory. The fiberglass fuselage and wing panels are premolded, while the landing gear and control system assemblies are prefabricated. It is claimed the aircraft can be built with everyday shop tools. Construction time is estimated at 200 man-hours.

Flying wise, the XTC appears to be the best of the group. It scored a 20 out of 20 in the ARV lightplane division fly off—the highest flight score of the competition. It features typical canard characteristics. Since it is amateur-built, prospective XTC flyers must have at least a student pilot's license.

The factory is busy developing a two-seater, which will enable interested pilots to get checked out by his dealer before purchasing the single seater. Options include both ballister and hand deployed parachutes.

Specifications

Wingspan	32 ft
Length	15 ft
Height	4 ft 8 in
Wing Area	147 sq ft
Engine Make, Model, HP	KFM, 107ER, 25 hp
Prop Diameter/Pitch	54 in/22 in
Reduction Ratio	2.1-to-1
Fuel Capacity/Consumption	10 gal/1.8 gph
Gross Weight	560 lbs
Empty Weight	330 lbs

Useful Load	230 lbs
Wing Loading	3.9 psf
Power Loading	23.2 lb/hp
Design Load Factors	FAR 23 Utility
Construction Time	200 man-hrs
Field Assembly Time	7 min
Pricing	$6,600

Flight Performance

Velocity Never Exceed	80 mph
Top Level Speed	68 mph
Cruise Speed	56 mph @ 55% power
Stall Speed (in free air)	32 mph
Sea Level Climb Rate	500 fpm @ 45 mph
Takeoff Run	150 ft
Dist. Req'd. to clear 50 ft	450 ft
Landing Roll	150 ft
Service Ceiling (100 fpm climb)	11,000 ft
Range at Cruise	300 mi
L/D (Glide Ratio)	14-to-1 @ 45 mph
Minimum Sink Rate	200 fpm @ 43 mph

XTC

Diehl Aero-Nautical
1855 No. Elm
Jenks, OK 74037
(918) 299-4445
Dan Diehl

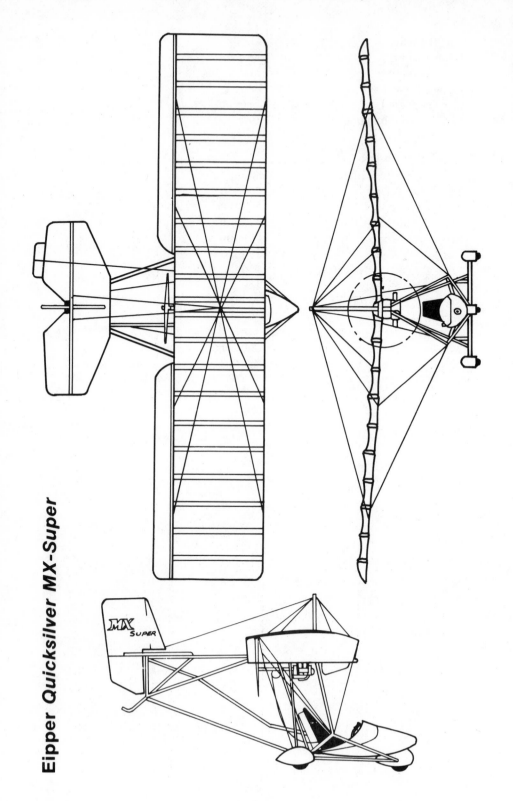

Eipper Quicksilver MX-Super

35

EIPPER *QUICKSILVER MX SUPER*

The Quicksilver MX Super is a tricycle landing geared, high wing pusher monoplane, which is a modification of the ultralight MX. The Super features a beefed-up airframe and a larger engine. It is capable of limited aerobatics.

The Quicksilver's airframe can only be described as simple and basic, to the point of being an almost irreduceable minimum. It is your basic end loaded tension structure. The airframe consists primarily of an anodized aluminum tubing structure, held together by stainless steel cables and covered with pre-sewn dacron sailcloth. The wing is constructed in a ladder type frame of leading and trailing edge tubes, with compression members serving as "rungs." A kingpost above the wing center supports the wing and tail against negative loads.

Fittings consist of stainless steel (tangs and brackets, and injection molded saddels and plugs). The Super is available, only as an amateurbuilt kit. It features a no-weld, bolt-together assembly. A unique adjustable telescoping kingpost eliminates the need for turnbuckles or other wire tensioning devices.

Fig. 3-7. The "Quicksilver MX-Super" in one of its more normal attitudes, under the able guidance of Lyle Byrum. Aircraft weighs 300 pounds, and is in amateur-built category, and is capable of limited aerobatics. It may look like an ultralight, but it is not.

A couple of aluminum tubing triangles just down from the wing center section (root tube), surrounding the pilot. The rear triangle picks up the main landing gear; while the front one is mid-way between the mains and nosewheel. A series of triangles make up the undercarriage and suspension system. Two tubular triangles are attached to the trailing edge and run aft to support the tail group. Another tubular triangle runs from the main landing gear to the trail, and a single tube from the leading edge center to the nose gear. These final members readily distinguish the Super from the ultralight MX.

The engine is hung below the root tube and drives a pusher propeller via an extension drive shaft and multi V-belt drive. The reduction drive is mounted at the rear of the root tube, turning the propeller between the booms leading to the tail.

The heart of the Super is its control system and powerplant. Elevator and ailerons are controlled by a side-mounted joystick, while the rudder is pedal driven via cables. The control system is, of course, quite responsive, compared to the ultralight MX version. The engine is the Rotax 503, which produces 46 hp, the kind of power needed to pull it through aerobatics. It is fitted with an inverted fuel system, as well.

Like the other Quicksilvers of the line, the Super features the same "Tricycle—tailgear," combining the taxiing stability of the tricycle, with the maneuverability of the taildragger. For taxiing on rough ground or making sharp turns, the pilot simply pulls back on the stick to lift the nosewheel to move into the taildragger mode. Propwash flowing over the tail surfaces allows the rudder to turn the aircraft as up elevator is applied. Only partial stick and partial throttle is required. Takeoffs and landings are, of course, made in the tricycle gear mode. A single nosewheel brake is standard.

The Super needs about 100 feet to become airborne, climbs out at 1000 fpm, and clears a 50 foot obstacle in 250 feet. Stalls are straight forward, preceded by a warning. The airplane will not drop a wing, unless desired. Final approach speed is around 40 mph, and she stalls at 29 mph. It cruises at 51 mph on 55% power.

The kit comes neatly packaged with all hardware shrink-wrapped onto printed cardboard parts boards, appropriately identified. Assembly requires 150 man hours, or over three times what it takes to build the ultralight version. The wing and tail surface coverings are pre-sewn stabilized dacron sailcloth, appropriately reinforced, that simply slips over the frame. Prefabrication is not as complete as the ultralight version, so the aircraft comes within the amateur-built ribs.

Standard equipment includes: pilot fairing, wheel pants, four-point compass, tachometer, CHT, G meter, Hobbs hour meter, inverted fuel systems, and ailerons. Nothing extra needs to be bought.

Specifications

Wingspan	30 ft
Length	18 ft 7 in

Height	8 ft 7 in
Wing Area	150 sq ft
Engine Make, Model, HP	Rotax 503, 46 hp @ 6,500
Prop Diameter/Pitch	52 in/34 in
Reduction Ratio	2-to-1
Fuel Capacity/Consumption	11 gal/2.3 gph
Gross Weight	616 lbs
Empty Weight	320 lbs
Useful Load	296 lbs
Wing Loading	4.1 psf
Power Loading	13.4 lb/hp
Design Load Factors	+6, -3
Construction Time	150 man-hrs
Field Assembly Time	30 min

Pricing: $7,995 F.O.B. Standard Equipment: Inverted fuel system, ailerons, pilot fairing, wheel pants, 4 point pilot harness, complete instrument package: altimeter, air speed indicator, compass, tachometer, cyl. head temp., G meter, Hobbs meter.

Flight Performance

Velocity Never Exceed	95 mph
Top Level Speed	75 mph
Cruise Speed	51 mph @ 55% power
Stall Speed (in free air)	29 mph
Sea Level Climb Rate	1000 fpm @ 41 mph
Takeoff Run	100 ft
Dist. Req'd. to clear 50 ft	250 ft
Landing Roll	75 ft
Service Ceiling (100 fpm climb)	10,000 ft
Range at Cruise	221.7 mi
L/D (Glide Ratio)	7.4-to-1 @ 41 mph
Minimum Sink Rate	500 fpm @ 41 mph

NOTE: MX Super is designed for *limited* aerobatics. Special aerobatic flight training required. FAA pilot and aircraft certification required. Available as a home-built kit.

Quicksilver® MX Super ®
Eipper Aircraft
1080 Linda Vista Dr.
San Marcos, CA
(619) 744-1514
Eric R. Gilliatt

Fishercraft Zippy Sport

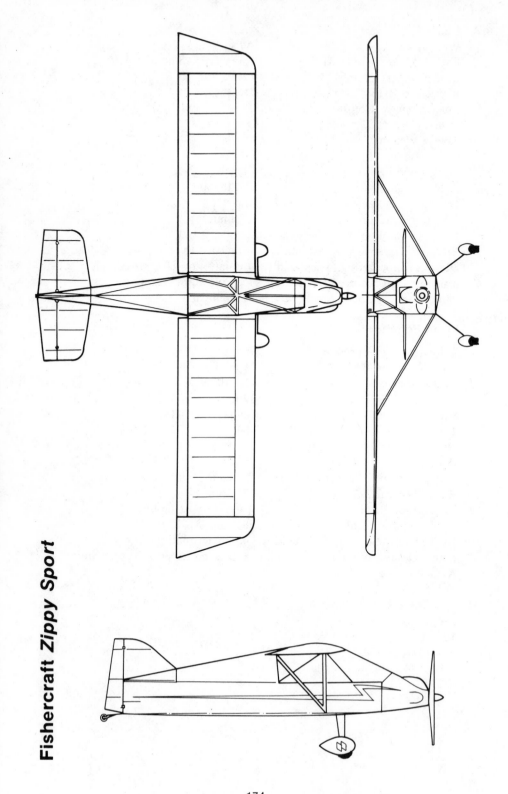

36

FISHERCRAFT
ZIPPY SPORT

Back in 1978, Ed Fisher began some original design work on a small aircraft for his own personal enjoyment. Prior to that he had built a Monnett Sonerai Formula Vee racing plane. The entire family had been interested in air racing but, Fisher's interest waned - the Formula Vee class was not developing very well. When Fisher finally did enter the 1980 Cleveland Air Races, he not only placed last but discovered it was no fun flying at 200 mph, 50 feet off the deck in heavy traffic. These experiences turned his interests to sport flying, and enabled him to establish some criteria for his own personal airplane: (1) easy to build, (2) economical, (3) strong, (4) sporty. It was also necessary that the new airplane offer good short field performance and decent cross-country capability.

Fisher began the design and construction of the Zippy Sport in the spring of 1980. Before building though, he had an aeronautical engineer do a complete stress analysis, as well as stability and control studies. He wanted the lightest airframe possible, consistent with Utility Category strength requirements.

Fisher elected to stick with conventional construction and the traditional configuration. He felt most prospective amateur builders could work with these better than composite and canards. He also believed he could achieve performance comparable to the Quickie (featured elsewhere in this book) with the basic highwing cabin monoplane layout.

Fig. 3-8. Fishercraft "Zippy Sport" features conventional construction in a traditional strut braced, high wing monoplane layout. Placed third in ARV fly-off lightplane division.

Economy was of utmost importance to Fisher because he felt too many would-be pilots as well as current pilots, were losing interest in flying because of soaring costs. Maintenance, hangar rent and high fuel use and cost needed to be addressed. The Zippy Sport minimizes these items. Maintenance is minimal and handled by the builder himself. It is not necessary to hangar the Zippy Sport because the wings are designed to be folded alongside the fuselage and the aircraft trailered home. Fuel consumption is a scant two gallons per hour of auto gasoline - not much expense here. Fuel costs will run only less than three cents per mile at cruise.

The first engine installed in the Zippy Sport was the Onan four-cycle, as used on the Quickie, but it failed to produce half of its rated power. Fortunately, by then, the ultralight movement had produced a lightweight, 30 hp two-stroke, the Cuyuna 430. The Onan was removed and the Cuyuna installed with a 2-to-1 reduction drive. The Zippy Sport now possessed the desired performance.

After the other minor changes were incorporated into the design, she was pronounced a success. Cruise was 85 mph at 60% power, and it could reach 100 mph flat out. At a fuel consumption rate of two gallons per hour, the economy was outstanding, while providing the originally specified decent cross-country performance.

Economy of construction was also achieved by using conventional materials and methods. The fuselage and tail surfaces are 4130 tubing, and the rudder and elevator are actuated via push-pull tubes. The wing features spruce spars, your choice of either wood or formed aluminum ribs, aluminum ailerons, and built-up 4130 wing tips. The entire airframe is covered with 1.702 dacron, built-up with butycate dope and finished off with acrylic enamel. The cowling and gas tank may be either sheet aluminum or fiberglass. The landing gear is a formed aluminum leaf spring with go-kart wheels and brakes. The windshield is lexan. The wings fold, allowing the Zippy Sport to be towed home.

While the current engine is the Cuyuna two-stroke, Fishercraft is constantly experimenting with others. One of these is the Carr VW twin, an 85 pound four-stroke developing approximately 27 hp. Several other four-strokes have been introduced, and some will, no doubt, be applicable.

The Zippy Sport has been flown by many different pilots with varying degrees of experience. None of these has had any difficulties, according to the factory. The controls are light but, not overly sensitive. Despite its short wheelbase, Zippy is said to land easy and roll out straight, thanks to the landing gear placement with respect to the CG.

Visibility in flight is reported to be excellent, with large side windows and a full skylight. The cockpit will accommodate a 6 ft 3 in, 220 pounder. The overall flight handling characteristics are comparable to a Taylorcraft or Luscombe, while it is gentler on the ground.

Performance is quite good, as listed below. Contact Fishercraft for plans and further information. The Zippy Sport placed third in the 1983 ARV Fly-Off Competition.

Specifications

Wingspan	26 ft 4 in
Length	17 ft 10 in
Height	5 ft
Wing Area	100.5 sq ft
Engine Make, Model, HP	Cuyuna 430 RR 30 hp
Prop Diameter/Pitch	54 in/36 in
Reduction Ratio	2.1-to-1
Fuel Capacity/Consumption	5.5 gal/2 gph
Gross Weight	600 lbs
Empty Weight	350 lbs
Useful Load	250 lbs
Wing Loading	5.9 psf
Power Loading	20 lb/hp
Design Load Factors	+4,4, -3.1
Construction Time	600 man-hrs
Field Assembly Time	30 min

Pricing: Plans-built Zippy can be built for approximately $4,000.00

Flight Performance

Velocity Never Exceed	130 mph
Top Level Speed	100 mph
Cruise Speed	85 mph @ 60% power
Stall Speed (in free air)	39 mph
Sea Level Climb Rate	800 fpm @ 70 mph
Takeoff Run	250 ft
Dist. Req'd to clear 50 ft	550 ft
Landing Roll	550 ft
Service Ceiling (100 fpm climb)	N.A. ft
Range at Cruise	250 mi
L/D (Glide Ratio)	10-to-1 @ 65 mph
Minimum Sink Rate	400 fpm @ 70 mph

Zippy Sport
Fishercraft, Inc.
4356 Narrows Road
Perry, Ohio 44081
(216) 259-4412
Ed Fisher

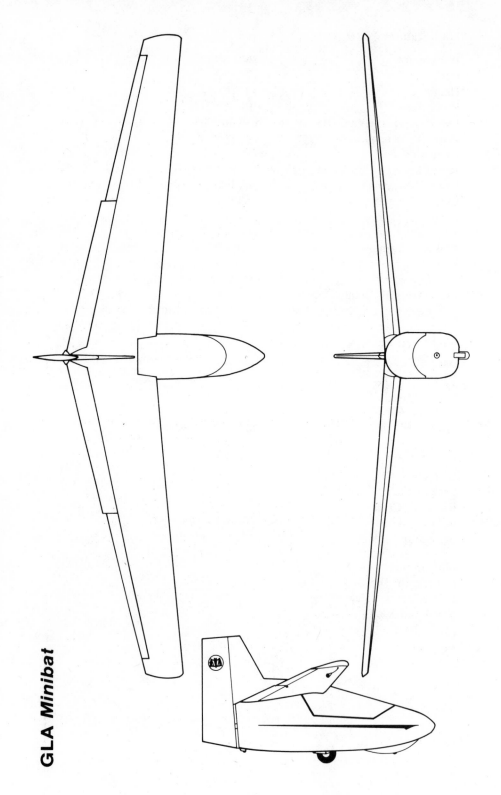

GLA *Minibat*

37

GLA *MINIBAT*

The Minibat is a tailless, swept forward sailplane, with performance comparable to the Schweitzer 1-26. An optional "sustainer" powerpack will turn it into a motorized glider capable of a slight climb. It can be launched by auto two bungee or gravity. It is the lightest of the ARV's.

The Minibat is constructed of a double walled composite monocoque utilizing Kevlar skins, S-glass spar caps and a pre-formed foam core. The spar caps carry all bending loads, the shear web carries all shear loads and the skins carry rib and torsional loads. The wing control surfaces are comprised of a single skin on a foam core with the skin and hinges carrying all loads.

The two fuselage halves are structurally tied by the seat, armrests and keel pieces, which are also double skinned Kevlar/foam composites. The wing halves are pin joined at the centerline, independent of the fuselage, and lift pins are used to transfer lifting loads to the fuselage. Landing gear, nose skid and tail skid loads are absorbed by the fuselage shell and transferred to the seat via the keel.

The rudder and fin are comprised of single skinned Kevlar/halves joined together with foam ribs and E-glass spars. Most fittings are 4130 steel stampings and/or weldments with aluminum fittings used only where significant weight savings were possible. The canopy is a fully framed, rear hinged, two piece optical quality plexiglass assembly with a clear vinyl taped joint between the two sections. It rests on the fin, when open. The main wheel is an unsprung 3.50" x 4" go-kart racing slick mounted on a molded nylon wheel with sealed ball bearings on a steel axle.

Fig. 3-9. The "Minibat" flying wing offers good performance in a tiny composite package. Features a 3 hp sustainer engine capable of limited climb, to be used essentially for producing zero sink between thermals. Propeller does not produce enough thrust for self-launching.

Cockpit ventilation is provided via a nose inlet which also serves as the pitot tube mounting. Basic instruments such as airspeed indicator, variometer, altimeter and compass are mounted in a fiberglass console between the pilot's knees. No provision for an oxygen system or a radio are included, although either may be accommodated with minor modifications.

The kit is complete, except for the engine package. All parts such as wing halves, spars, ailerons, elevators, fuselage halves, seat, rudder and fin halves, and canopy are supplied pre-molded and finished. All welded and/or machined parts are also supplied ready to use. Flat metal parts or parts that require only single bends are fabricated by the builders. Complex parts, such as the canopy frame, are supplied pre-bent by the factory.

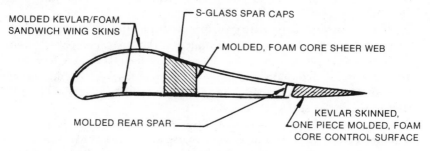

Fig. 3-10. Typical wing section as used on "Minibat" features composite construction using fiberglass, kevlar and foam.

All bonding agents, epoxies, chopped cotton, glass and microballoon fillers, filler strip Kevlar and glass fabrics are supplied as are all attaching hardware including nuts, bolts, pop rivets, rod ends, and cables.

Basic flight instruments such as airspeed, vario and altimeter are included set in cushion material, wheels, tires, tube and other necessary devices. The only items not in the kit are trim paint and interior fabric.

In addition to the engine package, other options include the Minibat's "Learn-to-Fly" tripod, extension wing panels, optional instruments, radios, bungee launching system and trailer plans. The factory may also offer a parachute system that could lower both pilot and plane to the ground.

The "Learn-to-Fly" tripod is a unique item which enables the neophyte to get the feel of the controls without leaving the ground. The main landing wheel is removed (it's located exactly at the CG) and replaced with the tripod. The tripod has a 12" to 18" limited vertical travel and provided with stops limiting both pitch and roll angles to about 20°. Initially, the student pilot can "fly" the Minibat while the tripod is securely anchored in a wind of from 12 to 35 mph. This wind is too low to develop vertical lift, but will allow the student to learn how to balance and control the aircraft and develop a feel for the control inputs required to maintain equilibrium. Later the tripod could be mounted to a truck or car top for practice while under motion when there is not enough wind.

After he has mastered the tripod training technique but before working on low altitude tows, the student must obtain a student certificate. At this point, it is also strongly recommended that dual instruction be taken before attempting towed or free flight.

Flight tests on the prototype have shown the Minibat to be stable about all axes, easy to control and very responsive to control inputs. Rudder control is said to be excellent and apparently, because of the tailless/forward swept wing arrangement, there is no limit to crosswind landing capability. The factory test pilot has successfully negotiated 90° gusting crosswinds of 20 to 35 mph without much difficulty.

The tailless design contributes a desirable feature in rough air. Whereas a conventional sailplane tends to pitch up, thus increasing the "g" loading on the wing when entering a thermal, the Minibat pitches down, unloading the wing and trying to maintain its original trim speed.

The Minibat's roll rate is considered outstanding due to the relatively short span and very low inertia wings.

The glide path control system is also unique to the Minibat, apparently having overcome the one real criticism of all flying wing designs, and that is higher landing speeds for the wing area. This is so because in landing, the elevators are deflected near their upper limit, effectively making them "negative" flaps and reducing the lifting ability of the wing. If they were deflected down like flaps, the nose would pitch down and a landing would be impossible.

The designer's solution to this "impossible" situation was to rig the control linkage to a "down" control handle so that when actuated, it converts the ailerons into up elevators. These "elevons" then provide a nose-up pitching movement which compensates the nose down pitching movement generated by the inboard flaps. This is an excellent drag configuration, what with the flap down and ailerons up, while at the same time increasing the lift of the wing and lowering the landing speed. As an added benefit, the up deflected ailerons introduce a high degree of tip washout reducing the possibility of tip stall at a time when it is most likely to occur.

Complete kits and accessories are available from GLA, Inc. An extended wing version is also available for improved performance. The L/D goes to 30, the sink rate to 138 fpm and the gross weight to 350 pounds.

Specifications

Wingspan	25 ft
Length	9 ft 4 in
Height	5 ft

Wing Area	65 sq ft
Engine Make, Model, HP	3 hp
Prop Diameter/Pitch	20 in/10 in
Reduction Ratio	1-to-1
Fuel Capacity/Consumption	½ gal/½ gph
Gross Weight	320 lbs
Empty Weight	105 lbs
Useful Load	220 lbs
Wing Loading	5 psf
Power Loading	107 lb/hp
Design Load Factor	+6, -6 (at a safety factor of 2)
Construction Time	40-60 man-hrs
Field Assembly Time	N.A.
Pricing	Send $10 for information kit

Flight Performance

Velocity Never Exceed	126 mph
Top Level Speed	88 mph
Cruise Speed	55 mph
Stall Speed (in free air)	39 mph (high sink rate mush at 38-42 mph)
Sea Level Climb Rate	50-100 fpm
Takeoff Run	N.A.
Dist. Req'd to clear 50 ft	
Landing Roll	N.A.
Service Ceiling (100 fpm climb)	N.A.
Range at Cruise	N.A.
L/D (Glide Ratio)	23-to-1 @ 55 mph
Minimum Sink Rate	3 fpm @ 43 mph

Minibat
GLA, Inc.
841 Winslow Court
Muskegon, MI 49441
(616) 780-4680
Larry Haig

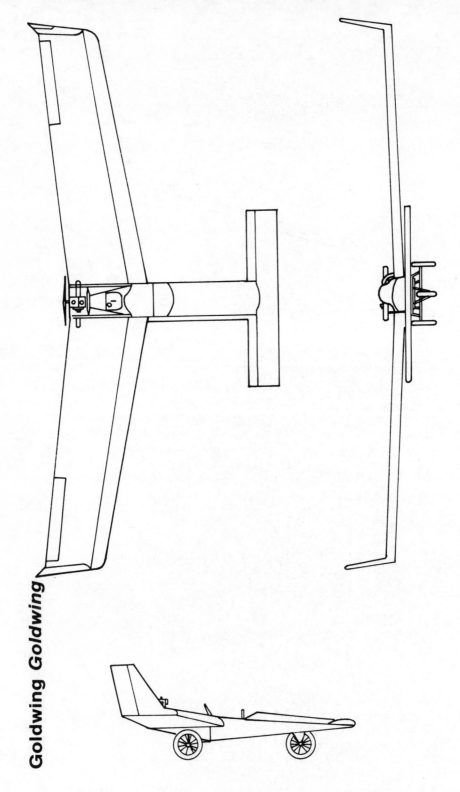

Goldwing Goldwing

38

GOLDWING *GOLDWING*

The Goldwing is an ultralight aircraft of the canard configuration. Conventional 3-axis controls are incorporated into the foam-fiberglass composite structured airframe. Handling is described as straightforward and docile with very forgiving characteristics. It is sold as a kit.

The nose-mounted canard not only provides lift, but also pitch stability and control. Winglets provide directional stability while increasing the effective aspect ratio, without a sacrifice in handling. Split rudders produce yaw while maintaining the winglet advantage. Spoilers and ailerons are used together for roll control at all speeds. The fully independent 3-axis control system enables the Goldwing to handle crosswind takeoffs and landings.

Power is provided by a two cylinder, electric start, 25 hp snowmobile engine. Full throttle at sea level gives a climb of 600 fpm at 47 mph, while power is pulled back to 75% throttle for a comfortable 500 fpm. At the economy cruise setting of 50% throttle, the airspeed holds at 50 mph while the fuel consumption drops to one gallon per hour. At higher power settings, the aircraft has been clocked at 85 mph in level flight.

High altitude performance at 9,000 feet density altitude resulted in a takeoff roll of 400 feet and a climb rate of 400 fpm.

During stall and spin testing, the Goldwing was capable of being flown with full aft stick at an indicated 27 mph, while maintaining full control at all power settings. The canard would not stall unless forced into an accelerated stall. In that case, the canard would rise above the horizon, make a gentle break at 24 mph, and then rise back up to the horizon where it would remain with full aft stick.

Fig. 3-11. Composite "Goldwing" canard began life as an ultralight, but weight and performance exceeded FAR 103, putting it into the lightplane category.

Spins were attempted repeatedly by forcing an accelerated stall, then kicking in full rudder. The nose dropped down to the horizon, while the wingtip dropped into a 30 degree bank, resulting in a slow speed turn. The Goldwing appears to be very spin resistant.

Specifications

Wingspan	30 ft
Length	12 ft
Height	5 ft (Winglet)
Wing Area	128 sq ft
Engine Make, Model, HP	Cuyuna 430, 30 hp
Prop Diameter/Pitch	36 in/24 in
Reduction Ratio	1-to-1
Fuel Capacity/Consumption	6 gal/1½ gph
Gross Weight	550 lbs
Empty Weight	300 lbs
Useful Load	250 lbs
Wing Loading	4.3 psf
Power Loading	18.3 lb/hp
Design Load Factors	+3.8, -1.8
Construction Time	170 man-hrs
Field Assembly Time	15 min
Pricing	$4895.00

Flight Performance

Velocity Never Exceed	70 mph
Top Level Speed	70 mph
Cruise Speed	65 mph @ 75% power
Stall Speed (in free air)	26 mph (Canard)
Sea Level Climb Rate	800 fpm @ 45 mph
Takeoff Run	160 ft
Dist. Req'd to clear 50 ft	N.A.
Landing Roll	200 ft
Service Ceiling (100 fpm climb)	13,000 ft
Range at Cruise	200 mi
L/D (Glide Ratio)	16-to-1 @ 42 mph
Minimum Sink Rate	325 fpm @ 35 mph

Goldwing ST
Goldwing, Ltd.
Amador Co. Arpt., Bldg. 3
Jackson, CA 95642
(209) 223-0384
Reklai Selazar

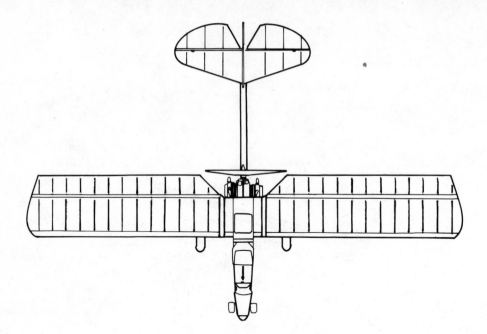

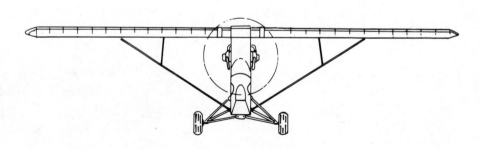

Hovey *Beta Bird*

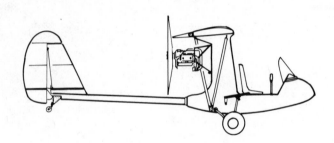

39

HOVEY *BETA BIRD*

The Beta Bird is an open air seating, strut braced wing pusher monoplane with taildragger landing gear, powered by a VW engine. It evolved as a follow-on to the designer's successful WD-II ultralight biplane of the early 70's. It is the result of correspondence with hundreds of amateur builders who wanted a higher performance, more rugged and useful airplane.

The criteria suggested by the various enthusiasts shaped up as follows:
1) Simple, fast construction methods for unskilled builders.
2) Low cost with readily available materials or kits furnished.
3) VW engine conversion power plant.
4) Short field take-off and landing capability.
5) Stability and control characteristics consistent with low time pilot skills.
6) Suitability for either on or off airport operation.
7) Range capability for cross-country flights.
8) Small size and light weight.
9) Folding wings for ease of transport and storage.

The open seating arrangement used on the WD-II was continued, however the fuselage width was increased from six to fourteen inches and, a nose fairing, instrument panel and windshield were added. The high wing monoplane configuration was used to simplify construction and to provide an improved lift-to-drag ratio. The aluminum tube boom tail support worked well on the WD-II, so it was used again on the Beta Bird. The

Fig. 3-12. Hovey "Beta Bird" offers decent cruise performance for an open air airplane. Its powered by a VW conversion, and can be operated out of unprepared fields, much like an ultralight.

formed aluminum tube design was used for wing ribs, with refinements using sheet gussets and pop rivets for attachments.

Large wheels and tires were added for rough field operations, while individual hydraulic toe brakes provide improved ground handling. Short field takeoff and landing characteristics are obtained by using drooperons (ailerons that can also be simultaneously lowered) to achieve a significant increase in lift coefficient. A much larger percentage of wing area is devoted to the full span drooperons than is normal practice. (This is acceptable because of the small speed difference between stall and cruise). A small droop angle of both drooperons thus produces the desired large change in lift, without appreciable loss of roll control. A simple mixer device coordinates stick roll control inputs with droop handle activation.

Excellent flight handling, stability and performance occur in the Beta Bird as a result of low power loading, light wing loading and large tail surfaces. The designer claims the feeling of mobility and freedom of flight, particularly at low altitudes, are indescribable.

Storage and transport are simplified by the wings being foldable. They rotate about a pin joint in the rear spar. The front spar joint is disconnected by putting a verticle pin at each joint.

Construction of the Beta Bird is unique. It not only utilizes aluminum tubing for its basic structure, but also combines wood frame, sheet aluminum, welded steel tube, and epoxy/fiberglass structure in local areas where simplicity and the strength to weight characteristics of a particular material are advantageous. Designs used in each of these areas do not require any special tools or advanced skills. None of the designs are said to be critical from a quality standpoint, except for engine mount welding. They will certainly expose the builder to a variety of construction methods.

Aluminum tubing, sheet gussets and pop riveting are used extensively for wing rib, tail group and tail boom installations. The high strength Monet "Break Stern" hollow blind rivets are easily installed by one person working alone using a common pop rivet puller tool. Fiberglass layups are used for the nose fairing, dome nose and, fuel tank. Detailed procedures are given for fabrication, and, in any event, these items are not critical for strength or aesthetics and can be patched extensively. Complete materials kits are available to the builder who wishes to make all the parts himself. Otherwise, most of the parts requiring metal cutting or welding may be purchased.

The basic fuselage pod is constructed of a spruce stringer and stick framework covered with ⅛ inch plywood skins. A four inch diameter aluminum tailboom is integrated into the aft end of the pod, and mounts the tail group at the other end. The nose fairing and instrument panel are constructed from sheet metal, fastened by pop rivets.

The wing is a basic ladder frame of spruce spars and compression members. Drag and anti-drag loads are taken internally by appropriate diagonal bracing. Wing ribs are simply formed out of ½" aluminum tubes. All can be made in a single evening. The wing leading edge uses one inch urethane foam stub ribs to support a wrap around aluminum sheet forward of the front spar. The drooperons are attached directly to the rear spar by three short sections of piano hinge. A two inch torque tube handles the loads from root to tip.

The tail group consists of a fin/rudder and stabilizer/elevator. The basic frames are aluminum tubing joined with aluminum gussets, pop riveted in place. Cable braces the fin to the stabilizer.

Ground handling is direct and positive with no tendency to ground loop, or nose over with application of brakes. Lift off occurs at 50 mph and climb out at 400 fpm is at 60 to 65 mph. Sixteen degrees of droop are used for takeoff and nine degrees for climb out. Cruise is at 80 mph and 3200 rpm. The windshield tends to form a streamline bubble of still air around the pilot with airflow pasing at the elbow line and the top of the head. The pusher prop tends to draw off base drag from the fuselage pylon and engine. The cruise drag of the Beta Bird is thus quite low for an open type configuration, allowing it to outrun an 85 hp Cub with two on board.

The drag increases noticeably with power off. The glide ratio with zero droop, power off appears to be about 6-to-1. Landing approach is made at 65 mph with slight power. Flare at 55 mph and chop power. Deceleration is rapid. Landing is made with 16 degrees droop in still air and 9 degrees with 10 mph or more wind.

It is difficult to reach the 40 mph stall speed without full power. At low power settings the aircraft will mush, at 45 to 50 mph. Slower speeds just increase the sink rate. No pitch down or roll-off on a wing has been detected under any condition. No spins have been attempted to date and, intentional spins are prohibited. The aircraft exhibits no tendency to enter unintentional spins.

Specifications

Wingspan	25 ft 6 in
Length	17 ft
Height	6 ft
Wing Area	86 sq ft
Engine Make, Model, HP	VW conversion, 1200-1600cc, 45 hp
Prop Diameter/Pitch	54 in/24 in
Reduction Ratio	1-to-1
Fuel Capacity/Consumption	7½ gal/3½ gph
Gross Weight	630 lbs
Empty Weight	405 lbs
Useful Load	225 lbs
Wing Loading	7.3 psf
Power Loading	14 lb/hp
Design Load Factors	+4, -1.5
Construction Time	N.A.
Field Assembly Time	N.A.
Pricing	$60 for plans (Contact Hovey for kit prices)

Flight Performance

Velocity Never Exceed	N.A.
Top Level Speed	N.A.
Cruise Speed	80 mph
Stall Speed (in free air)	45-50 mph (high sink rate mush)
Sea Level Climb Rate	400 fpm @ 60 mph
Takeoff Run	250 ft
Dist. Req'd to clear 50 ft	N.A.
Landing Roll	250 ft
Service Ceiling (100 fpm climb)	N.A.
Range at Cruise	250 mi
L/D (Glide Ratio)	6-to-1

Beta Bird
R.W. Hovey
P.O. Box 1074
Saugus, CA 91350
Bob Hovey

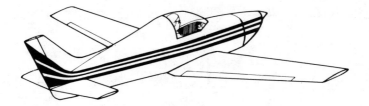

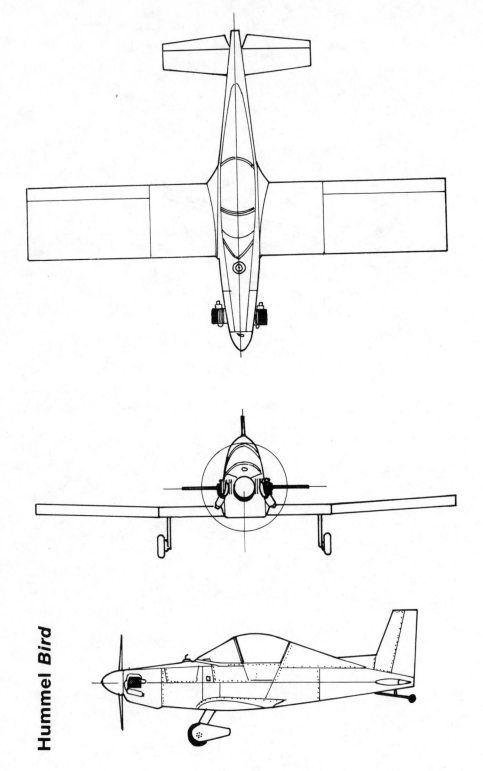

Hummel *Bird*

40

HUMMEL *BIRD*

The Hummel Bird is an all metal single place low wing monoplane with taildragger landing gear. It features a fully enclosed cockpit, and offers excellent cross-country capability. It is actually an extensive modification of the Watson Windwagon, featured elsewhere in this book.

The airframe is similar to the Windwagon, with the obvious differences being taildragger gear and an enclosed cockpit. Hummel also conducted a weight reduction program, eliminating more than 30 pounds. Things like lightening holes in spars and ribs, .016 skins on the leading edge, outer panels and the top of the wing, Dick Schreder's sailplane spar caps of 7075-T6, and an all aluminum tail spring, made it possible. The standard Windwagon weighs in at around 300 pounds, while the Hummel Bird checks in at under 270 pounds.

Hummel claims the bird can be built in only about six months of spare time, with no special tools. Also, the more difficult parts can be purchased. Hummel says there is no mystery to building a metal airplane. As an example, he forms leading edges simply by folding the sheet metal over on a carpet, without any jigs.

Hummel has apparently turned the Windwagon into a better airplane by increasing pilot comfort and protection, installing a more reliable engine and improving performance. The two front formers were heightened a couple inches to increase fuel tank capacity by one gallon, as well as improve toe clearance. The former immediately behind the pilot was heightened five inches allowing installation of a shoulder harness, while serving as part of a fairing aft the pilot. Cockpit width was increased two inches for added shoulder room, as well. One safety item lacking in the

Fig. 3-13. The Hummel "Bird" is an extensively modified version of the Windwagon, featuring pilot comfort, roll bar, and enhanced performance.

Windwagon is rollover protection. The Hummel Bird solves this problem with windshield and canopy frames of ½" square 6061-T6. The wheels were upgraded to the KR type with brakes.

The Hummel Bird kit includes essentially all materials and components to complete the aircraft, with the exception of paint. The designer intended the Bird to be polished to conserve weight and for aesthetic reasons. Painting is up to the builder.

The step-by-step construction manual is professionally drawn, and is said to be easy to comprehend. All the difficult to build parts are pre-fabricated. Parts which require welding are supplied pre-welded and parts needing extensive machining are finished. Sheet metal parts requiring elaborate forming are supplied pre-formed. It is not necessary to construct formblocks and fixtures. The primary method of construction is sheet metal with pop rivets, and the Hummel Bird can be built with basic metal working hand tools. No temperature or humidity criteria processes are involved in the construction, and a single car garage will provide all necessary room.

Hummel liked the Windwagon's curious little engine, consisting of two cylinders and half the crankcase from a VW. But, as with the airplane, he thought things should be done a little differently. He described what he did in *EAA's Sport Aviation.*

"I began my conversion by purchasing a VW engine that had thrown a rod through the case on the flywheel end. . . for $10! And I also bought some dual part heads from an engine that had swallowed a valve. . . for another $10 bucks. After cleaning and careful inspection, I found I had a low time engine that did not even require align boring of the case.

"I sawed off the case and had the required pieces welded in prior to machining the rear of the case. . . after which the pulley end became the front of the engine. Next, a piece of 6061-T6 a quarter of an inch thick was cut to form the back cover of the case. It was drilled and tapped for ¼ x 20 screws. The mag was mounted on this rear cover plate.

"The crank was magnafluxed to be sure I had a good one, then cut off as shown in the drawings. Afterwards, a ¼ inch projection was milled to drive the mag. I used a HAPI mag coupling. . . and found a two cyclinder Fairbanks Morse tractor mag in a salvage yard for $2 and had it rebuilt to like new condition for $68.

"The camshaft should be a higher lift job than stock and, I recommend the HAPI camshaft which can be bought for about $60. The timing gears are trimmed off 3/16" to make room for the flanged rear main bearing. Two are used—one in front, another in the rear.

"Using the damaged dual port heads, I cut off the damaged areas and welded the good portions together to complete the shape to fit the valve cover. The cover itself, was "sectionized" to size by cutting a slice out of the middle and welding the ends together; some with the retainer spring.

"I used a Monnet prop hub and spinner, however, a tapered shaft and hub are nice if you want to remove the hub for any reason.

"On the induction system, I used a Bendix Zenith float type carb with a

25 mm throttle plate opening. This might be too small, but Rex Taylor of HAPI says it is adequate for my 900 cc displacement. I used 92 mm cylinders, but I think 88 mm might have been sufficient—which would have eliminated the need to spend $40 to have the heads and case bored to match.

"The standard VW oil pump has plenty of volume for the two cylinders. My oil cooler is the commonly seen length of soft aluminum tubing wrapped around and epoxied to the outer section of the intake pipe. My oil temperature averages 180° to 190°. . . and an oil filter keeps the oil nice and clean.

"This nice running little two cylinder VW engine can be built for three or four hundred dollars, depending on how much you scrounge."

"How does the Hummel Bird fly, you ask? Pure joy, says Hummel. I take off in two runway lights and land in five (two on grass). This is good short field performance. In smooth air, it flys hands off and is not overly sensitive. The rudder and fin were enlarged to permit better slips and crosswind landings. It can handle 20 mph crosswinds.

"With full aft stick in a slow mush, you still have good aileron control. Stalls are clean. People who have flown it say it is just right—and that I shouldn't change anything. They especially like the rate of climb. It is the easiest to fly of any plane I have flown and, obviously, I am quite pleased with it. I am planning a pressure cowl and hope to come up with a better prop, which should improve the cruise speed.

"I flew N3765H to Oshkosh this past summer, a distance from my home in Bryan, Ohio of 345 miles, in three hours and 30 minutes. This is a block-to-block ground speed of 97 mph and includes some headwinds, crosswinds and airport patterns. I used 6.8 gallons of 100LL [Ed. 50.74 mpg]. About 45 pounds of baggage was handled with ease—including a tent, sleeping bag, air matress, food, thermos, tie downs, etc.

"I have $2400 in the airplane, including the engine, to give you an idea of the cost of building one yourself. If you want to build my version of the Windwagon, it is necessary for you to first buy the original plans for $50 from the designer, Gary Watson, Rt. 1, New Castle, TX 76372, phone (817) 862-5615.

"Then, you will need my modification drawings which I sell for $120. My address is given below. An information brochure is available for $3."

Specifications

Wingspan	18 ft 0 in
Length	13 ft 4 in
Height	3 ft 10 in
Wing Area	54 sq ft
Engine Make, Model, HP	VW Revmaster R-800, 2 cyl, 28 hp
Prop Diameter/Pitch	
Reduction Ratio	1-to-1
Fuel Capacity/Consumption	7 gal/1.8 gph

Gross Weight	520 lbs
Empty Weight	275 lbs
Useful Load	245 lbs
Wing Loading	9.63 psf
Power Loading	18.57 lb/hp
Design Load Factors	+6, -6
Construction Time	N.A. man-hrs
Field Assembly Time	20 min
Pricing	$70 for plans ($5995 for kit)

Flight Performance

Velocity Never Exceed	140 mph
Top Level Speed	122 mph
Cruise Speed	115 mph @ 70% power
Stall Speed (in free air)	45 mph (flaps down)
Sea Level Climb Rate	700 fpm
Takeoff Run	350 ft
Dist. Req'd to clear 50 ft	900 ft
Landing Roll	450 ft
Service Ceiling (100 fpm climb)	N.A.
Range at Cruise	420 mi
L/D (Glide Ratio)	15-to-1 @ 60 mph

Hummel Bird
James M. Hummel
509 E. Butler
Bryan, OH 43506
(419) 636-3390
Jim Hummel

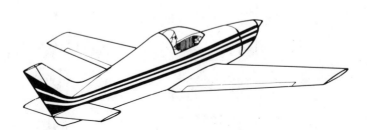

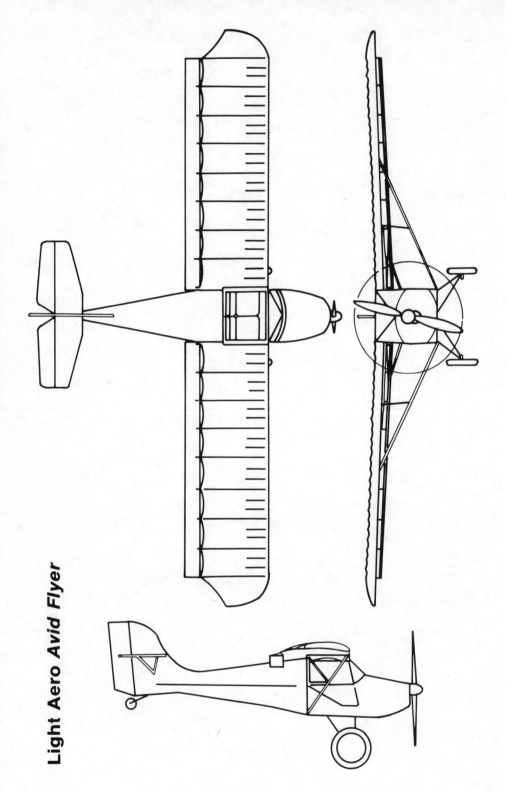

Light Aero Avid Flyer

41

LIGHT AERO *AVID FLYER*

The Avid Flyer is a high wing, two seater, cabin monoplane that can be built either in taildragger or tricycle landing gear versions. It features a conventional rudder and elevator controls, as well as unique full span, full flying flaperons. It did not enter the ARV competitions, but it is certainly a prime example of the type.

The fuselage is constructed of welded steel tubing, as are the tail surfaces. The engine is covered by a fiberglass cowl. The cabin area features large windows and a skylight. The undercarriage is steel tubing, with large wheels and tires for operation off unimproved fields. A six foot propeller is gear driven by a 43 hp Cuyuna engine.

The wings are constructed of an aluminum tubing frame with a leading edge spar, rear spar, diagonals and compression members. Wooden ribs with cap strips are bound to the leading edge and rear spar. The prefabrication full flying flaperons are hinged off of reinforced ribs. The entire structure is covered in dacron and doped.

The Avid Flyer is one of those rare cases where a dreamer's good idea is taken beyond mere drawings, and often a roughly-executed prototype. Most of the production refinements and polish are already on this little bird. All the production tooling is built and in place, and actual kits are complete and in stock. The kit meets the FAA's "51% homebuilt" requirement and is ready for shipment. With the demand for the pricey ($8,500 plus freight and about $120 in butyrate dope and finish) kits, this condition probably won't last long. However, the current production

Fig. 3-14. The "Avid Flyer" perhaps represents the epitome in conventional construction techniques in a two-place ARV.

capacity of sixteen units per month can be doubled simply by adding a second shift on the company's one fuselage welding jig.

Rick Matthiesen, owner of the *Actic Bluebird* taildragger which was also on display at Oshkosh, has an interesting rationale for buying an Avid Flyer. In the spring of this year Matthiesen left Anchorage for the Lower 48 to locate—and spend $20,000 to $30,000 on—a Super Cub that he could bring back to Alaska and outfit for bush flying. Somehow he chanced upon Dean Wilson and his Flyer, and Matthiesen's plans changed abruptly. "I got in it [and] I thought Dean was going to go flying with me the first time. he didn't know me from the Man in the Moon. [He said],... 'Just use 45 over the fence.' That's all he told me... I got in it and was a little nervous, [but] I took off...and I'm just an old Cub driver, you know, but by the time I had turned downwind I felt so good [about it] I was doing steep turns, climbs, dives and stalls. It's a very stable flying airplane!"

Matthiesen was so impressed that he abandoned his search for a Super Cub and immediately began work on his own Avid Flyer, in a rented building next door to Dean Wilson's facilities in Boise. He took around 350 hours to finish his kit, but this included time spent photographing the construction steps for the assembly manual, as well as engineering the first tailwheel model of the airplane.

As Rick explained it, wing spars are cut and factory jig-drilled for strut attachment. The wings are built on two leveled saw horses, with the rear one elevated at a prescribed point with a two-inch wood block. This sets the $4\frac{1}{2}°$ washout.

The wing's components are held together by a combination of pop rivets and 3M two-part construction epoxy. The adhesive giving three or four hours of work time before hardening. It is claimed to be a non-volatile, non-allergenic glue. The distinctively scalloped wing trailing edge is achieved when the 1.8 ounce dacron sailplane cloth shrinks tightly over a 1/16-inch aircraft control cable stretched the length of the wing. Both wings are usually ready for covering in 30 to 40 man-hours.

There is no rib stitching. Prior to covering, three coats of "Super Seam Cement" are applied to the one-inch rib cap strips, and to other contact areas, and let dry. Then, as the covering is attached, but before it is shrunk, another coat of cement is brushed over the fabric to wet through and bond with the previous coating of glue. After drying overnight, the covering is heat-shrunk. It appears to make for a very tight, smooth assembly.

Although the engine is factory red-lined at 7000 rpm, where a maximum 43 horsepower is developed from the dual-carbureted Cuyuna 430RR engine, Matthiesen claims the Flyer's performance figures are conservatively based on 6000 rpm, which presumably will increase engine life if run in this range. (Matthiesen thinks 500 to 700 hours' time between overhaul [TBO] is reasonable to expect.) Fuel is contained in an integral nine-gallon tank forward of the instrument panel, and gauged by sight from the cockpit.

The tail wheel and tricycle versions sell for the same price, but for the cost of the tail wheel assembly a builder can have a tricycle gear airplane that easily converts back and forth to the tail wheel configuration. The fittings are already in place to move the main gear for or aft, very much like converting a Tri-Pacer to a Pacer. Ten or twelve pounds can be shaved, however, by eliminating the nose gear attach fitting. Matthiesen had the *Arctic Bluebird* outfitted with some non-standard, oversized (and overweight) balloon tires, such as might be used on the tundra. But, he says, "I'll be putting mine on floats and skis as soon as I get it up to Alaska." Brakes are toe-operated, from the left side of the cockpit only.

Cabin heat is provided by ducting the flow from The Cuyuna's cooling fan into the cabin. There is definitely a large number of BTU's being produced by the engine. In Alaska, "I've frozen enough in Super Cubs to know, that this should be better," reports Matthiesen.

Cabin' doors are covered entirely in clear plexiglass. They hinge at the top, to swing outward and upward, and latch against the lower wing surfaces. This makes the airplane quite easy to get into and out of, especially compared to some other enclosed vehicles of similar size and weight.

With its empty weight of 360 pounds and a cruise speed of 80 mph, the Avid Flyer is, of course, a true airplane and must be licensed in the Experimental Homebuilt category. Production models will likely weigh in at less than 350 pounds. It is conceivable that a properly-selected climb prop could reduce the cruise speed enough to allow the craft to be operated under one of the ultralight flight instruction exemptions (EAA's or AOPA's).

Maybe the real appeal of the Avid Flyer, though, aside from the workmanship and design excellence evident in every detail, is that the aircraft really can be folded and towed away on its own main landing gear, *by one person,* easily, in five minutes or less. Rick Matthiesen demonstrated the procedure. He pulled a single retaining pin at the forward wing root, and swung the wing back faster that a photographer could wind film and snap the shutter. The photographer had to have Rick back up and hold his position long enough to get the shots! He then secured the wings to the tail for transport with a single bolt per side. (None of the controls are disconnected, and they are all safetied with AN grade hardware.)

A trailer hitch/tow bar then attaches to the tail, and the Flyer is ready to be towed up to 20 or 30 miles, at speeds approaching 50 mph. Common sense indicates that some sort of trailer would be easier on the airframe for longer distances and higher speeds. The very fact that it can be towed at all is quite unique, and could be one of the main essentials of sport flying.

The operating restrictions imposed at Oshkosh by the convention rulemakers prevented test flying the Avid Flyer at Whitman Field. According to Dean Wilson, though, "lots" of pilots with widely varying flight experience have flown the airplane easily. Apparently, its slow stall and landing speeds preclude its wanting to swap ends the way other taildraggers do.

As for the performance numbers themselves, anybody with a lick of sense should be suspect. How can an airplane with as high a wing loading as the Avid Flyer (over 6.5 pounds per square foot), not to mention high power loading (over 17 pounds per horsepower), achieve such low stall speeds, and correspondingly low takeoff and landing distances? Dean Wilson says he studied the NASA data on the old Junkers and Stuka aircraft, which had similar flaperons or ailerons that extended out beyond the trailing edges. He then did his own engineering to see if he could apply any of this German technology to his own design.

As it turned out, he certainly could. Where (according to Wilson) the best stock Cessna on a bright sunny day achieves a lift coefficient of around 1.6, the Avid Flyer--by some miracle of modern technology that Wilson does not pretend to understand entirely--at a 15° flaperon setting realizes the astonishing lift coefficient of *2.8.*

The kit does come complete with engine, but there are a few options available: floats, skis, and dual CHT and EGT gauges. Contact Light Aero for further details.

Specifications

Wingspan	29 ft 10½ in (wings folded 19 ft 9 in)
Length	17 ft 0 in (wings folded 7 ft 9½ in)
Height	6 ft 4 in
Wing Area	117 sq ft
Engine Make, Model, HP	Cuyuna 430 RR 43 hp @ 7000 rpm
Prop Diameter/Pitch	72 in/36 in
Reduction Ratio	3.111-to-1
Fuel Capacity/Consumption	9 gal/2.4 gph
Gross Weight	764 lbs
Empty Weight	360 lbs
Useful Load	404 lbs
Wing Loading	5 psf @ 580 lbs (6 psf @ 764 lbs)
Power Loading	13.48 lb/hp (solo) 17.76 lb/hp (dual)
Design Load Factors	+3.8, -1.5
Construction Time	200 man-hrs
Field Assembly Time	5 min (1 man)
Pricing	$8,495.00

Flight Performance (based on 6000 rpm)

Velocity Never Exceed	90 mph (flutter tested to 100 mph)
Top Level Speed	83 mph
Cruise Speed	80 mph @ 80% power
Stall Speed (in free air)	25 mph solo (30 mph dual)
Sea Level Climb Rate	1400 fpm solo (960 fpm dual)
Takeoff Run	75-200 ft (solo-dual)
Dist. Req'd to clear 50 ft	275-400 ft (solo-dual)
Landing Roll	100-150 ft (solo-dual, with brakes on blacktop)

Service Ceiling (100 fpm climb)	19,000 ft solo (12,000 dual)
Range at Cruise	300 mi
L/D (Glide Ratio)	8.5-to-1 @ 45 mph
Minimum Sink Rate	385 fpm @ 35 mph

Avid Flyer
Light Aero, Inc.
P.O. Box 45177
Boise, Idaho 83711
(208) 939-0221
Dean Wilson

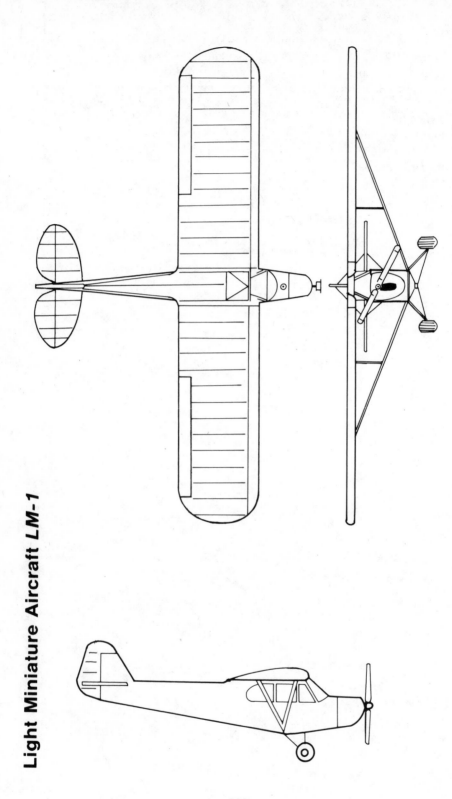

Light Miniature Aircraft *LM-1*

42

LIGHT MINIATURE
AIRCRAFT *LM-1*

The LM-1 is basically a scaled down replica of the classic Piper J-3 Cub. It placed fourth in the lightplane division of the ARV Competition. The wings fold for transport and storage.

While the LM-1 may look like a single seater Cub, its construction is entirely different - it's all wood. With an emphasis on construction technique and simplicity, the designers claim to have introduced a new approach to an all wood airframe. First of all, you don't have to work from full size drawings or even layout drawings. For instance, wing ribs are not built up, but are assembled in place as the wing is laid up, saving hours of work. Also, this may be the first all wood airplane to use zeroporosity dacron. Glue is applied to the structure and the fabric pressed into place. Later it is heat shrunk - no sealing is necessary. The designers claim the entire cover job requires only about 15 hours, half the time being used to wait for the glue to set before applying fabric.

The designers have also used a method they call "selective engineering and testing." They say they have been particularly careful in engineering the various critical components of the airframe, such as: wing spars, struts, wing attachments, elevator attachment, engine mounts and firewall, as well as the landing gear attachment. On the other hand, they have not spent too much time on seat and door design, the tailwheel, windows, windshield, wheels, instruments, etc. Testing was approached the same way. If a failure of some part could cause an accident, it was tested and

Fig. 3-15. Light Miniature Aircraft "LM-1" is essentially a scaled-down Piper J-3 Cub. Single seater features all wood construction and Cuyuna engine. Placed fourth in ARV fly-off, lightplane division.

retested to limit well beyond necessity, according to the designers. Non critical items were not tested, because the designers felt they have been tested and proven on other designs.

The designers firmly believe that aircraft such as the LM-1, will be the basis for a new wave of homebuilding far greater than anything yet seen. This idea is based on using powerplants developed in the ultralight movement, using inexpensive building materials such as wood and dacron. By using a tried and true design combined with selective engineering and testing, they feel they have found the key to developing sportsplanes that are inexpensive and not time consuming to build.

Contact Light Miniature Aircraft for further details.

Specifications

Wingspan	27 ft
Length	17 ft 6 in
Height	5 ft 7 in
Wing Area	118 sq ft
Engine Make, Model, HP	Cuyuna 430D 30 hp
Prop Diameter/Pitch	50 in/27 in
Reduction Ratio	2.1-to-1
Fuel Capacity/Consumption	5½ gal/1½ gph
Gross Weight	600 lbs
Empty Weight	345 lbs
Useful Load	255 lbs
Wing Loading	5.0 psf
Power Loading	20 lb/hp
Design Load Factors	+5.0, -4.5
Construction Time	500 man-hrs
Field Assembly Time	6 min
Pricing	Complete kit from Wicks $4,504.00

Flight Performance

Velocity Never Exceed	85 mph
Top Level Speed	70 mph
Cruise Speed	60 mph @ 75% power
Stall Speed (in free air)	25 mph
Sea Level Climb Rate	500 fpm @ 60 mph
Takeoff Run	250 ft
Dist. Req'd. to clear 50 ft	
Landing Roll	350 ft
Service Ceiling (100 fpm climb)	
Range at Cruise	185 mi with 30 min. reserve
L/D (Glide Ratio)	10-to-1 @ 40 mph

LM-1
Light Miniature Aircraft, Inc.
13815 NW 19th Avenue
Opa-Locka, FL 33054
(305) 681-4068   Fred McCallum

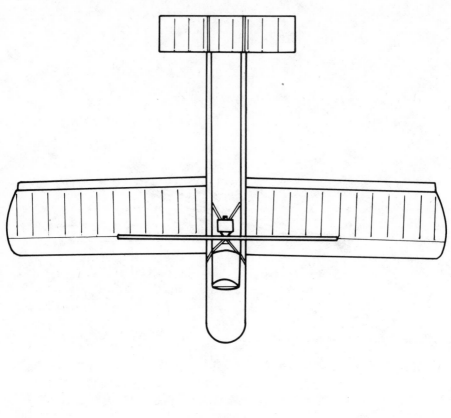

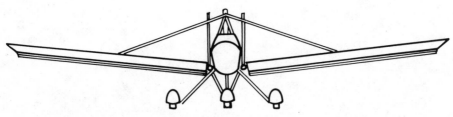

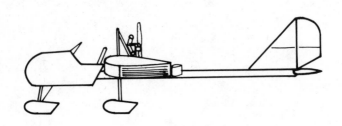

43
MITCHELL P-38 *LIGHTNING*

The P-38 is a tri-geared, twin boom, mid-wing pusher with full aerodynamic controls. It features twin vertical surfaces, an all-flying horizontal tail, and full span, detached flaperons. It is available in plans and kits.

The wing and tail are of built-up construction with the wing strut braced on top. The nose wheel is steerable and includes a brake. A reduction drive engine is mounted on a pylon behind the pilot. The pilot sits up front and steers the aircraft with a conventional aircraft control system. The landing gear is fiberglass, offering a shock absorbing feature that helps smooth out rough landings.

While not designed for speed or performance, the Lightning offers a good feel in the air. The controls are responsive, and all three axis are equally balanced with very light control pressures. Due to the Mitchell pioneered detached, full-span flaperons, the roll response is maintained, even near the "stall."

In general, the flight characteristics are described as docile, and the P-38 doesn't have much of a stall. At 32 mph, the airplane enters a light mush which progresses into a heavy wallowing at 34 mph, and the stall ends.

The aircraft is available in an economy kit, homebuilder's special and plans, as well as an engine package. Optional accessories include flight instruments, propellers, parachute and wheel parts. An agricultural version is available for crop dusting.

Fig. 3-16. Mitchell "P-38" prototype with wings tufted for airflow tests. The aircraft is capable of carrying agricultural spray equipment.

211

Specifications

Wingspan	28 ft
Length	17 ft
Height	5 ft
Wing Area	120 sq ft
Engine Make, Model, HP	Cuyuna 430R, 35 hp
Prop Diameter/Pitch	N.A.
Reduction Ratio	N.A.
Fuel Capacity/Consumption	6 gal/2½ gph
Gross Weight	700 lbs
Empty Weight	305 lbs
Useful Load	395 lbs
Wing Loading	5.83 psf
Power Loading	23.33 lb/hp
Design Load Factors	+4, -4
Construction Time	100 man-hrs
Field Assembly Time	10 min
Pricing	N.A.

Flight Performance

Velocity Never Exceed	N.A.
Top Level Speed	65 mph
Cruise Speed	55 mph
Stall Speed (in free air)	32 mph
Sea Level Climb Rate	500 fpm @ 40 mph
Takeoff Run	275 ft
Dist. Req'd to clear 50 ft	N.A.
Landing Roll	325 ft
Service Ceiling (100 fpm climb)	12,000
Range at Cruise	110 mi
L/D (Glide Ratio)	7-to-1
Minimum Sink Rate	400 fpm

P-38 Lightning
Mitchell Aircraft Corp.
1900 S. Newcomb
Porterville, CA 93257
(209) 781-8100
Tom Sawyer

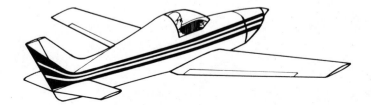

Mitchell U-2 Superwing

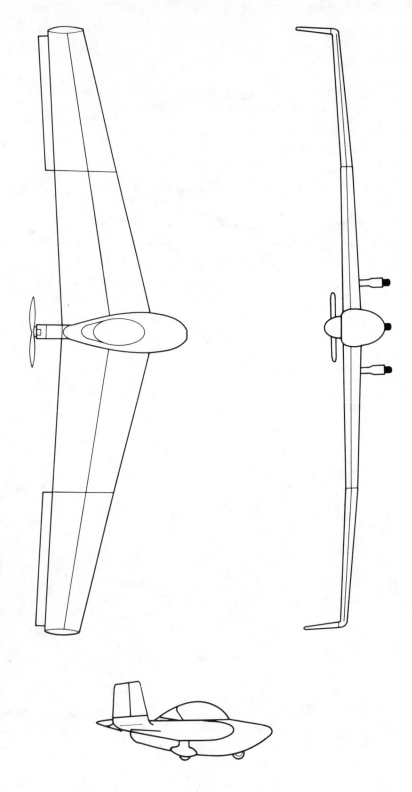

44
MITCHELL U-2
SUPERWING

The U-2 is a high performance flying wing of wood and foam construction, similar to the B-10. It features fully enclosed cockpit (an open cockpit is optional) and three-axis aerodynamic controls. It can be built from either plans or a complete kit.

Unlike the B-10, which is actually a hang glider modified for power, the U-2 is an all new ultralight designed around the powerplant. Its primary design goals included: improved performance without sacrificing safety, easily built with hand tools and inexpensive to purchase, good soaring performance, a safe and economical engine installation, and it features one-man operation — no groundcrew, loads and unloads with little difficulty, and taxis easily. The above design goals appear to have been met.

The construction techniques used in the U-2 are the same time proven methods as are employed in the B-10. The ribs are the standard truss type, each requiring about one man-hour to build. The spars are pre-cut, as are most all other components. The leading edge skins are one millimeter aircraft grade birch plywood, stiffened every 4½ inches with foam nose ribs, allowing for a nice smooth contour. The kit itself is reminiscent of a huge model airplane. The outer wing panels fold for transport and storage.

The completed wing frame, as well as the control surfaces, are covered with 2.7 oz. dacron after the structure has received several coats of clear dope. The fabric will adhere to the structure by application of dope over the contact areas. Rib stitching is not used. After the fabric has been attached to the airframe, about three coats of clear dope are applied to fill

Fig. 3-17. Mitchell U-2 "Superwing" completely encloses pilot in center section. The aircraft was a development of the Mitchell B-10 ultralight flying wing, and offers superior performance.

the pores. The fabric can then be tightened by moving an ordinary household iron near its surface. Color coats may follow.

The fuselage structure is a trusswork of one-half inch diameter chromoly tubing surrounding the pilot area. Two hardwood runners extend the full length of the cockpit underneath the pilot's seat, serving as protection in the event of a wheels-up landing.

The canopy is a one piece bubble which attaches forward and aft via lock pins, and it's easily removed for entry and exit. Visibility is virtually 360° horizontally, while clear mylar panels located in the lower area of the cockpit, allow viewing directly below while in a slight bank.

The seat is made of heavy, re-inforced canvas that attaches to the main spar and forward crossover member. It can be adjusted to various heights via eyelets and snaps. The pilot is held in by a seatbelt which is secured to the main frame and spar, while a shoulder harness can also be installed, if desired. The cockpit allows a chest-pack type parachute to be worn.

As on its predecessor B-10, the U-2 employs stabilators for both lateral and pitch control. Unlike the B-10 though, the U-2 vertical surfaces consist of a fixed fin and moveable rudder. Yaw control is accomplished by deflecting the appropriate rudder with a push on the corresponding pedal. Press both rudder pedals together however, and the glidepath can be controlled quite effectively. The tricycle landing gear consists of a steerable brake equipped nosewheel, with the mains tracking 58 inches, making for excellent ground handling manners. This set-up disallows asymmetric braking, while the nosewheel turns with the rudders. The mains attach just aft the main spar and carry the primary landing loads. The three 3.50" x 4" tires are mounted on nylon hubs for good service, and allow the aircraft to operate out of grass and dirt fields.

Each main wheel is framed in a one-half inch chromoly cradle, and retracts into the wing by a bellcrank arrangement. This is attached to a pushrod that locks the gear firmly in the up or down position via an overcenter mechanism.

The powerplant used on the U-2 prototype is the ubiquitous 10 hp McCulloch go-kart engine, fitted with a 3-to-1 reduction belt drive. The engine and drive are shock-mounted with the thrust line set at 7 degrees with respect to the wing chord. A tuned exhaust allows the engine to develop its full power, while yielding an adequate muffler effect at 8,600 rpm.

The engine burns a mixture of regular gas and synthetic two-cycle oil, giving reduced friction and excellent service life. The engine is stock "off-the-shelf" and not modified in any way. The engine mount is designed to accept engines of up to 25 hp and 50 pounds in weight, without sacrificing structural integrity.

The fuel tank is made of a translucent plastic and contains a useable 7 quarts, which is enough for almost two hours duration at cruise. It is located aft the main spar, with the filler cap within easy reach. The flexible urethane fuel line includes an in-line filter and pressure squeeze bulb for priming.

Flying the U-2 should be no problem for the current licensed pilot, as its characteristics can be described as docile. After unfolding and pinning the outer wing panels in place, a preflight is made to check the integrity of the craft. Entering the cockpit should be done with care—step on the sling seat or else you might put your foot through the floor! Once seated, your feet will come to rest right over the rudder pedals. The throttle is buried in the left wing root for the left hand to grasp easily. The joystick is between the legs.

The engine is started by pulling a rope end located behind the left shoulder—a compression release valve makes it a cinch. Prime may or may not be needed.

Call "clear," and a quick jerk on the starting rope sparks the mighty Mc to life. Idle is set at around 4,000 rpm, and it isn't as loud as you might have imagined. Scan the instrument panel. Set the sensitive altimeter and check the cylinder head temperature. Goose the throttle to 8,000 and roll.

The trike gear and steerable nose wheel make ground handling pleasant, however, the new U-2 pilot is urged to drive it around a bit until a good comfortable feel is developed. When ready for takeoff and lined up with the centerline of the runway and pointed into the wind, open her up to 8,000 rpm. The acceleration is a surprise—coming from 10 hp. At 30 mph the nose will unstick, and at 35 mph she'll be light on her feet and flying in ground effect. The tach should indicate about 9,000 rpm.

Forward visibility is good, as the nose slopes away. Let the speed build to 45 mph, ease back on the stick and climb out. Crosswinds can be countered by a normal crab. For cruise, you can throttle back as desired.

The airplane handles well and you probably won't realize it doesn't have a conventional tail. The U-2 has passed its stall and spin tests well, but the factory warns there is a tendency for the wing to drop in a power stall, although standard recovery will catch it before a large loss of altitude occurs.

Turns should be lead by rudder, and coordinated with "aileron." The rudder located way out on the tip causes the desired turn side to slow down, while the undeflected rudder wing speeds up, resulting in a roll and turn.

Landings are no real chore. Ease forward on the stick and throttle back. Set your glide at about 45 mph and drive it onto the ground, and touchdown carrying a good 10 mph above stall, lest a gust stall you out. In a calm, a three-point can be done—with the mains and a tailboom skid (for protection against prop damage) touching. Then ease forward on the stick and roll or brake to a stop. Braking force can be enhanced simply by leaning forward, putting more weight on the nosewheel.

Production units are available as an economy kit, homebuilder's special, and plans. Engine packages include the Zenoah G25-B and Cuyuna 430R. Options include flight instruments, and a parachute.

Specifications

Wingspan	34 ft
Length	9 ft

Height	3 ft	
Wing Area	136 sq ft	
Engine Make, Model/HP	Zenoah G25-B, 22 hp	
Prop Diameter/Pitch	N.A.	
Reduction Ratio	N.A.	
Fuel Capacity/Consumption	3 gal/1.0 gph	
Gross Weight	550 lbs	
Empty Weight	300 lbs	
Useful Load	250 lbs	
Wing Loading	3.67 psf	
Power Loading	25 lb/hp	
Design Load Factors	+7.8, -7.8	
Construction Time	350 man-hrs	
Field Assembly Time	15 min	
Pricing	N.A.	

Flight Performance (with 190 pound pilot) Zenoah

		Cuyuna
Velocity Never Exceed	N.A.	
Top Level Speed	85 mph	N.A.
Cruise Speed	75 mph	100 mph
Stall Speed (in free air)	33 mph	80 mph
Sea Level Climb Rate	475 fpm	37 mph
Takeoff Run	225 ft	750 fpm
Dist. Req'd to clear 50 ft	N.A.	210 ft
Landing Roll	300 ft	N.A.
Service Ceiling (100 fpm climb)	10,000 ft	250 ft
Range at Cruise	150 mi	12,000 ft
L/D (Glide Ratio)	24-to-1 @ 45 mph	80 mi
Minimum Sink Rate	150 fpm @ 42 mph	23-to-1 @ 49 mph
		180 fpm @ 45 mph

P-38 Lightning
Mitchell Aircraft Corp.
1900 S. Newcomb
Porterville, CA 93257
(209) 781-8100

Monnett *Monerai-P*

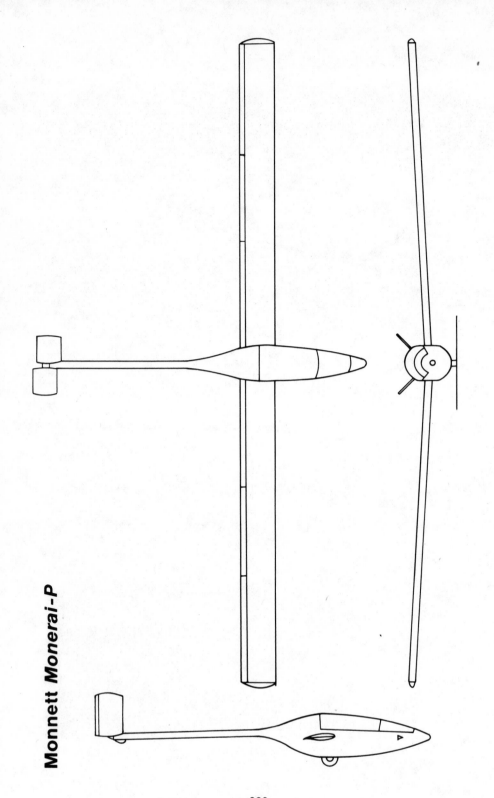

45

MONNETT *MONERAI-P*

The Monerai is basically a medium performance sailplane with a bolt-on power pod available to convert it into a motorglider. While not an ultralight per se, at least by wing loading standards, it is nonetheless ultralight in weight, tipping the scales at a mere 220 pounds. It's a dramatic demonstration of what can be accomplished with a given amount of materials. It is available only in kit form.

Construction time has been minimized by extensive use of special aluminum extrusions, formed fiberglass, plexiglass, and ABS plastic parts.

The extruded tailboom tube and its extruded attachment fittings slip into the rear of the formed fiberglass fuselage shell. A welded chromoly tubular truss is fabricated in a simple fixture and slipped into the shell from the top. The tailboom is bonded to the aft portion of the shell.

The instrument panel is designed to allow easy accessibility. A sling seat, adjustable rudder pedals, and adjustable headrest accommodate pilots from 5 feet to 6 foot-2 inches and 230 pounds.

A combination turn-over structure and power pod mount in the aft fuselage allows the transition to a powered sailplane by plugging in the power pod, hooking up the ignition switch, throttle cable, and pull starter.

The wing uses an extruded aluminum spar, tapered for structural efficiency. Wing spar root fittings are also extruded and milled for simple hand tool finishing.

Aileron and flap skins, rear spar channels and the wing ribs are formed at the factory and ready for assembly. A one piece aluminum wing skin is bonded in place with epoxy provided to produce a wing of uniform smoothness without the filling, sanding, and mess associated with

Fig. 3-18. Monnett "Monerai-P" offers sailplane performance with the convenience of an engine. Engine unit comes complete with cowling and strut fairing.

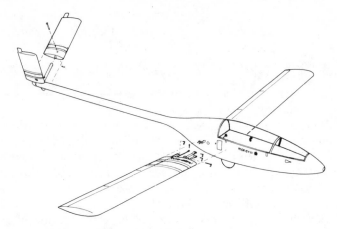

Fig. 3-19. Cutaway of the "Monerai," less engine.

fiberglass construction. Total wing panel construction time is about 20 man-hours.

Both V-tail surfaces also have completely formed ribs and single tube spar. They require only a few hours to assemble.

The Monerai has several features worth mentioning:

- Full span flaps, except for ailerons, designed for negative (up) settings for high speed flight, and positive (down) settings for thermaling and 90° down for landing.
- Automatic flap hook-up and one pin aileron hook-up.
- Single pin tail surface attachment.
- Fixed main wheel.
- Supine seating.
- Adjustable rudder pedals, control stick, headrest, and seat sling.
- Wheel brake on flap handle.
- Side stick with bungee trim system.
- 24 inch wide cockpit.
- Complete quick disconnect shoulder and seat belts.
- Provisions for oxygen and radio.
- Power pod mount for conversion to motorglider.
- Swing open canopy.

Rigging the ship for flight is quite simple, requiring but five minutes. The two tail surfaces are slid onto the tubes at the rear of the tailboom, and pinned in place. The wings weigh only 52 pounds per panel and are easily handled. Slide the root spars into their location, engage the flap drive and insert the shear and drag pins. Do the same with the other wing, then insert the two main pins. Last is the aileron connect pin and she's ready for flight.

The Monerai prototype was thoroughly flight tested and the F.A.A. flight restrictions were removed before kits were released for sale. During the flight testing stage, the aircraft was flown through all regimes of normal flight, including stalls from all attitudes, flap settings, insipient spins, high speed runs in excess of 140 mph, high "G" pull ups, 200 foot releases and slack line exercises. Thermaling flights of two hours duration were achieved on moderate lift days; 4400 foot altitude gains have been achieved in Illinois soaring conditions.

Basically, the Monerai prefers doing whatever it was doing when the stick was let go. Roll control was good, a 45° to 45° bank requiring 3.5 seconds—a comfortable rate.

Stalls are fast and clean, with a slight tendency for the left wing to drop, and a left spin to develop if at the aft CG location. This incipient spin condition is accompanied by a 20° nose drop which can be handled by the rudder.

In general, control coordination is good. Thermaling is done at around 51 mph indicated and 6 degrees of down flap, and the ship tracks well. At cruise, all is quiet except for vent noise. Landing with 90° flap capability makes approach control very good. Once touched down, the wheel brake gives you all the acceleration you need.

The Monerai Power Pod includes everything except instruments and paint, which are available as an option. In actual use, it is easily attached and removed, enabling the pilot to convert his sailplane into a motorglider at any time.

Specifications

Wingspan	36 ft
Length	19 ft 7 in
Height	2 ft 11 in (4 ft-4 in with engine)
Wing Area	78 sq ft
Engine Make, Model, HP	Zenoah G25B, 18 hp
Prop Diameter/Pitch	35 in/12 in
Reduction Ratio	N.A.
Fuel Capacity/Consumption	1 gal/1.5 gph
Gross Weight	450 lbs
Empty Weight	220 lbs
Useful Load	230 lbs
Wing Loading	5.76 psf
Power Loading	25 lb/hp
Design Load Factors	+6, -6
Construction Time	400 man-hrs
Field Assembly Time	5 min
Pricing	$5,200

Flight Performance

Velocity Never Exceed	120 mph
Top Level Speed	90 mph
Cruise Speed	60 mph
Stall Speed (in free air)	40 mph
Sea Level Climb Rate	400 fpm
Takeoff Run	500 ft (900 ft on turf)

Dist. Req'd to clear 50 ft	N.A.
Landing Roll	N.A.
Service Ceiling (100 fpm climb)	N.A.
Range at Cruise	30 mi
L/D (Glide Ratio)	28-to-1 @ 60 mph
Minimum Sink Rate	168 fpm @ 55 mph

Monerai-P
Monnett Experimental Aircraft, Inc.
P.O. Box 2984
Oshkosh, WI 54903
(414) 426-1212
John Monnett

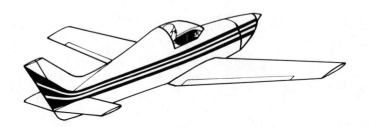

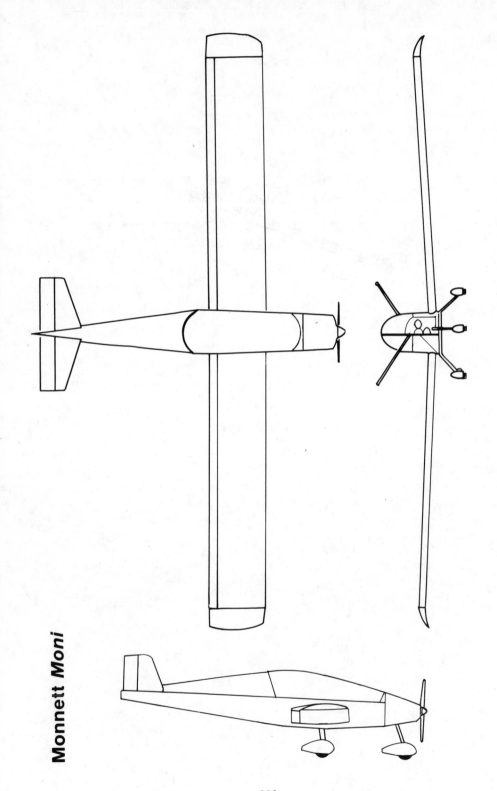

Monnett _Moni_

46

MONNETT *MONI*

The Moni is a single seater, cantilevered low wing monoplane with V-tail. It features an all metal airframe, and single wheeled main gear.

Essentially of all aluminum construction, the Moni's components come preformed, and are said to cut, trim and assemble with the ease of a model airplane. The kit comes complete with everything but paint, and only common home shop tools and an electric drill are required. Materials and components include: All formed aluminum components that require complex bending, shaping, or machining. These include wing ribs, spar, skins, spar fittings, fuselage bulkheads and formers, hinges, castings, etc. All are completely welded control assembly components. All instruments, including: airspeed, altimeter, compass, tachometer, and CHT. A KFM 107E, 22 hp electric start engine, propeller, spinner, battery, fuel tank, and exhaust system. Pilot support includes: seat sling, seat belt, shoulder harness, and head rest. Landing gear mains, tailwheel, and wing tip wheels. Plastic parts include: a molded plexiglass canopy, wing tips, stabilizer tips, wheel fairing, engine cowling, and ABS cockpit interior panels. Every nut, bolt, rivet and epoxy adhesive required. And finally, complete, concise, easy to follow construction plans, templates and assembly manual.

The original Moni features a unique single wheel main gear, steerable tailwheel and wing tip wheels. Below 5 mph, you taxi with one wing down. Above 5 mph, and the ailerons take hold. The 10½ inch main provides shock absorption. Monnett claims ground handling is very easy with this set up. On landing, simply fly it on and hold forward stick enough to keep the aircraft planted to the runway. The tail will remain up virtually until you stop. By the time one wing drops to the surface, your roll out is about finished. An optional tri-geared version is available for those who prefer.

Fig. 3-20 Monnett "Moni" offers 120 mph top speed, and gets over 80 mpg at cruise. It's powered by a KFM 107 opposed engine. Although prototype featured a unique mono-wheel landing gear, kits can be ordered with tricycle gear, as shown.

The Moni gets its go from the KFM 107E, a two cylinder, horizontally opposed two-cycle rated at 22 hp. It features a 12 volt, 60W alternator, double reduction clutched electric starter, shielded ignition harness, and solid state magneto. It turns a 38 inch diameter Warnke constant speed propeller, and has a tuned exhaust system. Mixture control is optional, while a diaphragm carburetor with adjustable jets is part of the package.

The wing is built up of an extruded aluminum spar, stamped ribs and one piece skins—all bonded together. A few rivets are used in certain areas to prevent bond linepeeling from starting. This method, of course, results in a very smooth, low drag wing. And incidentally, the full span ailerons are actually drooperons—they function as both flaps and ailerons.

While metal bonding is unusual in a homebuilt aircraft, Monnett says bonding preparation requires less time than for a composite wing, while the actual adhesive process takes only 45 minutes. "And there's almost no chance of having an allergic reaction as many people do with fiberglass resins," Monnett adds. Tail surfaces can be assembled in one evening, claims Monnett. He also says that fast and easy construction were prime considerations in the design of the aircraft.

Even though the Moni is small, its cockpit is large and will accommodate a 6 ft - 4 in, 235 pounder. The seating position is supine, as in a sailplane and is, perhaps, the biggest difference between the Moni and a conventional lightplane. Otherwise, the airplane offers no surprises. Pitch and yaw are controlled by the v-tailed rudder vators via a mixer assembly in the fuselage. Plans for building a trailer/storage unit are also included with the kit.

Short wings (16 ft span) are available to convert the airplane to a Mini-Moni. It yields a higher top speed (140 mph) and a much higher roll rate for aerobatics. (Keep in mind the KFM 107 has a built-in inverted system.) Essentially, the short wings use half the components of the longer wings. Both wings are interchangeable. Empty weight goes down to 230 pounds, while the gross weight remains unchanged.

Flying the Moni should be easy for anyone with a private ticket. Four to five hours of pattern work should get you used to it. If you have sailplane experience, you'll feel at home with the Moni. A stick, located under the right canopy sail, controls pitch and roll. Pitch forces are light, and trim is accomplished by pushing a button located on top of the stick—a spring does the trick. Roll is not as quick, using three seconds to go from 45 to 45. The aircraft stalls straight ahead without dropping a wing. With controls crossed however, a wing could drop. The factory has spun the Moni in both directions, with good recovery characteristics. However, Monnett does not recommend spins, and has placarded the aircraft against them.

Specifications

Wingspan	27 ft 6 in
Length	15 ft
Height	3 ft 3 in

Wing Area	75 sq ft
Engine Make, Model, HP	KFM 107E, 22 hp electric start
Prop Diameter/Pitch	38 in/12 in
Reduction Ratio	1-to-1
Fuel Capacity/Consumption	4 gal/1 gph
Gross Weight	500 lbs
Empty Weight	260 lbs
Useful Load	240 lbs
Wing Loading	6.67 psf
Power Loading	22.73 lb/hp
Design Load Factors	+6, -4
Construction Time	350 man-hrs
Field Assembly Time	10 min
Pricing	$6,000

Flight Performance

Velocity Never Exceed	150 mph
Top Level Speed	120 mph
Cruise Speed	110 mph @ 75% power
Stall Speed (in free air)	38 mph
Sea Level Climb Rate	500 fpm
Takeoff Run	400 ft (turf)
Dist. Req'd to clear 50 ft	N.A.
Landing Roll	500 ft
Service Ceiling (100 fpm climb)	13,000 ft
Range at Cruise	320 mi (@ economy cruise at 90 mph)
L/D (Glide Ratio)	20-to-1 @ 50 mph
Minimum Sink Rate	200 fpm

Moni
Monnett Experimental Aircraft, Inc.
P.O. Box 2984
Oshkosh, WI 54903
(414) 426-1212
John Monnett

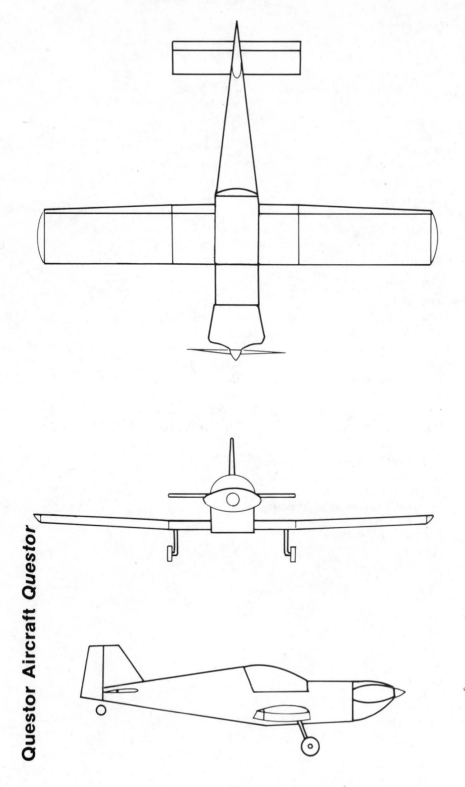

Questor Aircraft Questor

47

QUESTOR AIRCRAFT
QUESTOR

The Questor is an all metal, low wing, single-seater monoplane. It features a completely enclosed cockpit and a 120 mph cruise. The wings may be removed for transport and storage in a one car garage.

The fuselage is constructed simply of sheet aluminum sides and tubing frames. The tubing is cut to length, fitted to the side skins with double sided tape, and pop riveted together. Special pop rivets with steel mandrels are provided that may be used on varying thickness of material without loss of strength. Cherry max rivets are used at stress points for maximum strength. All inside fittings and parts are riveted to the sides prior to joining them together.

The wing is a two spar affair of three main sections: a straight stub section that runs under the fuselage, and two dihedral panels. The main spar of each outer section attaches to the stub with two bolts, whereas the rear spars get connected with one bolt. The spars are made with backed rivets at the factory, to assure their quality.

The airfoil is a slightly modified NACA 4415 which produces a gentle stall and very docile characteristics. According to the designer, there is no tendency to roll off or break sharply. Ailerons run the entire length of the trailing edge, even though they are split at the stub and outer panel separations. The Questor does not have flaps.

Fig. 3-21. The "Questor" features very simple, all metal construction techniques, and a 120 mph cruise.

The airplane was designed to accommodate someone as large as 6 ft-3 in, weighing 235 pounds. Even so, a 135 pounder can get in and still be within the CG envelope.

Landing gear may be either tricycle or taildragger. In either case, no shock absorption is used because the 10 inch wheels and tires have enough give. Hydraulic brakes are fitted to the mains, and enable steering the free castering tri-gear version. Takeoffs and landings are supposed to be a snap with either model—the aircraft sort of levitates off the runway rather than rotating.

The factory says construction is handled much like a model airplane. The kit contains all parts and components needed to finish and fly the Questor except for paint. This includes: all welded parts, seat belts and shoulder harness, engine, prop, exhaust, all instruments, welded fuel tank and all fittings, hardware, wheels, hydraulic brakes, cowling, canopy and wheel fairings. All difficult to form structures such as elevator, ailerons, bulkheads, ribs and spars have been preformed. All placards, the data plate, decals and complete instructions for building and acquiring certification are included. Rivets are supplied, as needed, for structural component assembly.

Specifications

Wingspan	18 ft
Length	15 ft 6 in
Height	3 ft 8 in
Wing Area	55 sq ft
Engine Make, Model, HP	GMT, 2 cyl-4 stroke, 37.5 hp
Prop Diameter/Pitch	54 in/32 in
Reduction Ratio	1-to-1
Fuel Capacity/Consumption	10 gal/1.8 gph
Gross Weight	530 lbs
Empty Weight	270 lbs
Useful Load	260 lbs
Wing Loading	9.64 psf
Power Loading	14.13 lb/hp
Design Load Factors	+6, -3
Construction Time	250 man-hrs
Field Assembly Time	10 min
Pricing	$7,500

Flight Performance

Velocity Never Exceed	135 mph
Top Level Speed	135 mph
Cruise Speed	120 mph @ 75% power
Stall Speed (in free air)	50 mph
Sea Level Climb Rate	600 fpm @ 95 mph
Takeoff Run	300 ft

Dist. Req'd to clear 50 ft   500 ft
Landing Roll   450 ft
Service Ceiling (100 fpm climb)   N.A.
Range at Cruise   600 mi
L/D (Glide Ratio)   15-to-1 @ 75 mph

Questor
Questor Aircraft
Aero Valley Airport
Rt. 4, Box 16F. Roanoke, TX 76262
(817) 491-9497
Bob Counts

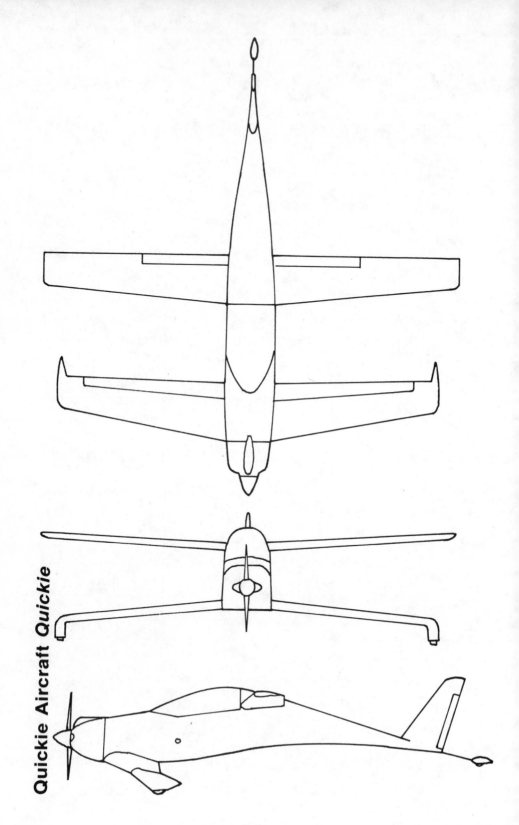

Quickie Aircraft Quickie

48

QUICKIE AIRCRAFT
QUICKIE

The Quickie is a tandem wing, single seater tractor taildragger. It is built of all composite construction and offers fuel economy in excess of 100 mpg. Power is supplied by a converted four-cycle industrial engine. The airplane will accommodate pilots up to 6 ft-6 in and 215 pounds. It won the EAA's 1978 Outstanding New Design Award.

When the development of a new homebuilt aircraft is undertaken, it is often closely followed by the public. Prototypes can even be viewed on static display at fly-ins and airshows during the construction period, at which time its performance and cost estimates are echoed by the developers. This was not the policy of the little skunk works at the Mojave Airport. The development of the Quickie was one of the best kept secrets in aviation. Until its first flight on November 15, 1977, its existence was known only to a handful of people.

The Quickie story began in early 1975 when Gene Sheehan and Tom Jewett began looking for a reliable 12 to 25 hp engine that would be suitable for powering an efficient, single place, sport aircraft. The search included two-stroke and four-stroke engines used in chainsaws, garden tractors, motorcycles, and automobiles. It was very frustrating because engines that were light and powerful lacked reliablity, and those engines that promised reliability were either too heavy or not powerful enough.

Fig. 3-22. The unique tandem-winged "Quickie" was one of aviation's best kept secrets. It didn't appear until it was ready for market. Offers outstanding performance on 20 hp.

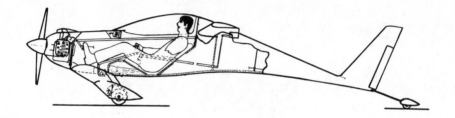

Fig. 3-23. Inboard profile of Quickie shows seating and main components of diminutive craft.

Finally, in January 1977, Gene located an engine that appeared to be reliable, possess sufficient power, and possibly light enough to serve the purpose. It was an opposed two cylinder, direct drive, four-stroke engine that produced 16 hp from 40.3 cubic inches of displacement and weighed 104 pounds in stock configuration. It was used in various industrial applications at a continuous 3600 rpm. Deciding to thoroughly investigate this engine, Tom purchased one and Gene set out to strip off the unnecessary weight and convert it to turning a propeller on a ground test stand.

By early April, the engine was ready to run on a test stand. For the next two months, Gene and Tom sorted out cooling, induction, and vibration problems associated with the aircraft applications while building running hours to verify its reliability.

By early May, both individuals were convinced that this 16 hp engine was a viable aircraft powerplant. The problem at hand then, was to design an airplane that was light enough and clean enough to provide good performance and unequalled fuel economy using this engine. It was a considerable challenge to combine the required low drag aerodynamics with a structural weight of less than 100 lb.

Tom and Gene contacted Burt Rutan, an old friend, who was noted for developing efficient designs and lightweight structures. Burt was impressed by the demonstrated reliability of the engine and set out to develop a suitable airplane configuration. Early attempts were unsuccessful, because obtaining low enough drag necessitated a retractable landing gear that increased the weight and the complexity. Most pusher configurations analyzed would balance properly only within a narrow range of pilot weights. Finally, the tractor canard/tailless biplane concept was discovered. This solved many problems. The pilot sits near the center of gravity, and the combined canard and landing gear is simple, has low drag, and is weight efficient. This configuration allows a design goal of safe stall characteristics. Its compactness allows a "glue together" airplane, saving weight on wing attachments. It was decided to place a full-span elevator/flap on the canard, inboard ailerons on the rear wing, and to use the tailwheel fairing as the only rudder. Later a rudder was added.

Once this concept was established, a detailed plan to develop the Quickie was agreed on. It involved Tom and Burt doing the detailed design work in June and July while Gene conducted further engine development.

236

Construction work on the prototype began on August 13, 1977. The construction phase, including tooling for the cowling and the canopy, took 400 man-hours over a three month period. First flight occurred on November 15, 1977. Burt, Tom, and Gene all flew 77Q on the first day, and it compiled over 25 flight hours within the first month.

The construction of the Quickie is a sandwich of high strength fiberglass, using low density, rigid foam as the core material. This structure is fabricated directly over the shaped foam core so that expensive tools and molds are not required. Composite sandwich structure offers the following advantages over conventional wood or metal: less construction time requiring fewer skills, improved corrosion resistance, improved contour stability, better surface durability, a dramatic reduction in hardware and number of parts, and easier to inspect and repair.

Keeping the structural weight of the aircraft to a minimum was necessary because the Quickie uses an engine of low horsepower and relatively heavy weight. While other designers have obtained low structural weights, it has usually been necessary to compromise the durability of the surfaces by using very light gage aluminum. This results in an aircraft that can become wrinkled and dented within a short time of entering service, unless extraordinary care is taken during the ground handling operations. In fact, it is not unusual in an ultralight aircraft to find that the ground handling loads are far in excess of the loads seen during flight.

The Quickie was designed to provide durable outer surfaces that would remain intact for years, with only normal precautions. For example, the canard can be walked on without damaging the structure in any way! Composite construction necessitates only a small weight penalty be paid to gain this important feature.

Gene Sheehan, who did most of the work on the prototype, had no prior experience with composite construction. He rapidly acquired the necessary skills, thus demonstrating that the first time builder is at very little disadvantage to the experienced composite worker.

Life with the Quickie is unique. Cockpit entry is easy because the main instrument panel is part of the canopy and is, therefore, out of the way when the canopy is open. The fuselage longeron is only 34 inches above the ground (about the same height as the seat of a motorcycle), allowing even short pilots to climb in without a step. Once in, the pilot finds a very comfortable semi-supine seat with good thigh and lumbar support, and a headrest. Throttle and sidestick locations allow the pilot to rest his forearms on the side consoles (armrests) to further reduce fatigue on long flights.

Ground handling is a real pleasure. The Quickie's very positive tailwheel steering, together with its wide landing gear stance, allows a pilot to make zippy taxi turns that would tip over the average lightplane! Since the tailwheel is not forced off the ground during the takeoff roll like a conventional taildragger, positive tailwheel steering is available all the way to lift off speed. Still, The Quickie's handling characteristics are enough like a taildragger that the Owners Manual will recommend some taildragger time before flying one. However, the Quickie is possibly the most docile taildragger around and has little tendency to ground loop.

Flight handling is the Quickie's most attractive feature. In spite of its unique configuration, the handling qualities are quite good. For example, the Quickie has less adverse yaw, better stall characteristics, and improved visibility over the average lightplane. Its control harmony and dynamic damping are superb, which makes it an easy aircraft to fly, even for low time pilots. There is no portion of the flight envelope that can be considered "sensitive" in any way. The Quickie will hold airspeed within 5 knots when flown hands-off-the-controls, even in turbulence.

Takeoff is a bit different than the conventional taildragger or nosegear aircraft. Because of the location of the elevator, the airplane does not rotate for takeoff. If the pilot holds full aft stick during the takeoff roll, the airplane will lift off at about 49 mph. If pitch control is held neutral, the airplane lifts off at about 58 mph. In both cases, the pilot has the impression that the airplane "levitates," or rises level, rather than "rotating." If the pilot holds the stick full forward during the takeoff roll, the tailwheel will raise at about 50 mph and the aircraft will not takeoff. With the tailwheel raised (not a normal maneuver), the directional sensitivity is increased, but it is still easily controlled as it is very similar to a Piper Cub during its takeoff roll.

Attitude reference is much better than other small airplanes since the canard and long nose are in the pilots peripherial vision. This makes the Quickie easier to land than other small airplanes since the height above ground as well as the roll attitude are very obvious to the pilot during the flare. Everyone who has flown the Quickie has remarked at how comfortable and confident he felt, even on the very first landing.

Smooth turns can be accomplished with ailerons, rudder, or both—all giving more than adequate roll rate. Sideslips are conventional. Even though the Quickie has low horsepower, it can perform continuous 60-degree bank turns without losing altitude—something a 108 hp Grumman Trainer has difficulty doing.

The Quickie's lift-to-drag ratio of 13 is better than conventional lightplanes, giving it a relatively flat approach without a high sink rate, even with power at idle. The recommended final approach and best climb speeds are the same—75 mph indicated. We generally fly the pattern at 80 mph, slow to 75 mph on final, and touch down at 55 mph.

Stall characteristics are supposed to be safer than a conventional aircraft. With any power setting, the airplane can be flown at full aft stick without a departure from controlled flight. The airplane generally exhibits a mild to moderate "pitch bucking" (an up and down pitch motion) when near full aft stick. The airplane will drop a wing if the rudder is uncoordinated while at full aft stick, but recovery is easy and immediate. Trim change with increasing power is a mild nose up tendency. Roll and yaw trim changes are negligible.

Takeoff acceleration is initially quite normal but bleeds to somewhat lower than you're used to with high-horsepower airplanes, while accelerating from 40 mph to the liftoff speed of 50 mph. This, combined with the relatively low climb rate, is the only indication the pilot has that he is flying with 16 hp. Once he accelerates out to above 100 mph indicated, he has the feeling that he is flying a 100 mph lightplane! Even though the climb rate is low, the airplane will climb at a very wide range of speeds. At gross weight, at sea level, with the 16 hp engine, the airplane will climb at any speed between 55 mph and 121 mph.

Specifications

Wingspan	16 ft 8 in
Length	17 ft 4 in
Height	4 ft
Wing Area	53 sq ft
Engine Make, Model, HP	Onan 4-cycle, 18-22 hp
Prop Diameter/Pitch	
Reduction Ratio	1-to-1
Fuel Capacity/Consumption	8 gal
Gross Weight	480 lbs (520 with 22 hp)
Empty Weight	240 lbs
Useful Load	240 lbs (280 with 22 hp)
Wing Loading	9.06 - 9.81 psf
Power Loading	26.6 - 23.6 lb/hp
Design Load Factors	N.A.
Construction Time	400 man-hrs
Field Assembly Time	None
Pricing	N.A.

Flight Performance	**(18 hp engine)**	**(22 hp engine)**
Velocity Never Exceed	N.A.	
Top Level Speed	127 mph	140 mph
Cruise Speed	121 mph	133 mph
Stall Speed (in free air)	53 mph (49 mph power on)	
Sea Level Climb Rate	425 fpm	550 fpm
Takeoff Run	660 ft	450 ft
Dist. Req'd to clear 50 ft	N.A.	
Landing Roll	835 ft	600 ft
Service Ceiling (50 fpm climb)	12,300 ft	14,800 ft
Range at Cruise	550 mi	
L/D (Glide Ratio)	13-to-1	

Quickie
Quickie Aircraft Corp.
Mojave Airport, Hangar 68
Mojave, CA 93501
(805) 824-4313
Gene Sheehan

Rutan Solitaire

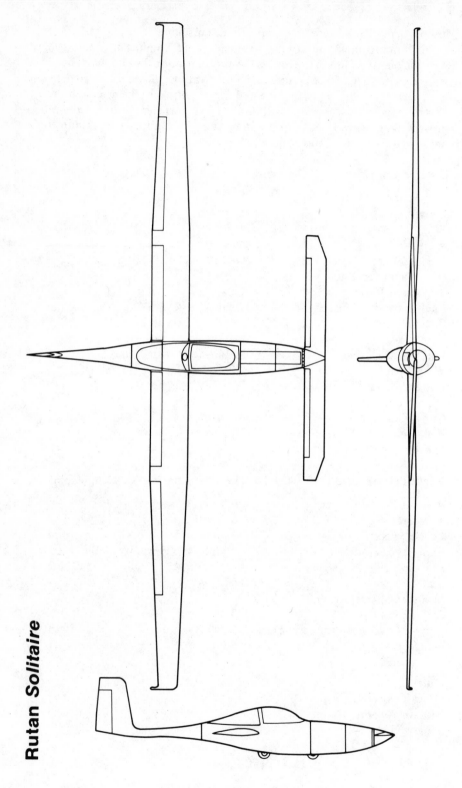

49
RUTAN *SOLITAIRE*

The Solitaire is a single-seater, self-launching, sailplane with retractable engine and propeller. It features all composite construction and a bicycle land gear. It won the Soaring Society of America's competition for a self-launching sailplane.

The development of the aircraft was quite exciting and was chronicled, by Rutan test pilot Mike Melvill, originally in the EAA's *Sport Aviation,* as presented below.

During August of 1980, personnel of the Rutan Aircraft Factory (RAF) were building the Grizzly STOL plane in a shop which was closed to the public. We knew people were speculating as to what was going on in our skunkworks. . .and that if someone about to buy plans for a Long-EZ got the idea we were developing a new, more advanced model, he would likely hold off on his purchase. Although the Grizzly was strictly a research project, we were concerned it would be mistaken for a new homebuilt. So, when the Soaring Society of America announced its competition for a homebuilt self-launching sailplane in November of 1980, we saw this as a means of killing two birds with one stone. For a long time Burt had wanted to design a sailplane, so we announced that we were entering the competition. People would assume it was the sailplane prototype under construction in our skunkworks. . .which would give us some breathing

Fig. 3-24. The Rutan Aircraft Factory "Solitaire" is a self-launching sailplane with retractable engine/propeller. It won the 1983 Soaring Society of America design contest.

space to work on the Grizzly and Burt would have time to start designing the sailplane.

I feel very fortunate that Burt includes me in a lot of the facets of conceptualizing, aerodynamic and structural design. It is fascinating to watch Burt at work. He got out his yellow legal pad and began to sketch. Should it be a canard? What about a forward swept wing? A tractor or a pusher? What engine should we use?

Burt initially settled on the Zenoah engine, however, we changed to a Robin within a few weeks and, still later, switched to a single cylinder 215cc Cuyuna. Of 7 or 8 conceptual sketches, Burt liked the canard or tandem wing, with the canard mounted right on the forward end of the fuselage, with its leading edge in line with the tip of the nose. This produces a very efficient wing-to-body juncture. Done right, it can theoretically reduce interference drag to zero. For the same reason, the main (rear) wing is mounted at the widest vertical point of the fuselage, which does not start to taper in planform until well behind the trailing edge. The parameters of the original 3-view were assessed and revised, using computer programs for stability and performance to refine the planform and control surfaces. The aircraft was designated as Model 77, the 77th design by Burt.

A small sailplane demands special airfoil sections. For the best possible performance commensurate with the small size of the sailplane, Burt turned to John Roncz. John is a leading low Reynolds number airfoil designer. He came up with three excellent airfoils for our application. The canard has to develop a very high lift coefficient at a Reynolds number of only 370,000 for takeoff, landing and thermaling. As John told me, most birds fly at a higher Reynolds number!

For the canard Burt selected a Roncz 1052-177 from butt line 0 to butt line 60 and a Roncz 1052-155 from b.l.60 out to the tip. The main wing is a Roncz 517-177 from the fuselage side out to b.l.93.5 and a Roncz 515-140 from b.l.93.5 outboard to the wing tip. The main wing is very carefully optimized for maximum performance. Because there is down wash behind the canard and upwash outboard of the canard tip, Burt "broke" the main wing with a -2° incidence change, which occurs over 11" of span between b.l 82.5 and b.l. 93.5. This allows optimum span-wise lift distribution for the main wing to provide its maximum capacity while flying in air already influenced by the canard.

Glide path control on a canard design is a real challenge. Flaps or spoilers cannot be easily used due to the large pitching moments produced by such devices. Spoiling or increasing lift on the back wing of a tandem wing or canard type will pitch the aircraft, possibly beyond the control authority of the elevator. This dictated a "spoilflap," a main wing trailing edge device that is tailored to provide high drag without a lift change. The flap on the bottom increases lift while the spoiler on the top kills lift. This one-piece, simple surface is designed to not pitch the aircraft. Burt built the spoilflap and we built a full scale section of the main wing, four feet long including Burt's trailing edge spoilflap. An outrigger device was built to mount the section of wing about 8 feet away from the side of our van while we were measuring lift. An airspeed indicator was also set up with pitot/static out on the wing section. We drove the van up and down the 9600 foot runway at Mojave at speeds varying from 40 to 90 knots while Burt actuated the spoilflap. From these tests he was able to verify that the spoilflap design was correct.

Burt initially elected to install the single cylinder Cuyuna engine, buried in the fuselage. The prop, driven by two V-belts, was mounted atop a steel tube arm that pivoted up and out of the top of the fuselage. A test stand had been utilized earlier to break in the engine and look at our folding prop mechanism. With a 2.4 to 1 reduction drive and a 42″ diameter prop, we measured right at 100 pounds of thrust.

To design the fuselage, Burt wrote a program for his Apple computer which could loft the complex compound curved shape. Task Research (see May 1983 *Sport Aviation*) made the male plug and from it pulled the female molds. The prototype fuselage was made from oriented prepreg glass skins with PVC foam cores.

One of Burt's major design goals was to put the pilot right at the CG, thus eliminating the requirement for ballast, depending on pilot weight, normally associated with sailplanes. This requirement is primarily what dictated the canard configuration, with the cockpit to be located between the wing and canard, allowing the pilot's "bellybutton" to be right at the CG of the sailplane.

We started construction on the sailplane in December of 1981 and it was completed and ready to fly on May 28, 1982. I was the test pilot for the project. All the taxi tests and initial lift-offs from Mojave's long runway were documented with video tape shot from a van. The first few runs were devoted to checks of ground handling, a cursory airspeed check and flights in ground effect to evaluate control authority and response. After several runs, I just kept climbing and flew around the airport for 15 minutes with the engine running. Solitaire handled well. We were particularly happy with the spoilflap drag device. Later the same day, we flew again and this time I climbed to 2500 feet AGL with Burt chasing me in the Grizzly. Stalls, power on or off, were as predicted: no tendency for wing rock or altitude loss, just a mild pitch bobble. A low altitude turn back to the airport with full aft stick will not result in a stall/spin. This is a common sailplane hazard due to rope breaks, etc. At altitude, I shut down the engine for the first time and folded the prop away to fly as a pure sailplane; it was intoxicating! I then extended the prop and, using a rope pull, restarted the engine and climbed back up to 3000 feet AGL. I did not know it at the time, but this was the only successful air restart ever to be made with the buried Cuyuna installation. Later attempts were unsuccessful due to various engine problems which made it clear to us that we would need either a very easy starting engine or an electric start capability. During one of the flights, we had a fuel leak that spilled gasoline into the engine compartment. Only five flights were made with this engine before we decided that the fire hazard with it buried in the fuselage was too great. Later design work would focus on extracting the entire engine. In the meantime we worked on airplane tow launch development.

We removed the engine, installed ballast to account for its missing weight and with the loan of a towplane and pilot from Fantasy Glider Port in Tehachapi, were ready for our first attempt at towed flight. We did this on June 6, 1982 in spite of gusty crosswinds right up to the limit of the Super Cub tow ship. On the first try, I aborted due to an unexpected pitch sensitivity. On the second try, I got to 300 feet—and the rope broke!

I turned, made an abbreviated pattern and landed into the wind (which was gusting to 30 knots). The third try was the charm; we towed to 3000 feet AGL and spent an enjoyable 30 minutes evaluating the "door closed" clean sailplane configuration.

Since we felt we needed to tow the sailplane ourselves, we worked with our local FAA to get the Grizzly signed off as a tow plane and get Burt checked out as a tow plane pilot. This sent the local FAA into a bit of a whirl since they had never licensed an experimental to tow another experimental! With these goals accomplished, we made our first Grizzly tow on June 23. By now we had officially named the new bird "Solitaire," a name suggested by RAF employee Roger Houghton. We towed many flights with the Grizzly and some were to 10,000 feet AGL in order to obtain L/D data, with and without spoilflaps, and to open the envelope. These were great flights. Early morning over the desert, cool, crystal clear air and very smooth conditions. Our remaining problems were the lack of a good self-launch capability and an overly sensitive pitch control system. The basic static stability of the aircraft was excellent (stable, smooth elevator versus C_L curve). The control system was the culprit, needing lower friction and gearing revisions.

On June 27, 1982, we felt confident enough to invite an experienced sailplane pilot, Hannes Linke, to try Solitaire and give us his opinion. Hannes liked Solitaire, though it was a bit pitch sensitive and that its L/D was more than enough for an entry level sailplane. He was particularly complimentary about the spoilflap system. On July 1 the FAA signed off our area restrictions, so we were ready to take Solitaire to Oshkosh.

We obtained a prototype Normal/Aire Garrett, two cylinder, two stroke engine, recommended to us by Englishman Colin Chapman of Lotus auto fame. This was installed on a fixed pylon for evaluation purposes and the first flight in this configuration was on July 21. All of the next ten flights were to get carburetion, exhaust system length and prop to the best we could, to see if it was promising enough to develop a retraction capability.

Michael Dilley and Doug Shane towed the Solitaire to Oshkosh behind our van. . . and Burt towed me aloft with the Grizzly on four different afternoons during the air show periods. One afternoon I took off under power to participate in the fly-bys . . . and had a short trip, indeed. I took off on Runway 18, turned crosswind over the woods near Steve Wittman's home—and had the engine seize solid! I turned for the airport with barely 200 feet under me. I did not believe I could make it back to the runway, but I had under estimated the Solitaire's glide capability. Even with the engine mounted on a fixed pylon, I made it back easily, flying downwind, base and turning final to line up with the taxiway. At the last minute, I decided my wings would strike the tall taxi lights, so I closed the spoilflaps, pulled up and glided over to make a smooth landing on the grass between the taxiway and the runway.

The factory representative tore the engine down and rebuilt it with new pistons and barrels, and we were able to make several successful demo flights under power in the fly-bys.

Soon after returning to Mojave, Burt made his first flight in the Solitaire, It was getting close to contest time. The rules of the SSA contest stated that although proof of structural integrity by analytical means (stress analysis) is normally acceptable to the FAA, this would not be acceptable for the purposes of the contest. A static load test was the only basis acceptable to prove the structure. The contest rules defined the limit load for our category of sailplane as a minimum of 4.67 G's. Because the Solitaire was considered by the judges to be "unconventional," we were required to proof load to 4.67 x 1.5 = 7.0 G's. This load was defined as "ultimate." Tests to ultimate generally yield or destroy structure, making it unairworthy, however, the Solitaire had sufficient margins to allow using the prototype for the load tests.

On August 20, 1982, we mounted Solitaire upside down on foam block supports on top of a strong work table. The main wing tips were 48″ above the floor. We static loaded the canard first, using 25 pound bags of lead shot. These were carefully placed, simultaneously one on each side at exactly the butt line Burt had called out. We took the canard to limit (4.67 G's) in bending, then limit load in both bending and torsion by moving the lead shot bags aft 3.5 inches. At this point, all weight was removed to check that the canard tips returned to their original position. Then it was taken to "ultimate" (4.67 x 1.5) in bending and torsion combined. For the canard this required careful symmetrical hand loading of 910 lbs. of lead shot. No noise or signs of stress were apparent, so we off loaded and went on the main wing.

The main wing at ultimate bending and torsion looked quite scary! The tips bent to within 2½″ of the floor, meaning they had deflected 45½″! Of course, the "downhill slope" of the wings means that in order to get the lead shot bags to stay in the correct position, each bag had to be duct taped into place. This is a tricky operation because any bouncing induced can apply massive overloads. Putting the last lead bag on the wing tip brought the total weight on the wings to 1932 lbs and was really a teeth gritter. As it turned out, like the canard, the wing did not make a sound and returned to its normal relaxed position as soon as the weight was removed.

The fuselage was then jigged on its side and braced at the main wing and canard attach areas, after which the vertical tail was loaded with 168 lbs to test it to ultimate.

While this static load was very interesting to all of us who participated, it is not a task to be taken lightly and I for one would not even consider doing a static load such as this to an airplane of mine without having a qualified engineer present.

245

Flying the Solitaire early the next morning, I must say I felt a tremendous confidence in the structure. Even when I opened the dive speed out to its present 120 KIAS and pulled out full spoilflaps at the dive speed, I had no doubts at all. Loops (4 G's), rolls, split S's and wing over turns all seemed easier now that I had seen the airplane at 7.0 G's.

The SSA contest was held in Tehachapi, California on September 3, 4 and 5, 1982. Tehachapi is only 20 miles west of Mojave, so we elected to fly in. Burt and Grizzly towed Solitaire and me over the ridge where I released and soared around out of sight of the crowd at the Fantasy Haven airport. Burt landed and parked the Grizzly and then called me in on the radio. Of course, I had to show off a little, so I did three consecutive loops and a series of wing over turns while losing altitude to make a high speed low pass, entered the pattern and landed.

We took the Solitaire apart for the contest judges and the public to inspect the insides. We later flew with power and tow. Two of the contest judges, Einar Enervoldson and Walt Mooney, flew the Solitaire, as did Larry Barret, owner of the Fantasy Haven facility. Burt also flew at Tehachapi, his first flight under tow. Monday, September 5, the final day of the SSA contest, Solitaire was declared the winner. The whole purpose of our design was realized: that it is the best homebuilt available to promote soaring.

Later that afternoon, I fired up the Normal/Aire Garrett and flew my first powered cross country back to Mojave. The same week, Sally Melvill, an RAF employee, and Burt's brother, Dick Rutan, flew the Solitaire. Both were delighted. On September 23, 1982, we were invited to fly the Solitaire at a Society of Experimental Test Pilots air show, a prestigious event and quite an honor.

By now, we were close to freezing the design. We had, in the course of testing, increased the span of the elevators and reduced elevator system friction. We had increased the span of the ailerons (better roll), had reduced the height of the vertical tail (directional stability was more than needed) and had tested several different wheel brakes. We had not figured out a way to fold the engine. The Normal/Aire Garrett simply would not physically fit into the available space. Besides, it did not have a starter, a mandatory requirement in our opinion.

At this point a KFM 107E was obtained from Don Black in New York. We mounted it on the fixed pylon for evaluation and soon decided that this was the way to go. We had to rotate the KFM 90° to place the cylinders vertically instead of horizontally as they normally are, and also had to come up with an exhaust system that would allow us to fold the engine/prop/exhaust assembly into the nose. Dale Fischer of Fischer Engineering put our KFM on his dyno and developed a super exhaust system that has done the job.

Our first flight with the KFM mounted on a fixed pylon was on October 1, 1982. Many flights were conducted in this configuration developing props, carburetor jetting, etc. During December 1982, Einer Enervoldson asked if he could conduct an extensive flight test of Solitaire with a view to writing an article for *Soaring*. Burt readily agreed.

Einar installed his own calibrated instruments, an eight foot long pitot boom and conducted eight towed flights ranging from 35 minutes to over an hour duration. Einar is a NASA test pilot and is going to publish his pilot report in an upcoming edition of *Soaring* magazine.

Meanwhile, Michel Dilley and I were alternately working on the Solitaire plans and trying to make the KFM engine retract. We settled on an electro hydraulic unit used as a trim motor on an outboard speedboat, with a double acting ram. This does the job beautifully. It is so simple, and has been flawless to date. First flight with the retractable engine, but with no doors to close it in, was on February 24, 1983. It worked great and was quite a kick to be able, finally, to retract and extend the engine with just a flip of a switch! The next several flights were used to clock the prop so it would stop vertically oriented, or nearly so. We installed a small cam that could be manually extended so that the prop would windmill to the vertical and a lobe on the prop hub would engage the cam, at which point the engine could be retracted.

At this point, the Soaring Society held its annual convention at the MGM Grand in Reno, Nevada. Sally and Michael Dilley drove the van towing Solitaire up to Reno while Burt and I took the easy way by flying up in Burt's Defiant. We put the Solitaire together in the display area and had a good response from the crowd of several thousand soaring enthusiasts. Michael and I can easily put Solitaire together or take it apart in under 10 minutes. We did not see any other sailplanes up there that could be assembled any faster. The Convention was fun and the location excellent! We were proud to have the SSA present Burt with an "Outstanding Achievement" award for the design of the Solitaire.

Back at the shop, Michael and I got busy on the last item not yet worked out—the engine compartment doors. These are split in the middle and held closed by bungee cords. The engine pushes them open as it comes out and holds then open while it is out and running. We have limit switches that stop the motor at its upper and lower limits of travel, as well as micro switches that disable the starter and ignition *unless* the engine is all the way up and in the proper position for running.

First flight with the engine cover doors was April 14, 1983. Test results showed a reduction in directional stability with the doors open and engine out. The added vertical surface ahead of the CG was the culprit. We went back to the original vertical tail height and now have the required stability for powered launch.

On April 17 I flew the Solitaire to the California City air show with surface winds gusting to 40 knots! I arrived there at 2500 feet AGL and gave the customary couple of loops and a few wing over turns before making a high speed low approach with the engine folded away. I pulled up to downwind where I extended and started the engine, flew base, final, landed and taxied around several aircraft and many people to my tiedown spot, unaided with no requirement for any ground crew. The following day we flew back to Mojave and in even worse wind conditons with no problem.

A few days ago I climbed to about 3000 feet AGL, shut down and folded the engine and worked a little lift over the Mojave Airport. I was up for over two hours before an over full bladder forced me to land. Several flights have included over two hours unpowered. Burt flew a self launch flight, working weak lift for over two and a half hours, using the engine for about 25 minutes. I plan to use Solitaire to achieve several of the altitude gain and duration pins offered by the Soaring Society of America.

May 5, 1983, Peter Lert, editor of *Air Progress* magazine, arrived to fly Solitaire. After a brief cockpit check out, he taxied out for the first of four flights. Conditions were very weak but Peter managed to stay up for over an hour on one flight and enjoyed our Solitaire very much. Look for a Solitaire article in a future *Air Progress*.

Our most recent refinements have been to add a bob-weight to improve pitch handling, increase the tire size for better gravel and grass field operation and we also installed the neatest hydraulic disc brake in the back wheel. Ken Brock Manufacturing designed and built the new brake. Ken Brock will be the source for all the prefabricated metal parts. Literally every single metal part in the airplane will be available, or a person could buy some of them and make the remainder. The choice is up to the builder.

Aircraft Spruce and Wicks Aircraft are the sources of all raw materials and hardware. This system has worked well for us with our previous homebuilt designs, the VariEze and Long-EZ.

Task Research will be manufacturing and marketing the prefabricated fiberglass parts. These parts will be the most advanced state-of-the-art components offered to homebuilders. The fuselage halves consist of skins of prepreg fiberglass, carefully oriented for optimum efficiency, with Nomex honeycomb cores and utilizing high tech film adhesive to bond the sandwich together. This is vacuum bagged into female molds and cured at 220° F in a large oven. The main wing spars have "S" glass roving spar caps and are molded in metal molds and cured at 220° F. The metal machined fittings are jigged in place and drilled and fitted. The spars and fuselage halves will be required items, since they are not readily homebuildable. Task Research will also be supplying the seat pan, the canopy in its frame and the turtledeck premolded. In addition, optional pieces include prefab fuselage bulkheads, wing root fairings, wheel fairings, wingtips, even pre-hot wired foam cores for wings and canard.

Specifications

Wingspan	41 ft 9 in
Length	19 ft 2 in
Height	5 ft 7 in
Wing Area	102.44 sq ft
Engine Make, Model, HP	KFM 107E 25 hp
Prop Diameter/Pitch	30 in/15 in
Reduction Ratio	1-to-1
Fuel Capacity/Consumption	5 gal/2.4 gph at 100%

Gross Weight	620 lbs
Empty Weight	380 lbs
Useful Load	240 lbs
Wing Loading	6.05 psf
Power Loading	25.8 lb/hp
Design Load Factors	+7, -3
Construction Time	400 man-hrs
Field Assembly Time	15 min
Pricing	$7,000 - $9,000 (depending on amount of prefabricated parts)

Flight Performance

Velocity Never Exceed	143 mph
Top Level Speed	89.7 mph
Cruise Speed	80 mph @ 90% power
Stall Speed (in free air)	36.8 mph (minimum flying speed)
Sea Level Climb Rate	350 fpm @ 46 mph
Takeoff Run	950 ft
Dist. Req'd to clear 50 ft	N.A.
Landing Roll	300 ft
Service Ceiling (100 fpm climb)	12,000 ft
Range at Cruise	120 mi
L/D (Glide Ratio)	32-to-1 @ 50 KTS 57.5 mph
Minimum Sink Rate	150 fpm @ 40 KTS 46 mph

Solitaire
Rutan Aircraft Factory, Inc.
Bldg. 13, Airport
Mojave, CA 93501
(805) 824-2645
Trish

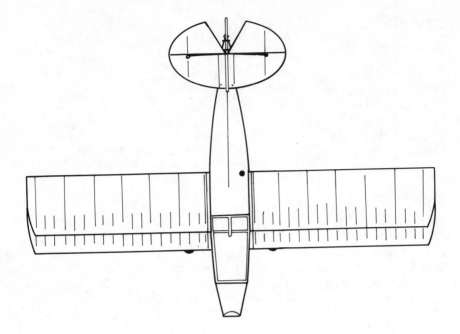

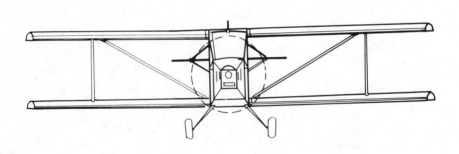

Sorrell Guppy

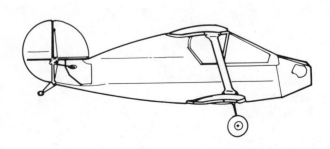

50

SORRELL *GUPPY*

The Guppy is a totally enclosed, single place, negative stagger biplane. It features all wood construction covered with 1.7 oz. dacron and doped.

The fuselage uses a box girder frame of spruce and plywood. Landing gear legs and the tailwheel spring are 6150 spring steel rod, while the engine mount is 413 welded steel tubing.

The wings are single spar with a plywood "D" section leading edge and single I-strut per side. The ribs as a solid balsa web with spruce cap strips. Alternately, the ribs could be sawed plywood or build-up stick and gusset. Most attach fittings are aluminum slate. The drag member is 6061-T6 tubing. The ailerons are sheet aluminum pop riveted to an aluminum torque tube. The wings on the prototype were not designed to be foldable. However, they can be removed.

Cockpit entry is accomplished by a step on top of the left wing root, and over the left side of the cockpit. The top and left side forward window hinges to the right, allowing easy access. A 220 pound, 6ft-2in person should fit inside without any problem.

The current Guppy uses the Revmaster R-800 (a converted Citroen of 25-28 hp), or the more popular Rotax 377 of 35 hp. However, the prototype flew fine on an 18 hp Cushman, which proved very reliable.

In the air, the Guppy is very controllable yet, it is not at all sensitive. It is definitely a rudder airplane, due to significant adverse yaw, and neutral yaw stability. Because of its low speed however, it is "baby-carriage-like" in

Fig. 3-25. The original Sorrell "Guppy" was powered by an 18 hp Cushman four-cycle engine. Single-seater was all wood, fabric covered.

its difficulty rating. Installation of a skid ball is a big help in slip and skid control, and is recommended.

Many people ask if there is any difficulty operating without brakes. According to Mike Kimbrel, Guppy owner, "I have flown it in many different conditions (crosswinds, gusts, tall grass, pavement, soft fields, etc.) and have found it to be no problem. When I first flew it out of the Sorrell's 900 foot airstrip, the airplane presented no difficulty taking off or stopping."

"If I am operating on pavement, I don't land downwind. If I wish to stop on pavement while taxiing downwind, I either put one tire on the grass, turn into the wind, or turn off the engine. There are no other problems as long as I plan ahead."

"The Guppy rates as a very easy airplane to fly and only requires the pilot to be gentle and modest in his demands. It will reward him with economical, useful performance."

Specifications

Wingspan	21 ft 3 in
Length	15 ft 5 in
Height	5 ft 3½ in
Wing Area	129 sq ft
Engine Make, Model, HP	Revmaster R-800(28) or Rotax 377
Prop Diameter/Pitch	N.A.
Reduction Ratio	1-to-1, R-800 — 2-to-1 Rotax
Fuel Capacity/Consumption	6 gal/2 gph
Gross Weight	600 lbs
Empty Weight	340 lbs
Useful Load	260 lbs
Wing Loading	4.7 psf
Power Loading	21.4 R-800, 17.1 Rotax
Design Load Factors	+6, -4
Construction Time	400 man-hrs
Field Assembly Time	N.A.
Pricing	$5,979 with R-800 (Approx. $5,300 Rotax)

Flight Performance	90 mph
Top Level Speed	85 mph
Cruise Speed	75 mph @ 60% power
Stall Speed (in free air)	30 mph
Sea Level Climb Rate	575 fpm @ 55 mph
Takeoff Run	225 ft
Dist. Req'd to clear 50 ft	N.A.
Landing Roll	200 ft
Service Ceiling (100 fpm climb)	10,000 ft
Range at Cruise	225 mi

L/D (Glide Ratio)	12-to-1 @ 45 mph
Minimum Sink Rate	375 fpm @ 45 mph

SNS-2 "Guppy"
Sorrell Aviation
16525 Tilley Rd. So.
Tenino, WA 98589
(206) 264-2866
Mark or Tim Sorrell

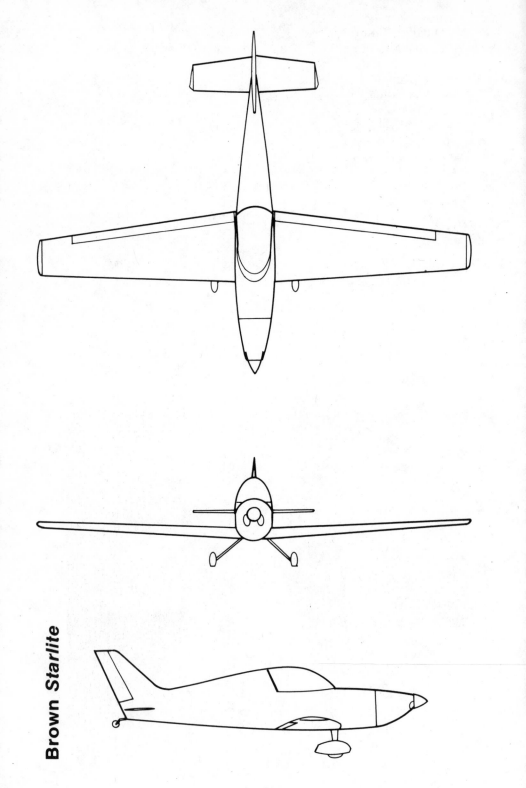

Brown Starlite

51

STARLITE AIRCRAFT
STARLITE

The Starlite is a single seat, low wing, tractor monoplane with taildragger gear. It features a mixture of composite and wooden construction in a sleek, sophisticated shape. It won first place in the lightplane division of the 1983 ARV Competition, as well as the Outstanding New Design at Oshkosh '83

The Starlite was designed specifically to lower the cost of sport flying. This was accomplished through very detailed engineering so that every part of the airplane was reduced to its absolute simplest and most efficient form. At an empty weight of only 225 pounds, it is one of the lightest aircraft ever flown. The result, of course, is performance on low power. Burning 1.2 gallons of regular auto gasoline an hour, the Starlite takes off in 300 ft., climbs at 800 fpm, and cruises at 110 mph.

Simplicity was the Starlite designer's other major design goal. Simple

Fig. 3-26. The composite construction "Starlite" won first place in the 1983 ARV Competition Fly-Off. Production kits feature the Rotax 277, with a cruise of 110 mph.

construction and simple systems were a must. Accordingly, the kit includes prefabrication of every part requiring a special building skill. Simple design was also a major contributor to keeping the cost down. This goal was aided considerably because of advancements in structural materials. The vacuum molded, sandwich composite materials and techniques are much more common now, driving the cost and availability in the right direction for amateur-built aircraft enthusiasts. The sandwich composite not only allows a much lighter fuselage, but also provides the builder with

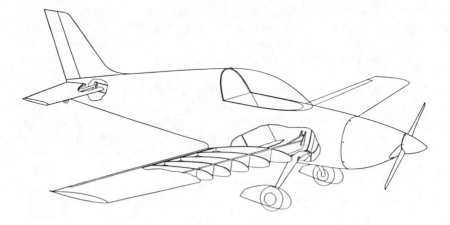

Fig. 3-27. Cutaway of the "Starlite" shows simple, efficient structure. Aircraft weighs only 225 pounds.

other advantages. The vacuum bagged surfaces are ready for paint, meaning you don't have to spend time sanding.

The wings are constructed of wood and foam. The two spars are spruce, the ribs foam, and the skin is plywood. According to Mark Brown, the designer, plywood has one-third the density of fiberglass, is relatively inexpensive and strong. Furthermore, unlike the compound curves of the fuselage, the wings have simple curves that lend themselves well to being covered with flat, rectangular stock—with little waste.

The wing kit includes the following components: double-tapered main spar, tapered rear spar, pre-cut ribs, wing skins, ailerons, flight controls, horizontal stabilizer material, rudder, and a wing construction manual.

The compound curved components of the fuselage are pre-molded from a sandwich composite of ⅛ inch Klegecell with a 120-type fiberglass skins. This costs a little more than supplying materials, but allows for quality control and assured structural integrity.

The fuselage kits consist of the following components: sandwich composite fuselage shell with wing fillets and vertical stabilizer molded in, composite landing gear, wheels, brakes, axles, canopy, fuel tank, epoxy resin, fiberglass cloth, tailwheel, seat and bulkhead panels, and a fuselage construction manual

Brown claims that his mixed methods of construction have some distinct advantages over an all-metal airplane. Chief among these are economy, ease of construction, and in many cases, better crash survivability. Furthermore, the higher costs of the pre-molded composites and prefabricated parts are offset by the lower costs of the wooden wing and its simplified construction.

Much needs to be said about the Starlite's light weight engine, for without it, the airplane would not have been possible. Thanks to the growth of the ultralight industry, several engines were already on the market that offered enough reliability for a sportplane like the Starlite.

So far, all the engines that have succeeded in the light weight category have been two-cycle, due primarily to their inherent high power-to-weight ratio. The real surprise to many conservative engineers is how dependable the two-cycles have performed in typical ultralight, off-airport conditions. In fact, two-cycle engines are operating by the tens-of-thousands, while providing the foundation for the extraordinary growth of the ultralight industry.

The main reasons for the acceptance and success of the two-cycle aviation engine are threefold: its inherent simplicity, a wider familiarity of how to take reasonable care of a previously misunderstood powerplant and, low cost. The simplicity of the two-cycle can be readily observed by taking one apart. A complete overhaul can be done in a couple of hours. The parts count is about half that of a four-cycle, because there are no valves, camshafts, or oil systems. Owners of two-cycle engines can care for them thanks to the existence of a book called *Ultralight Propulsion* (see list of books available at the rear of this book). Two-cycles are inexpensive because of their simplicity, and high volume production. They were, after all, developed from the snowmobile engine.

The primary cause for engine failure in the past has been negligence by the operator. A two-cycle engine depends on the oil and fuel mixture for lubrication and cooling. Consequently, if the operator neglects to mix oil with the fuel, the engine is in trouble. This requirement seems rather obvious and, in fact, doesn't appear to be a problem when the operator is properly informed. A more subtle requirement, however, is proper control of the fuel-to-air ratio. The two-cycle engine derives much of its cooling from a slightly rich fuel mixture. However, this actually detunes the engine away from its maximum power. Since the two-cycle engine is typically chosen for its inherent high performance (low weight with high power) the situation is a natural set-up for operator abuse. Not realizing the importance of proper fuel-to-air mixtures, the operator tends to keep leaning the engine more and more, because the power keeps getting stronger and stonger. The only limit to this process is when the piston gets so hot that it expands beyond the limits of the cylinder, shortening engine life and possibly seizing.

The solution to the problem of mixture mismanagement is actually very simple. An EGT (Exhaust Gas Temperature) gauge tells the operator exactly and immediately how the mixture is set. This simple gauge eliminates the guesswork and allows a very precise mixture adjustment.

Even though the mixture is usually set when the engine is first installed, the EGT is invaluable in insuring the mixture remains correct.

A two-cycle engine is a natural for aircraft applications, with its inherent power-to-weight advantage. With any civilized treatment at all, it should function at least as reliably as a four-cycle engine. Consequently, the powerplant selected for the Starlite is the two-cycle Rotax 277 single cylinder. It is the industry standard for ultralights and has an outstanding record for reliability and smooth, quiet performance. It is available with either electric or manual starters and is rated at 28 hp.

One of the most important considerations in recreational flying is handling qualities. The Starlite's aerodynamic configuration is strictly conventional, which implies no surprises in flight. The long fuselage and large tail areas provide static stability and a wide CG range. The wings incorporate generous washout, providing for a fully controllable stall. The NACA 2415 airfoil provides excellent low Reynolds number lift, while not being sensitive to surface imperfections as for many new airfoils.

Flyingwise, the Starlite's handling characteristics are quite conventional and docile. The ailerons give good roll control up to a full stall, aided by the wings 1½° washout—the wing roots stall before the tips. Landing speed is high enough to require attention, but the adjustably damped tailwheel aids the neophyte taildragger pilot greatly in taxiing straight ahead. Later on after confidence and experience is gained, the tailwheel can be loosened, allowing for greater ground maneuverability. The stick is side-mounted.

The Starlite is also designed for trailability. Because of the aircraft's light weight and simplicity, one person can unload and assemble it in ten minutes.

The airplane can be purchased in three separate kits: the fuselage, engine and wing and control surface kit. A separate plans manual comes with each kit. The plans manuals can be bought alone for $60, which is refundable when the kit itself is purchased.

Specifications

Wingspan	21 ft 6 in
Length	16 ft 5 in
Height	4 ft
Wing Area	56 sq ft
Engine Make, Model, HP	Rotax 277, 28 hp
Prop Diameter/Pitch	48 in/51 in
Reduction Ratio	3-to-1
Fuel Capacity/Consumption	5 gal/1.2 gph
Gross Weight	450 lbs
Empty Weight	225 lbs
Useful Load	225 lbs
Wing Loading	8 psf
Power Loading	16.1 lb/hp
Design Load Factors	+4, -2.6
Construction Time	300 man-hrs

Field Assembly Time	10 min
Pricing	$6,500

Flight Performance

Velocity Never Exceed	N.A.
Top Level Speed	110 mph
Cruise Speed	100 mph
Stall Speed (in free air)	42 mph
Sea Level Climb Rate	800 fpm
Takeoff Run	300 ft
Dist. Req'd to clear 50 ft	N.A.
Landing Roll	300 ft
Service Ceiling (100 fpm climb)	10,000 ft
Range at Cruise	300 mi
L/D (Glide Ratio)	
Minimum Sink Rate	

Starlite
Starlite Aircraft Company
2219 Orange Blossom
San Antonio, TX 78247
(512) 494-9812
Mark Brown

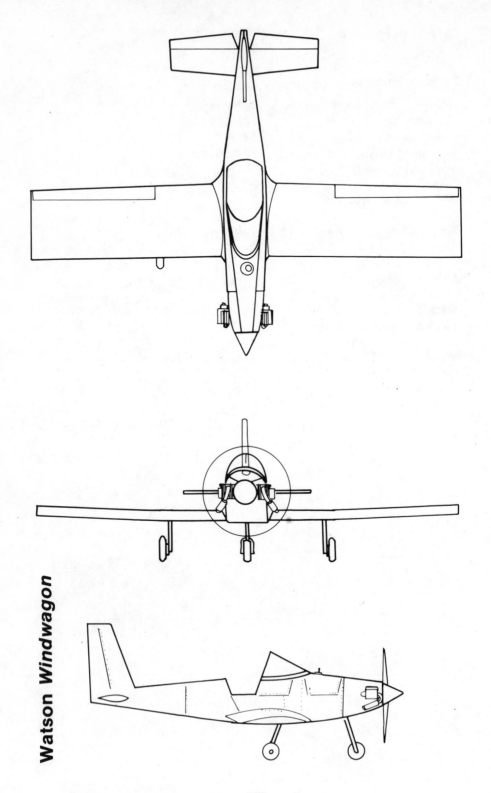

Watson Windwagon

52

WATSON *WINDWAGON*

The Windwagon is an all metal, single seat open cockpit monoplane with tricycle landing gear. It is powered by a sawn-in-half VW engine, and was the inspiration for Hummel Bird, as featured elsewhere in this book.

The cockpit is designed to accommodate tall pilots, with seating being a semi-supine position. The control stick is center mounted. The fuselage is formed by wrapping sheet aluminum around bulkheads. They are made by bending tabs over plywood formers, then drilling a hole and pop riveting.

The wing ribs are identical, and made all at once. They cut from sheet aluminum, clamped together and all tab bending holes drilled through the entire stack. They are then separated and each rib is clamped between the two plywood rib formers and the tabs bent over. The entire set of ribs can be made in one evening.

The spar is made from aluminum angle caps with a flat aluminum center shear web riveted to them. No bending is required.

The whole airplane is simple to build, and no bending brake or sheet metal experience is necessary, according to Watson. All you need is a couple of 2 x 4's, a pair of "C"-clamps, a plastic hammer, drill, bits, tin snips and a file for smooting the rough cut edges. All bending that must be done can be clamped between the 2 x 4 and bent over with the plastic hammer.

Some welding is required on the steel landing gear and the control system. Your local welding shop can do the job.

The entire airplane can be built in a single or double bay garage. The wing tip panels are removable, leaving a six foot wide center section on the

Fig. 3-28. Watson "Windwagon" is powered by a sawn-in-half VW. All metal single seater inspired Hummel "Bird," featured previously.

landing gear. It can also be stored in the garage to save on hangar rent, or even parked under the wing of another airplane.

The engine is quite unique, being obtained from your local VW wrecking yard. Basically, the rear cylinders are sawn off and an aluminum plate bolted on to cover the opening in the crankcase. All modifications to the engine are included with the plans.

The plans include full size bulkhead and rib patterns, and are very detailed and easy to understand, according to Watson. A list of materials needed and where to obtain them is also included.

The designer talks about the first flight of the prototype. "A tornado had been spotted about five miles south of the airport. The air was a bit bouncy with a 15 knot crosswind at 30 degrees to the runway.

"Previous taxi tests had been made. Ground handling was a joy with plenty of rudder and nosewheel control. On takeoff, rpm was a little low. At 40 mph, a gentle pull on the stick brought the nose up. Accelerate to 45 mph and it flys off the ground. Lower the nose and accelerate to 60 mph for climb out. Because of the low rpm and power available, I used a low rate of climb. At 400 feet, I made a shallow left turn. Ailerons have good control— positive but not at all sensitive.

"I made a few turns left and right, ensuring ailerons were alright, then made a pass back over the runway to check rudder control. This is the first airplane I have ever flown where the ball stays right in the middle without effort. Next, I climbed up a bit and cut the power back. I pulled back gently on the stick to see how it would flare power off. Lowering the nose at about 10 degrees and gently pulling back the stick would level it out at 50 to 55 mph. Next, at about half throttle, I dived to 100 mph over the runway and pulled up. Everything is okay, but power. I turned final at 55 mph indicated over the fence. Throttle back and a gentle flare levels off about a foot above the runway. At 45 mph, the main gear touches and, at 40 mph, the nose gear comes down. There is no backing or pitching.

"I am very pleased with the performance of the world's smallest conventional (in 1977) airplane. All in all, the Windwagon is the easiest airplane to fly that I know of. The takeoff and landing speed is low and the wing has lots of lift. It's very positive and stable, and an absolute joy to fly.

Specifications

Wingspan	18 ft
Length	13 ft
Height	3 ft 1 in
Wing Area	54 sq ft
Engine Make, Model, HP	½ VW, 30 hp
Prop Diameter/Pitch	50 in/28 in
Reduction Ratio	1-to-1
Fuel Capacity/Consumption	4 gal
Gross Weight	485 lbs
Empty Weight	273 lbs

Useful Load	212 lbs
Wing Loading	8.98 psf
Power Loading	16.17 lb/hp
Design Load Factors	N.A.
Construction Time	N.A.
Field Assembly Time	N.A.
Pricing	$50 (plans)

Flight Performance

Velocity Never Exceed	N.A.
Top Level Speed	100 mph
Cruise Speed	90 mph
Stall Speed (in free air)	40 mph
Sea Level Climb Rate	N.A.
Takeoff Run	N.A.
Dist. Req'd to clear 50 ft	N.A.
Landing Roll	N.A.
Service Ceiling (100 fpm climb)	N.A.
Range at Cruise	N.A.

Windwagon
Watson Windwagon Company
Rt. 1
Newcastle, TX 76372
(817) 862-5615
Gary Watson

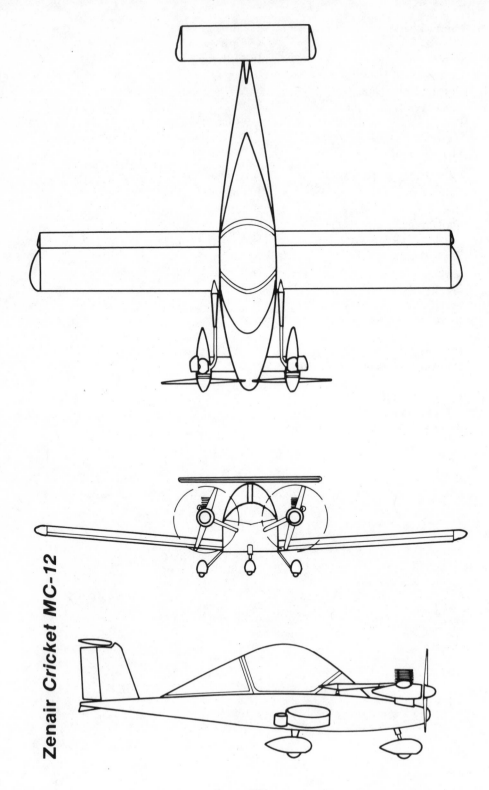

Zenair Cricket MC-12

53

ZENAIR *CRICKET*

The Cricket is a twin engined low wing monoplane with tricycle landing gear. It is capable of full aerobatic performance.

Each wing is a high strength structure with absolutely no internal systems. The four flap/aileron support arms are bolted to the rear end of the wing with nothing to interfere with the air flow over the smooth surface obtained by the construction method. The flap/ailerons are of the "junkers" type. The skins is bonded to rigid foam ribs and a few sheet metal ribs.

The wing spar is made up of inverted aluminum sections, with 32 rigid foam ribs bounded to it. Each rib is strong enough to withstand the aircraft's weight. The wing skins are thin sheet aluminum bonded to the spar/rib frame. The necessary bonding pressure is obtained by simply enclosing the wing in a sealed vinyl bag connected to a household vacuum cleaner.

The fuselage has a rectangular cross section with a bubble canopy over the cockpit. The forward fuselage has four single curved panels with rigid foam stiffness blind riveted to four angle members. The loads from the wing, pilot, gear and engines, are transferred through formed metal bulkheads. The rear fuselage consists of two straight sheets blind riveted to two sheets with formed edges. This provides for high strength and quick construction.

The horizontal tail is the all moving "T"-type with two hinged bearings at the top of the vertical fin spar. It is a single rectangular panel with no controls or trim tab, and is built similar to the wing. The vertical tail features a swept back fin and rudder, also constructed like the wing.

Fig. 3-29. Zenair "Cricket" is French all metal, single-seater with two 15 hp, two-cycle engines. The 160 pound aircraft is fully aerobatic, and cruises at 115 mph.

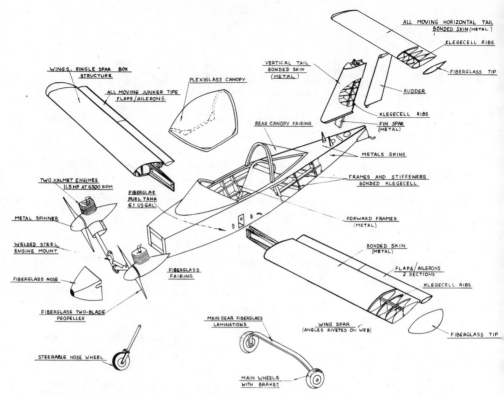

Fig. 3-30. "Cricket MC-12" cutaway shows how simply the aircraft is designed. It is surely the world's lightest airplane.

The nose gear is steerable. Suspension is provided by two telescoping tubes connected by bungee shock absorbers. The main gear is a single leaf spring attached to the fuselage via foam rubber donuts. Wheels are 3.00 x 3 with brakes on the mains.

Pitch is controlled by push-pull rods with built-in artificial "feel" provided by rubber springs connected to a trim control lever. This is said to avoid the "over loose" feeling so common among lightweight aircraft.

The flap/ailerons are controlled through a mixer, with quick release ball joints connected to the inboard end of the control surfaces. Short push-pull rods run to the stick.

The rudder controls yaw via pedals and cables. The pedals are adjustable in flight to accommodate pilots as tall as 6 ft 3 in.

On the ground, the nosewheel allows a turning radius of 14 feet, and the brakes are effective. In the air, the Cricket is stable, and the control response is immediate and crisp. The controls are firm at low speeds, and the Cricket can handle 20 mph, 90 degree crosswinds. Cruise is at 110 mph. Noise levels are said to be low because of the tuned exhaust system and engine mountings. There are said to be no vibrations.

Flight on one engine at cruise is reportedly no problem—there is no adverse yaw. The designer says this is due to the position of the engines which are very close to aircraft centerline and, the propeller slipstream, which is deflected by the canopy. This creates an incidence on the vertical tail, compensating for the asymetric thrust of one engine. The prototype has repeatedly been flown and landed safely on one engine. Also, the airplane will maintain just over 90 mph, and still climb on one engine.

The slotted flap/ailerons extend under the trailing edge of the full wing span. These, combined with a thick, high lift airfoil, allow for a stall speed of 42 mph, which is low for an airplane with a wing loading as high as the Cricket's. At moderate deflections, this type of flap provides low drag and roll control. In fact, the roll rate is 180 degrees per second. The relatively high wing loading of 11.2 psf makes the Cricket relatively insensitive to turbulence.

Assembly and disassembly of the Cricket is one of the Cricket's strong points. Each wing panel is attached with two main handled pins and four secondary self-locking pins. The flap/aileron control is connected with a quick release ball joint. The best time clocked from getting out of the car, unloading the aircraft from its trailer, and assembling it, is two minutes. Disassembly takes an equal time—by one person. All this is said to be greatly simplified by the trailer, which incorporates its own ramp and the light weight and small size of the wings.

The Cricket's own hangar—trailer measures 5 ft x 13½ ft, and weighs 500 pounds fully loaded. It can be easily towed by any car.

The aircraft can be built from plans, where you gather all the materials, or from a complete kit. Most drawings are full scale, consisting of 42 blueprints. They cover all details and every part and assembly. The construction manual is in three parts. It begins with general information detailing such items as blueprint reading, working with rigid foam, sheet metal, riveting, degreasing, etching, bonding, etc. Detailed procedures then follow the plans with a step-by-step procedure for construction. Instructions for testing the aircraft on the ground and in the air, plus many useful instructions for taxi tests and the first flight, are included. A powerplant manual with chapters on engine installation and adjustments, general operations, the propellers full and electric system, powerplant controls, etc. is quite useful. Finally, a complete list of materials and recommended supplies is presented.

Once your project is completed and you have sent in the last page of the construction manual, along with a photograph of the completed aircraft, a Cricket Flight and Maintenance Manual will be sent to you.

Specifications

Wingspan	16 ft
Length	12 ft 10 in
Height	4 ft
Wing Area	34 sq ft
Engine Make, Model, HP	2-PUL, 15 hp each
Prop Diameter/Pitch	34 in

Reduction Ratio	1-to-1
Fuel Capacity/Consumption	6 gal/1.5 gph
Gross Weight	380 bls
Empty Weight	168 lbs
Useful Load	212 lbs
Wing Loading	11.2 psf
Power Loading	12.67 lb/hp
Design Load Factors	+9, -4.5
Construction Time	600 man-hrs
Field Assembly Time	2 min
Pricing	$3,560

Flight Performance

Velocity Never Exceed	N.A.
Top Level Speed	N.A.
Cruise Speed	115 mph
Stall Speed (in free air)	42 mph
Sea Level Climb Rate	1200 fpm
Takeoff Run	480 ft
Dist. Req'd to clear 50 ft	N.A.
Landing Roll	N.A.
Service Ceiling (100 fpm climb)	16,000 ft (3,500 ft on one engine)
Range at Cruise	300 mi
L/D (Glide Ratio)	11-to-1 @ 62.5 mph

Cricket MC-12
Zenair, Ltd.
236 Richmond Street
Richmond Hill
Ontario, L4C 3Y8
Canada

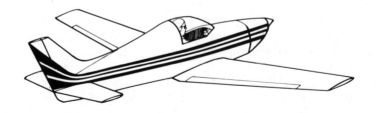

Section IV

ARVs Of The Future Composite Construction And Unusual Configurations

The future of the ARV is excitingly bright. In fact, ARV appears to be the long sought for answer to the high cost of flying.

The appearance of the ultralight has proven the public's interest in and enthusiasm for flying. Even so, it probably represents only the mere "tip-of-the-proverbial-iceberg" of popular flying. With the development of the ARV, and the establishment of the Recreational Pilot's License, the stage has been set for a boom in sport aviation.

Those who started flying ultralights will want to "move up" to an ARV, so they can go somewhere at no more expense than their ultralight. Those who are already licensed pilots, will now be able to afford to fly, while realizing decent cross-country performance with low turbulence sensitivity. The number of designs will proliferate because of an increasing demand. Prospective ARV pilots have a good number of designs to choose from now, but more are on the way.

Advances in two-cycle engine technology and increased reliability, will make them a more acceptable aero engine. Improved understanding of their operation will make pilots more comfortable with them. The development of lightweight four-cycle engines will also expand, meeting the needs of those who are convinced of their superiority. The Eipper-Lotus, Global, Pong, Dawn Star and others, are leading the way towards that dream—ultimate economy, performance and reliability.

Advances in structural materials, particularly the composites, will be a boon to kit manufacturing. Optimum aerodynamic shapes are now possible at minimal cost. The new aircraft will go together practically like large model airplane kits. The FAA will probably relax its "51% rule," and allow tremendous advances in kit design and packaging—all to the benefit of the consumer as well as safety. Conventionally constructed aircraft will still be built, but in lesser numbers.

Tomorrow's pilots will be looking for low initial cost, low operating expenses, creature comforts, good turbulence penetration, and decent cross-country performance. They'll want superior control response, reliable engines and durable structures. The ARV certainly looks like the answer—it offers the pilot all these things. The ARV appears to be the class of aircraft most likely to lead to the great popularity in sport flying that has had so many false starts in the past.

In this section, we will present a few new designs that are either in the design or prototype testing stages—the ARV's of tomorrow. Interestingly, all are of composite construction, and non-conventional in configuration. The direction of the development of the ARV is obvious. You don't have to be a soothsayer to see what is likely to happen.

These are very exciting times to be involved in sport aviation. Welcome aboard as we take a peek into the near future to see what we might be flying before too long.

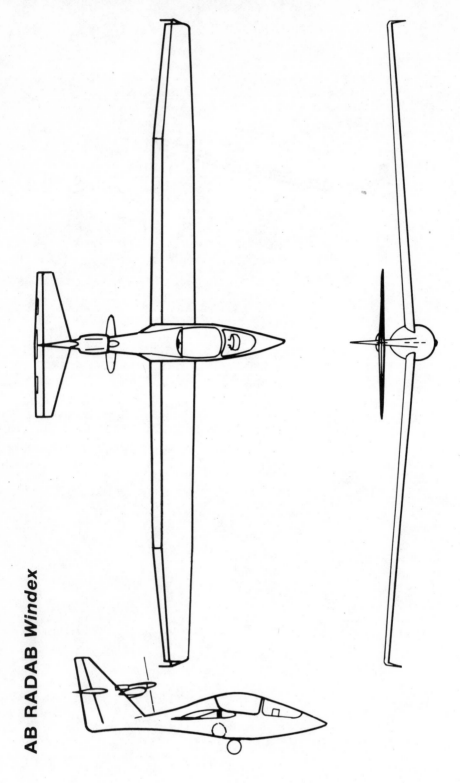

AB RADAB *Windex*

54

AB RADAB *WINDEX 1100*

The Windex is a single seater, powered sailplane of composite construction. It features a unique tail mounted engine, and complies with German Airworthiness Requirements.

The airfoil is a 17% thick, forward loaded laminar flow section designed at RIT (KTH), Stockholm, Sweden. The trailing edge flap is 22½% of the chord. It can be deflected from—5°(up) for low drag at high speed, and down to 70° for landing and glide path control. Ailerons grace the outer panel trailing edges.

The engine/propeller installation is quite unique. The propeller operates in comparatively undisturbed air, which should reduce prop noise and allow for higher propulsive efficiency. The propeller shaft is tilted 3° in order to lower the resultant thrust vector axis—due to the deflection of the slipstream by the horizontal tail. The propeller has a manually operated variable pitch control that permits feathering for soaring. It allows optimum efficiency in takeoff and cruise, as well as making for easy restarts. The prop is driven through a 1.6-to-1 reduction by an air cooled two stroke, horizontally opposed engine of 22 hp.

The landing gear is typical sailplane—a single wheel with shock absorber, supplemented by wing tip mounted skids.

The projected performance of the Windex is quite good, with a cruise of 97 mph on one gallon per hour. Rate of climb is a respectable 980 fpm. See Flight Performance figures below for further details.

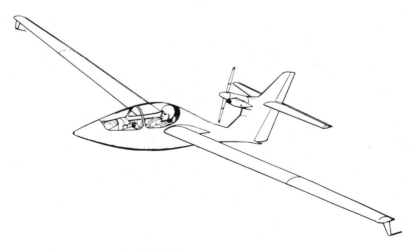

Fig. 4-1. Artist's sketch of the "Windex" reveals its sleek sailplane-like lines, and unique tail-mounted engine.

Specifications

Wingspan	36 ft 1 in
Length	14 ft 9 in
Height	4 ft 1 in
Power	22 hp
Gross Weight	408 lbs
Empty Weight	198 lbs
Top Speed	149 mph
Cruising Speed (30% power)	97.5 mph
Landing Speed (with flaps)	33.5 mph
Ceiling	19,000 ft
Climb	980 fpm

For further details, contact: AB RADAB, P.O. Box 81054, S-10481 Stockholm, Sweden.

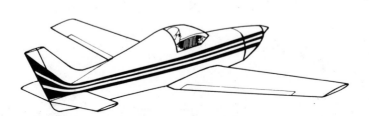

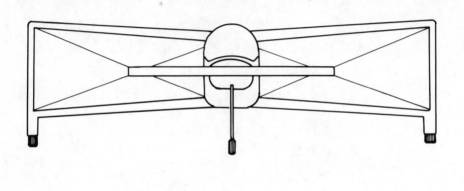

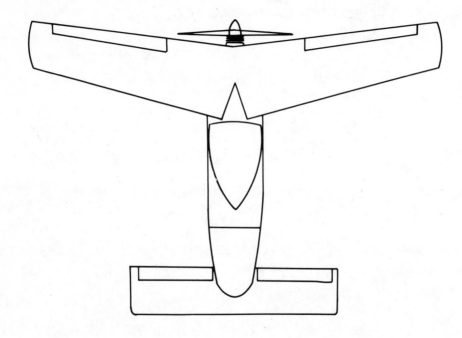

Catto Acro-X

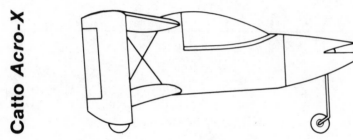

55

CATTO *ACRO-X*

Looking like something out of "Star Wars," the Acro-X actually is a composite construction canard with biplane wings. It was put on static display at the ARV competition, but was not flown because its restrictions had not been flown off. No word on its development was available at press time.

Specifications

Wingspan	16 ft 4 in
Length	10 ft 5 in
Height	5 ft 3 in
Power	30 hp
Gross Weight	530 lbs
Empty Weight	300 lbs
Top Speed	N.A.
Cruising Speed	105 mph
Landing Speed	36 mph

For further details, contact Craig Catto, Box 1104, San Andreas, CA 95249.

Fig. 4-2. The Catto "Acro-X" is truly a blend of the old and the new — a wire braced biplane in a composite construction canard configuration.

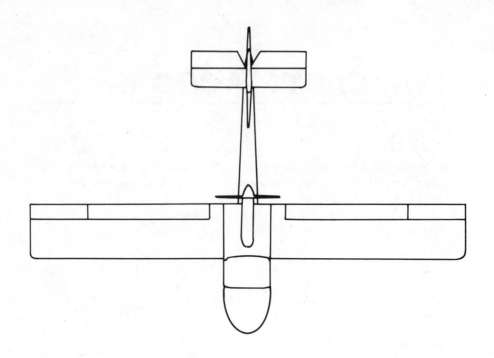

Devore Affordable Airplane

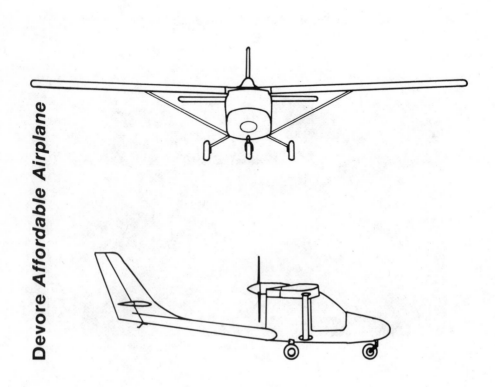

278

56

DEVORE *AFFORDABLE AIRPLANE*

The "Affordable" is a two-place, composite construction training and cross-country airplane. It features a strut braced high wing, pusher propeller, tricycle landing gear, and full FAR 23 certification.

According to company press releases, it is a state-of-the-art design, providing a large canopy for outstanding visibility. It's two-cycle, 55 hp four-cycle engine will burn premium automotive gasoline. Operating costs are to be less than half that of current two-place machines.

The prototype was scheduled to fly in the fall of 1984, while FAA certification and initial deliveries will begin in early 1986. The company plans to produce 125 units the first year, building up to 900 to 1,000 in the fourth year.

The primary market is seen as flight schools who can't really afford today's trainers, pilots who can't afford to fly today's airplanes, and ultralight pilots moving up.

Specifications

Wingspan	34 ft
Length	23 ft
Height	8 ft 2 in
Power	55 hp

Fig. 4-3. Full-scale mock-up of the Devore "Affordable" airplane. It's a thoroughly modern approach to two-seat training aircraft, incorporating state-of-the-art thinking and composite construction.

Gross Weight	950 lbs
Empty Weight	500 lbs
Top Speed	127 mph
Cruising Speed	115 mph
Landing Speed (with flaps)	38 mph
Ceiling	N.A.
Climb	825 fpm

For further information, contact: De Vore Aviation Corp., 6104 Kircher Blvd., N.E., Alburquerque, NM 87109. Tel: (503) 345-8713.

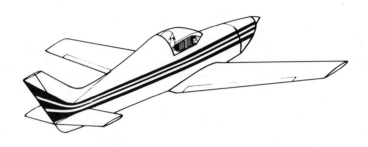

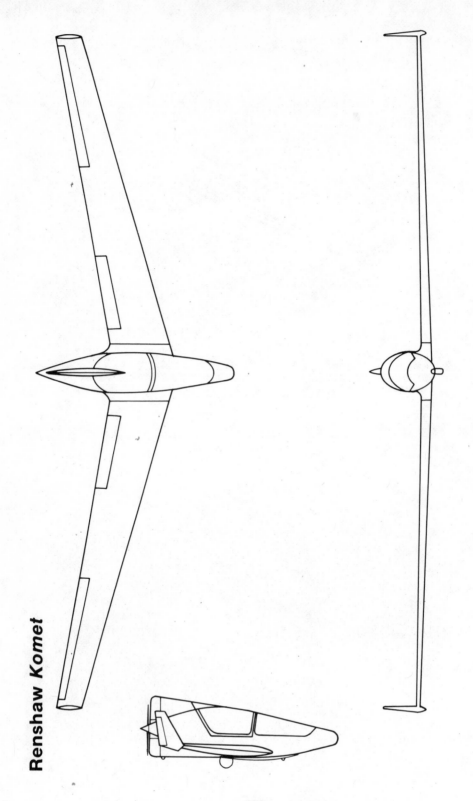

Renshaw *Komet*

57

RENSHAW *KOMET*

The Komet is a tailless pusher, powered sailplane designed to be constructed by homebuilders either from plans or from largely prefabricated kits. The primary concerns in designing this aircraft were to develop a configuration which could be built quickly and relatively inexpensively, yet be safe to fly and provide performance at least on the level of the Schweizer 1-26 sailplane.

The Komet is intended to be a licensed aircraft in the Experimental category so, at least a student pilot license would be required in order to fly it. The projected empty weight of the aircraft is 265 pounds, well above the 254 pound limit definition of ultralight aircraft. It is recommended that a potential pilot follow the current SSA training syllabus at least as far as the solo phase before moving on to any of the homebuilt sailplanes.

The general design of the Komet traces its origin back to the Horten brothers tailless aircraft of the late 1930's. The Hortens realized that tailless aircraft can offer a considerable reduction in parasite drag with a corresponding increase in performance. Indeed, their sailplanes were among the top performers of their day before their development was halted by the war.

In the past, many people thought of tailless aircraft as unstable or difficult to fly. This is not true, as many of the most popular ultralight aircraft of today have shown. The Mitchell Wing series of ultralights and all of the Rogollo derivatives have done much to change the way in which people think of "flying wings." A higher performance tailless sailplane

Fig. 4-4. A radio controlled model of the Komet was made to test the configuration's stability and control, as well as performance.

design could become popular once the homebuilder realizes the advantages inherent in this type of design.

The initial advantage of these aircraft comes during the building stage. Not only is the construction time shortened by the elimination of the conventional tail surfaces, but the size of the fuselage is drastically reduced. Thus, less material is required and the cost to build this type of design is lower. This reduction in size has a snowball effect; that is, the reduced size of the aircraft means that the wings can be smaller, further reducing the building time and cost. After the building is finished, the smaller size makes transporting the sailplane less cumbersome and assembly at the field less of a chore.

The size of the Komet was established on what was felt to be a good "soarable" wing loading combined with a maximum wingspan that could be built in two panels in a standard garage. Initial studies suggested that the aircraft could be built, including the self-launching capability, with a gross weight of under 500 pounds. A wing loading of between 4 and 5 pounds per square foot was desired, and this led to a wing area of 100 square feet. These wing loadings were selected to be higher than the current crop of ultralights, as experience has shown that a wing loading of much below 3.5 pounds per square foot limits the number of flying days due to ground handling difficulties and lack of wind penetration ability. Wing loadings of above about 6 pounds per square foot require either a sophisticated high lift system or unacceptably high landing speeds. An aspect ratio of 15 was chosen as this gave a span of 38.72 feet, which meant that each wing panel would be approximately 17 feet long. This size wing could be easily built in a 20 foot garage and would not require an especially long trailer to transport.

The combination of wing sweep and twist was chosen to provide stability, as opposed to using a straight wing with a large amount of airfoil reflex. The twisted swept wing can be designed to be stable with a smaller trim drag penalty, and the twist in the wing tip assures that the outer part of the wing is the last to stall, thus providing better roll control at low speeds. The wing is also tapered to produce a more desirable lift distribution across the span.

The Wortman FX-67-K-150 was chosen for the root airfoil due to its proven behavior at low Reynolds numbers and, the availability of data on the airfoil with various flap deflections. The airfoil was modified to remove some of the undercamber in the flap section since it would be used as a control surface rather than as a high lift device. The tip airfoil is an NACA 64-A012.

The Hortens felt that the best position for the pilot was lying prone over the wing spars with only a small bubble for visibility. While this may have been the most efficient design for a maximum performance ship, it probably would not prove to be too popular among sport fliers. The primary concern in laying out the fuselage for the Komet was to develop a cockpit which would allow a wide range of pilots to fly in comfort and safety. The question of cockpit size was of particular importance since the designer of the Komet is well over six foot tall. Many of the homebuilt designs currently on the market severely limit the size of the pilot they can accommodate. The Komet's cockpit size is designed to fit the full MIL spec range of pilot sizes. This means that pilots between 64 and 76 inches in height can be accommodated with only small changes in seating position (i.e. adjustable rudder pedals, extra seat cushions, etc.) The set is reclined back similar to that in many of the current high performance sailplanes in order to minimize the frontal area of the fuselage while providing a very comfortable environment for long flights. The pilots knees are slightly elevated so that the main wing spar can pass through the fuselage under the seat. The area immediately aft of the seat is reinforced to take the loads from the main landing gear well.

The design of the aft fuselage was directed by the inclusion of a self-launching system. It was felt that a true self-launching capability should be included as opposed to a "sustainer" type which requires some other type of ground launch assistance. Many fields where glider operations are conducted have obstacles at the ends, which makes immediate establishment of a substantial positive climb gradient absolutely necessary. The idea of using an auto tow to get airborne, and then using a sustainer engine to hunt for thermals at low altitude in the vicinity of the field can be very hazardous, particularly if the field has an established traffic pattern. The Komet incorporates a twenty horsepower two-cycle engine driving a pusher propeller via a belt drive reduction system. By using a pusher arrangement, the drag of the stopped propeller is minimized, since the turbulent flow off of the prop cannot cause flow separation on any part of the aircraft, as a tractor or overwing prop can. The short vertical surfaces immediately ahead of the prop serve to further reduce the drag of the aircraft when the engine is shut down. The lower surface also protects the propeller from striking the ground in case of over-rotation on takeoff.

The ultralight movement has done much work in developing lightweight engines in the ten to thirty horsepower class. The twenty horsepower figure given above is used only as a representative figure. There are several engines currently available which would provide adequate power for the Komet. The Normal Air Garrett 25 hp two-cycle is the prototype's powerplant.

Specifications

Wingspan	38 ft 9 in
Length	11 ft 9 in
Height	4 ft 3 in
Power	25 hp
Gross Weight	475 lbs
Empty Weight	265 lbs
Top Speed	N.A.
Cruising Speed	N.A.

Landing Speed	40 mph
Ceiling	N.A.
Climb	500 fpm
L/D	28

For further information contact: Kevin Renshaw, 10056 Farmers Branch Road, Ft. Worth, TX 76108. Tel: (817) 246-5666.

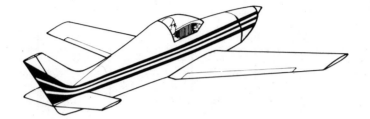

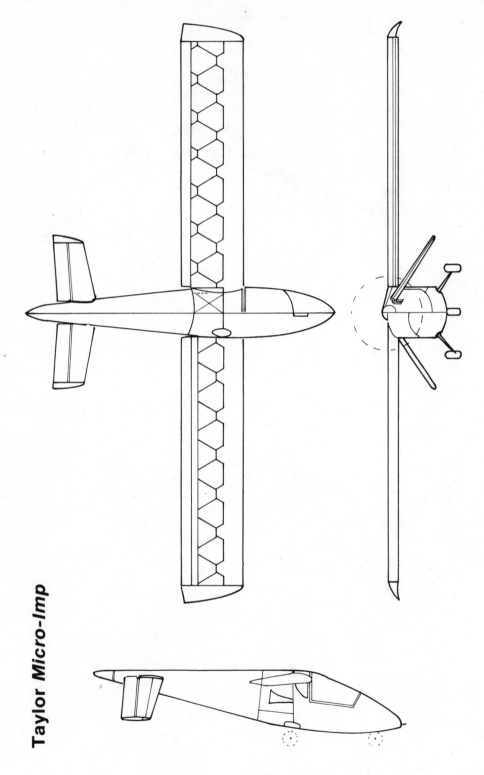

Taylor Micro-Imp

58

TAYLOR *MICRO-IMP*

The Micro-Imp is a high shoulder wing cantilever monoplane with inverted V-tail and tail mounted pusher prop. Besides being well streamlined, its main feature is the method of construction—paper core/fiberglass composites.

Molt Taylor, the designer, wrote about the conception and development of his paper/glass method, and its application to the Micro-Imp in *Sport Aviation* and in a memo, from which the following was derived.

To begin with, a solution was sought to the high cost of aircraft building materials as well as for gasoline and hangaring. Since gasoline prices can't be controlled, the desired aircraft must burn very little, implying lightweight and efficiency. Hangar fees can be avoided if the airplane is designed to be stored at home. The material part is a little tougher—something new would have to be developed.

In recent years, several new materials have been developed, all quite successful, but most requiring messy, critical, time consuming procedures. Taylor was looking for a "new" material that could be easily cut, formed, sheared, finished, etc. Spruce was getting almost as expensive as aluminum, so its use was to be minimized. Epoxy resin requiring special temperature, humidity, and other special working conditions, were out. Furthermore, it was desired to get a decent exterior finish without countless hours of labor. Of course, the new material would have to be light, as well.

Numerous types of composite construction were investigated, including the model airplane technique of using thin balsawood sheets over foam cores covered with Monocoat (a thin, self-adhering plastic). Naturally,

Fig. 4-6. Prototype Taylor "Micro-Imp" was used to prove viability of the Taylor Paper-Glass method of composite construction. Many parts are based on a core of Kraft-type paper.

balsa was out, because of its expense. Monocoat wasn't strong enough. Fortunately, the designer knew several paper industry engineers in his local area and discussed the problem with them. The solution was found in a common paper product called "solid fiber box board," available from any paper vendor. This material is an unbleached Kraft paper which is tan and available in a great variety of thicknesses. It is used for supermarket shopping bags and is commonly used in corregated paper boxes. In its simplest form it may be commonly known as 90 pound "linerboard." This is a single layer material about .025 inches thick.

Once the material was developed, Taylor decided to base the new aircraft design on his previous Mini-Imp. He felt that his was a nice flying airplane with a structural arrangement well-suited to paper-composite construction. The Mini-Imp uses flat sheet material throughout, except for the simple molded, fiberglass nosecone that slips on over the structure—this would also be used on the Micro. It was further possible to reduce the length of the fuselage. A simple, lightweight, manually operated tricycle landing gear was also worked out.

The heart of the Micro-Imp is the pilot's seat, to where all loads go. The upholstery simply snaps on. The flight control system of the Mini-Imp was simplified and lightened. It features a side stick, rudder-vator mixer and flaperon controls.

The Micro-Imp is fitted with the Citeron 2CV engine which is normally rated at 37 hp. However, the engine was modified and limited to a 3000 rpm "red line," and derated to 25 hp for aircraft use. It burns only 1.2 gallons per hour of regular automotive gasoline, which translates into a 500 mile range with the Micro's built-in 7 gallon fuel tank. The drive line features the flexidyne dry fluid coupling that was FAA "certificated" in similar application back in the fifties. It eliminates shaft problems and system vibration. The flexidyne has been suitably modified to permit hand cranking of the prop if desired. However, the engine can also be equipped with a starter and alternator. The modified engine is also equipped with a new Condenser Discharge Magneto type ignition system which has no points or distributor.

The new mags feature electronic spark retard for easy starting and smooth engine idling. The ignition system is fully shielded for radio reception and the solid state magneto provides an exceptionally "hot spark" for starting. The engine uses surface gap "ignites" instead of sparkplugs, precluding the possibility of fouling or failure. The four stroke engine is very light and has been modified to aircraft standards throughout. A special intake manifold and exhaust system are fitted along with an "injector" type carburetor featuring automatic altitude compensation. The engine is completely disassembled, magnafluxed, and dye-checked prior to reassembly, and the crankshaft is modified for the output flange while the engine is torn down.

Another feature of the drive system is the Micro-Imp's propeller. It's a Taylor designed all metal two blader, with baldes that bolt on. But, the most significant thing is that pitch is completely variable, including reverse. The unit weighs almost ten pounds, and is machined out of 2024-T4 aluminum bar stock. It is completely mechanical, being controlled by a push/pull cable aided by counterweights.

One of the most interesting features of the future kit, will be that all the parts that must be fabricated, will be printed full size on the basic building paper. Thus the builder will merely cut the parts out. They are then suitably "greased" using furnished glass and resin. The parts are joined mainly by using simple triangular wood "battens" and a hand staple machine. Corners are glassed with glass tape on both sides to finish corners and edges.

The kit will contain all instruments, hardware, engine, shaft system, propeller, landing gear, canopy, and the exterior skin in pre-molded fiberglass. All structures are the basic reinforced paper, including the tail boom, tail surfaces, and wings.

The wings are removable by one person and light enough to be handled once off the fuselage. Wing covering will be Ceconite or Razorback over diagonal ribs. The tail surfaces are done similarly.

The designer claims his method of construction is not only much lighter than metals or glass-over-foam composites, but is also easier to make and finish. The reinforced paper is suitably protected from ultra-violet rays prior to covering, and colors other than white may be used.

Taylor says that the development of the paper composite method has already proven to be of such potential as to cause considerable enthusiasm among other designers. He hopes that other designers will want to adapt their designs to his intriguing "new" material for light aircraft construction.

The prototype has been flying, and the following specifications are actual.

Specifications

Wingspan	27 ft
Length	15 ft
Height	4 ft
Power	25 hp
Gross Weight	750 lbs
Empty Weight	390 lbs
Top Speed	120 mph
Cruising Speed	100 mph
Landing Speed	45 mph
Ceiling	10,000 ft
Climb	450 fpm
L/D	25

For further details, contact: Molt Taylor, P.O. Box 1171, Longview, WA 98632. Tel: (206) 423-8260.

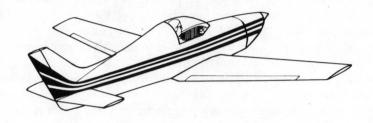

Section V
Appendices

A-1
Glossary

Aerodynamics is the science that deals with the relative motion of objects through the air and the interactions developed therein. It is central to anything that flies. As theories have evolved over the years, terms have been developed to describe various phenomena. We will explain the more important terms to make the text more meaningful.

aerobatic FAR (Federal Aviation Regulations) 91.71 defines aerobatic flight as an intentional maneuver involving an abrupt change in an aircraft's altitude, and abnormal attitude or abnormal acceleration not necessary for normal flight. Aerobatics are characterized by maneuvers such as loops, rolls, spins and inverted flight. An aircraft must be able to withstand ultimate load factors of +9.0 and -4.5 to be considered aerobatic. Ultralights are generally not designed for aerobatic flight.

aerodynamic center The point on an airfoil where the pitching moment coefficient is constant from zero lift up to near the stall. It is usually located one quarter of the chord length behind the leading edge, and the lift and drag are assumed to act through it.

aerodynamic coefficient A non-dimensional number which is the ratio of an aerodynamic force or moment, divided by the dynamic pressure and the wing area (and chord for moments), principally the coefficients of lift, drag, and pitching moment.

aerodynamic damping The aerodynamic forces that resist rotations about an aircraft's axes, and those that reduce rotations after a gust or control input is made.

aerodynamic force The force generated by a body's motion through the air.

aileron Plain flap control surfaces located at a wing's outer trailing edge. They deflect asymmetrically to rotate an aircraft about its longitudinal axis.

air A mechanical, not chemical, mixture of gases that comprise the earth's atmosphere. The main components are oxygen (78%) and nitrogen (21%) the rest being made up of several inert gases. The exact content of the mixture varies with altitude and latitude.

aircraft Any and all structures that are supported in the air either by its dynamic reaction with the air or by a buoyant gas. More specifically, the term applies to free and tethered balloons, blimps, dirigibles, kites, ornithopters, flying model airplanes, hang gliders, ultralights and other fixed wing aircraft, helicopters and autogyros.

airflow The movement of air. Its flow is measured as a mass of volume per unit time.

airfoil   Any structure designed to gain a useful reaction from the airflow around it. More specifically, the cross sectional shape of a wing, tail surface, or propeller.

airframe   The structural and aerodynamic components that support the loads transmitted to it by the parts in contact with the air. They include: fuselage, wings, tails, landing gear, tail booms, fairings, nacelles, and control surfaces.

airplane   Any engine powered, heavier-than-air, fixed wing aircraft that generates lift solely by the dynamic reaction of the air with its surfaces.

airscoop   The open end of a duct, hood, cowl or nacelle that projects into the airflow to carry a portion of that airflow to another part of the aircraft, such as an engine cooling air intake.

airspace   The air above a certain area on the earth, typically identified by some sort of boundary.

airspeed   The speed with which an aircraft moves relative to the air.

airstream   The airflow.

airworthy   When an aircraft is suitable for safe flight.

altitude   The vertical distance of an aircraft above the surface. Altimeters are usually set with sea level being zero, and all navigational charts are zeroed to sea level.

amphibian   An aircraft capable of operating off land and water.

angle of attack   The angle a wing chord line makes with respect to the relative wind.

angle of climb   The angle between the local horizon and the climb path of an aircraft.

angle of incidence   The angle the wing chord line is set with respect to an airplane's longitudinal axis.

aspect ratio   The slenderness of a wing defined as wingspan squared divided by wing area. Wingspan divided by average chord also yields aspect ratio.

atmosphere   The gaseous envelope surrounding the earth through which flight occurs. It extends up to about 700 miles above the surface, thinning out with altitude.

attitude   The orientation of an aircraft's axes with respect to the horizon.

aviation   The art and science of manned flight, especially with heavier-than-air vehicles.

axes   Three imaginary straight lines that pass perpendicularly through an aircraft's center of gravity, around which the aircraft rotates. The axes include: vertical (yaw axis), longitudinal (roll axis), and lateral (pitch axis).

balloon   The momentary, inadvertent rise of an airplane as it tries to touch down for a landing. It is normally caused by the pilot over-controlling the landing, and can be amplified by ground effect.

bank   The tilt of an aircraft about its longitudinal axis, which is necessary to turn.

Bernoulli's Principle   This most fundamentally important aspect of low speed aerodynamics was discovered in 1738 by a Swiss physicist named

Daniel Bernoulli. He found that in any given airflow, the sum of the static and dynamic pressures was always the same, everywhere in the flow. What this means is that for any streamline flow wherever the velocity is high the pressure is lowered and, wherever the velocity is lowered the pressure is raised. For example, the air striking the leading edge of a wing is stopped at the stagnation point, resulting in a higher pressure. Also, whenever an airflow meets with a restriction, as in a venturi, the velocity must increase to move the same volume of air.

biplane   An airplane with two sets of wings, one set above the other.

boundary layer   The thin layer of air immediately adjacent to a surface over which air flows, composed of decelerated velocity air—the slowest air being nearest the surface. The boundary layer can be laminar—where the velocity deceleration is gradual, or turbulent—where the various velocities mix with one another.

burble   The airflow condition above and behind a stalled wing. Turbulence.

camber   The depth of an airfoil's mean line, expressed as a percentage of the chord.

canard   Aircraft with a small lifting wing located ahead of the main wing. The small lifting wing itself.

ceiling, absolute   The highest altitude attainable by an aircraft.

ceiling, service   The altitude where the maximum rate of climb is 100 feet per minute.

center of gravity   The point where an aircraft balances and, through which the force of gravity is considered to act. It is also the point where the three axes meet perpendicular to one another, and around which all motions are considered to occur.

center of pressure   The point on a surface where the resultant of all the aerodynamic forces can be considered to act.

centripetal force   The acceleration on a turning aircraft that causes it to turn. Specifically, it is the inward tilt of the wing's lift vector which counteracts the centrifugal force tending to prevent the aircraft from turning.

chord   The length of an airfoil or wing section, as measured from leading edge to trailing edge.

circulation   The motion of air rotating about an axis. Specifically, the air rotating about a lifting airfoil as a theory of lift.

Coanda effect   The tendency of an airstream to attach itself to and follow the surface over which it flows. The surface should be smooth and rounded.

control surface   Aerodynamic surfaces that move to control the altitude, speed and direction of an aircraft. These include: elevator, ailerons, rudders, flaps, spoilers, trim tabs and drag brakes.

crab   Technique used to maintain course in a crosswind. It is established by a turn done in the normal way with aileron, while rudder is used to correct any adverse yaw. The aircraft will appear to be travelling sideways with respect to the ground but, it will be going straight with respect to the wind. Controls are then neutralized.

cruise speed The speed, below top speed, at which an aircraft normally flies for reasons of fuel economy and engine life. It generally occurs at throttle settings of 65% to 75% of wide open throttle.

delta wing Triangularly shaped wing with swept back leading edges and a straight trailing edge.

dihedral Small angle made between the horizontal and the wing panel chord plane.

downwash The downward flow of air behind a lifting wing.

drag The total aerodynamic force tending to retard the motion of an aircraft in a direction parallel to the airflow.

dynamic pressure The pressure developed when air comes to rest at the front of an object. It is measured in pounds per square foot and is often referred to as "q," which is the product of one-half the air density times the velocity squared.

dynamic stability The oscillating motion an aircraft exhibits in returning to its original flight trim condition.

eddy A small rotational turbulence within an airflow.

elevator The aft hinged portion of the horizontal stabilizer, or canard, which controls pitch, attitude and airspeed.

elevon Dual purpose control surface on flying wings, used for both pitch and roll control.

empennage The horizontal and vertical tail group.

empty weight The weight of an aircraft unloaded and unoccupied, including: usable fuel, undrainable oil, engine coolant, hydraulic fluid and attached ballast weights.

engine cowling A fairing positioned around the engine, designed to direct cooling air through the engine in an aerodynamically efficient manner.

equilibrium A condition of balance. An aircraft is in equilibrium when lift equals weight and thrust equals drag.

fairing A streamlined shell placed over a structure or component to reduce drag.

fin The fixed leading portion of the vertical tail.

fineness ratio A body's length divided by its thickness. Optimal fineness ratios develop minimal drag for a given thickness.

fixed-pitch propeller A propeller with blades that are unadjustable in flight, as is typical for ultralights.

fixed-wing aircraft An airplane with a stationary wing and not a helicopter or rotary winged aircraft.

flap The hinged, moveable inboard trailing edge portion of a wing used to alter camber, and therefore lift and drag, especially during landing.

flight Movement of an aircraft through the atmosphere.

flutter A harmonic oscillation or vibration of an aircraft part or control surface caused by aerodynamic forces acting on a too flexible or improperly balanced component.

fluid Any liquid or gas.

flying wing An aircraft that houses all essentials for flight within the wing. It does not have a horizontal tail.

flying wires Cables located beneath the wing that support it against positive flight loads.

free stream The airflow outside the region affected by the passage of an aircraft.

fuselage The part of the airframe that houses the pilot, with wings, tail and landing gear attached to it.

g The accleration subjected to an airplane by gravity and abrupt maneuvers. One g is generated in straight and level flight, due to the acceleration of gravity, which is 32 feet per second, acting on the mass of the aircraft.

gas The fluids that expand indefinitely, having no definite shape or volume.

glide Flight with little or no thrust, characterized by a loss in altitude.

glider An engineless aircraft that derives its thrust from gravity.

glide ratio Numerically equal to the lift over drag (L/D) ratio, it is the horizontal distance an aircraft will travel (engine-off) for every foot of altitude lost.

gross weight An aircraft's total flying weight, including: empty weight, fuel, oil, pilot, passengers and cargo.

ground effect The tendency for an aircraft to "float" when within a half wingspan of the runway. It's caused by a reduction in induced drag.

hang glider Engineless aircraft from which the pilot is suspended in a harness or swing seat. It is typically controlled by weight shifting, but may incorporate aerodynamic controls as well. They are normally footlaunched and landed.

induced drag That portion of the drag due to the generation of lift. It is associated with wing tip vortices and is most important at low speeds.

joystick The control stick. It is connected to ailerons and elevator on three axis controlled aircraft and, to rudder and elevator on two control aircraft.

kilo One kilogram, which equals about 2.2 pounds.

kinetic energy The energy possessed by a body due to its motion.

kite Generally, an aircraft flown while tethered to the ground or a ground based vehicle. It flys solely by the relative wind pressure against its surfaces. Also, colloquilly, a Rogallo-type hang glider.

laminar flow Airflow characterized by streamlines that move smoothly over one another, without mixing.

landing gear The undercarriage on which an aircraft rests while on the ground. Typically wheels, it can be floats and skis, as well.

landing speed The airspeed with which an aircraft touches the ground, typically equal to the stall speed.

landing wires Cables located above the wing that support it against landing and negative flight loads.

lateral axis The imaginary line passing from wingtip to wingtip, through the center of gravity. Pitch motions occur about it.

lateral stability   Stability about the roll axis.

leading edge   The front of a wing.

lift   The total aerodynamic force developed to support an aircraft perpendicular to the airstream.

lift coefficient   The non-dimensional number which represents the lift of a wing or airfoil. It is obtained by dividing the lift by the free stream dynamic pressure and wing area.

limit load factor   The number of g's an aircraft is designed to handle in flight.

load factor   The total g load on an airplane from gravity and other accelerations.

longeron   The primary longitudinal structural member of a fuselage.

longitudinal axis   The imaginary line passing from nose to tail through the center of gravity. Rolling motions occur about it.

longitudinal stability   Stability about the pitch axis.

maneuvering speed   The highest allowable speed for abrupt maneuvers or very rough air. It is typically set at twice the stall speed and is designed to protect against structural failure. Here, the aircraft could receive a maximum 4 g load, where the wing would stall before loading the airframe further.

mean aerodynamic chord (MAC)   The average chord of the wing, or wings, which can be used to represent an aircraft's center of aerodynamic forces.

mean line   The center line of an airfoil section equidistant between the upper and lower surfaces.

minimum flying speed   The lowest airspeed attainable, out of ground effect.

moment   A force times its distance from the center of action (rotation).

momentum   The quantity of motion, expressed as mass times velocity.

monocoque   A type of fuselage construction in which the skin carries all or most of the stresses.

mush   A nose high condition of flight between minimum power required speed and minimum level speed. It is flight on the "back side of the power curve."

navigation   Act of directing flight from point to point.

negative g   A condition that loads an aircraft from the top.

oscillation   Vibration or movement to either side of a neutral point.

parasite drag   Drag caused by components that do not contribute to lift. It becomes more important with speed.

parasol wing   A monoplane with its wing mounted above the fuselage.

pitch   A rotation about the lateral axis, as in nose-up, nose-down.

pitching moment   The moment about an aircraft's lateral axis. A nose-up pitching moment is positive.

phugoid   A long period longitudinal oscillation where an aircraft flies along a "roller-coaster" path with little or no change in angle of attack.

planform   The top view of an object, particularly a wing.

power loading   Pounds gross weight divided by horsepower.

potential energy   The energy possessed by an object due to its height.

pressure altitude   Height in the atmosphere as measured from the standard pressure datum of sea level.

profile   The cross section of a body, especially the airfoil section of a wing.

propeller   Airfoil shaped rotating wing used to convert torque into thrust. Larger diameters and lower tip speeds are more efficient.

propeller pitch   The distance a prop moves forward for each revolution.

range   Maximum distance an aircraft can fly at a given cruising speed, with a 45 minute reserve.

rate of climb   Vertical speed of an aircraft. Typically quoted as a maximum at standard sea level conditions.

relative wind   In the study of aerodynamics, it makes no difference whether an aircraft is flying through still air, or air is being blown past a stationary aircraft. The aerodynamic forces generated are identical.

Reynolds number   The basic law of airflow similarity which is the ratio of dynamic forces divided by viscous forces. Airflow patterns are the same for similar Reynolds numbers.

rib   The part of a wing that provides the airfoil shape.

Rogallo wing   A flexible membrane sail-type wing as used on most hang gliders.

rudder   Moveable part of vertical tail used to yaw aircraft. It balances adverse aileron yaw in independent three-axis control aircraft. Helps steer the aircraft while taxiing. It is NOT analogous to a ship's rudder and is not used like one!

ruddervator   Dual purpose surface on V-tailed aircraft used to control pitch and yaw.

sailplane   High performance glider with a glide ratio of 25 or better.

scale effect   The affect of size on aerodynamic reactions. Generally, the larger an aerodynamic body, the more efficient it can be.

seaplane   Aircraft designed for operations off water only.

separation   When air fails to follow the contour of the object over which it is flowing. It occurs behind bluff bodies and more important, on the upper surface of wings at high angles of attack.

sink rate   The vertical speed of descent, typically quoted as the minimum rate for the aircraft.

slat   High lift device, located at the leading edge, that directs high velocity air over a wing to delay the stall.

slot   The gap between a slat and a wing.

slope lift   Wind striking vertical terrain generates this vertical wind on which gliders soar.

span   Wing length from tip to tip.

spar   A wing's primary load bearing member.

spin   An aerobatic maneuver or a condition where an aircraft is stalled and rotating in a small radius about a vertical axis. The nose is pointed well below the horizon, as well.

spoiler   Control surface located on wing's upper surface, which normally lies flush. When deflected, it reduces lift and increases drag. They roll the aircraft when deflected singly, and control glide path when deflected simultaneously.

square-cube law   As a body is increased in size, its mass grows as the cube of its increase, while its area grows only as the square. In other words, doubling the linear dimension of an airplane will result in eight times the weight, and only four times the wing area, provided the construction and materials are similar. This also implies a doubling of the wing loading.

stagger   On a biplane, the relative longitudinal spacing between leading edges. Positive stagger is when the top wing is forward, while negative stagger is when the bottom wing is forward.

stagnation point   The forward location on a body where the airflow comes to rest, as on the leading edge of a wing section.

stall   A breakdown in the lift of a wing which occurs when the airflow separates from the upper surface at an angle of attack peculiar to the airfoil section, Reynolds number and aspect ratio.

static pressure   The ambient pressure of the atmosphere, normally 14.7 psi at sea level.

streamline   The path traced by air molecules as they move over an object.

sweepback   The angle the wing leading edge (or quarter chord line) makes with the lateral axis.

taildragger   An aircraft with main wheels in front and a tail wheel, or skid.

thermal   A parcel of heated air that breaks away from the ground and rises, usually generated over dark areas of the earth. Gliders use the updraft to gain altitude.

thrust   The propelling force generated by a propeller, needed to overcome drag.

thrust line   The imaginary centerline of the thrust, which is typically near or at the aircraft's centerline.

tip dragger   Wing tip control on some ultralights used to yaw the aircraft when actuated singly, and to control glide path when actuated simultaneously.

tip stall   The stalling of a wing tip. It could occur at higher lift, coefficients and develop into a spin. A properly designed wing should not tip stall—the stall should begin at the center of the wing.

trailing edge   Aftermost portion of a wing.

tricycle landing gear   Aircraft landing gear with a nose wheel and two main wheels aft the center of gravity. This is the most popular type, and it is stable.

turbulence   The mixing of streamlines in an irregular "eddying" motion, such as is found behind bodies that have experienced a flow separation. Also, uneven movement of the atmosphere found mostly near the surface and behind obstructions. It can be strong enough to destroy an aircraft.

ultralight   An aircraft with an empty weight under 254 pounds, a stall speed of 27 mph, and a top level speed of 63 mph, according to the FAA definition.

vector A force or speed that has both magnitude and direction. They can be added graphically by joining heads to tails or mathematically by trigonometry.

velocity never exceed (Vne) The red-line speed of an aircraft, beyond which structural damage may occur in calm air.

venturi A tube with a smaller diameter in the center than at the ends. When air, or any fluid, moves through a venturi, the velocity increases in the center, while the pressure decreases.

vertical axis Imaginary line which passes vertically through the aircraft's center of gravity and about which the aircraft yaws.

viscosity The "stickiness" of air as evidenced by its tendency to adhere to surfaces over which it flows, as well as to itself.

vortices Organized circular flow of air caused by pressure differences in an airflow. Examples include the "bound vortex" equivalent of a wing in circulation theory, and vortices developed at a wing tip.

washout Upward set of wing tip trailing edge to minimize tip stall.

weight and balance The practice of keeping an aircraft's gross weight and center of gravity within prescribed limits as established by the designer. Deviation form this results in poor performance and possibly catastrophic instability.

wind milling A propeller being turned by the airstream and not the engine.

wind tunnel Basically, a tube with a fan installed in one end to draw air over an object mounted inside the "test section." The object is connected to a sensitive balance system in order to measure aerodynamic forces and moments.

A-2

The Recreational Pilot License Proposal

Summary:
This notice proposes to establish a new concept in the certification of pilots. If adopted as proposed, the new rule would permit the issuance of a Student Recreational, a Recreational, a Student other than recreational and a Private Pilot Certificate. Each class of certificate would have its own minimum requirements and limitations. It also proposes requirements for the pilot with less than 400 hours of flight time.

Background

The last major change to the pilot certification rules in Federal Aviation Regulations (FAR) Part 61 was completed in 1973 when amendment 61-60 was adopted. This change, the results of over 7 years of development, provided new requirements for the issuance of student, private, commercial and flight instructor certificates. Additionally, changes were made to the recency requirements as they apply to certificate holders. Changes were also made to the ratings that could be added to pilot certificates. One of the new recency requirements was the Biennial Flight Review, a procedure wherein all pilots who are not required by other operating rules to take proficiency flight checks, are required to fly with a flight instructor every 2 years. This flight provides the opportunity for the flight instructor to comment on the pilot's flying and to determine if the pilot is knowledgeable of the general operating flight rules and that he/she is competent to safely operate the aircraft.

The adoption of revised Part 61, with its requirements for instrument training, flights into airports with operating control towers and the use of radio for VFR navigation, virtually eliminated the use of airplanes, such as the Piper J-3, Aeronica, 7AC, Taylorcraft BC-12D or a homebuilt airplane as a trainer. These rules, therefore, required the individual to learn to fly in a more expensive, more complicated airplane even though his/her ultimate goal was to fly and carry a passenger in a non-complex airplane. The added time in flight necessary to acquire the aeronautical knowledge and skills to pass the flight test, place the private pilot certificate out of the financial reach of many persons who have the mental and physical ability to be a safe pilot. While the minimum required flight time for the issuance of a private pilot certificate has remained at the 40-hour level, (a flight time that was established in the '30s), by the late '70s, the average flight time to acquire the certificate exceeded 66 hours because of the added requirements.

There is a need to provide a level of pilot certificate for those persons who desire to fly and carry a passenger in a relatively simple class of airplane and who would not object to certain limitations as the holder of such certificate. This proposal, therefore, describes a new class of certificate for the student recreational and the recreational pilot.

Need for a Regulation Change

As discussed in the background, there is a need for various levels of pilot certificate. These needs may be seen as economical needs, aviation promotional needs or safety needs. This proposal would allow a beginner, if he/she desired, to take training and receive a pilot certificate using a "simple" airplane as was permitted in the '40s, '50s and '60s. Such a pilot would be permitted to carry a passenger but would have specific operating limitations on where and when he/she could fly. If desired, the pilot could take additional training at a later date and upgrade to the less restrictive private pilot certificate.

There is also a need to amend the regulations to provide guidance to flight instructors in the training of students. A recent review of student and private pilot fatal and nonfatal aircraft accidents has indicated that there are weaknesses in operational skills in take-off and landing directional control, go-around procedures, stall recognition and recovery, emergency procedures and a general lack of flight precision and proficiency.

In this proposal, specific minimum flight times are not described nor are arbitrary mileages specified for cross-country legs. The instructor will be required to provide training in specific maneuvers and procedures and the student will be required to demonstrate proficiency to a specific performance level. There is also a requirement for the student to pass a pre-solo written test administered and graded by the flight instructor. It will be necessary, prior to implementation of the new rules, to develop and publish Advisory Circulars for the guidance of students and flight instructors.

Proposed New Pilot Certificates

This proposal contains the requirements and limitations for two new certificates referred to as Student Recreational and Recreational pilot certificates. The authors of this proposal considered many different names for these certificates, such as, Limited, Restricted, Provisional, Personal and Amateur student and private pilot. None of these names were believed to be as appropriate as the name recreational. Comments are requested on the preferred name for the certificate with the reasons for the selection.

Discussion of the Proposed Rules.

Subchapter C - Student Recreational Pilots.

Proposed 61.83 Eligibility requirements.

This section specifies the minimum requirements for the issuance of a student recreational pilot certificate. It proposes a minimum age of 14 years, the age that has been permitted for the issuance of a student pilot certificate limited to glider operations. The proposal would also permit the applicant to certify that he/she had no known medical defect that would make him/her unable to safely pilot an airplane. This concept has been utilized for many years for the operation of gliders and there has been no evidence of problems. As proposed, the Student Recreational Pilot certificate would limit the holder to flying one or two place single engine airplanes with a powerplant of not more than 200 horsepower.

Proposed 61.87 Requirement for solo flight.

Paragraph (b) of this section contains a requirement that the student must satisfactorily complete a written examination administered and graded by the flight instructor who is to endorse the student's certificate for solo flight. There is a need to have the student complete such an examination to assure that he/she has the basic knowledge of the flight rules and the operating parameters of the airplane. Prior to adoption of this rule, an Advisory Circular must be developed and published to provide guidance to fight instructors in the development and administration of the pre-solo test.

Paragraph (c) prescribes the maneuvers and procedures that the instructor must teach the student before authorizing solo flight and that the student must demonstrate proficiency to an acceptable performance level as judged by the instructor. An Advisory Circular must be developed and published to provide guidance to flight instructors so that they can properly evaluate the student's performance. Specific minimum maneuvers and procedures are proposed as the result of reviewing aircraft accidents involving student and private pilots. This increased emphasis will help to reduce the number of accidents.

Proposed 61.89 Cross-country flight requirements.

Basic minimum cross-country flight requirements have been specified. Since there is no requirement for instrument flight instruction, use of radio for navigation or communications for the recreational pilot, the training requirements can be less than for the less restricted student pilot.

The new recreational pilot would be permitted and be capable of flying an airplane from one uncontrolled airport to another and therefore appropriate cross-country training and practice is required. A new item, recognition of operational problems associated with the terrain features in the geographical area, has been added to alert instructors of the need to assure that students are aware of local conditions that can cause an accident.

Proposed 61.91 Limitations.

The student recreational pilot, as with other student pilots, would not be permitted to carry a passenger or operate an airplane for compensation or hire. A student recreational pilot would not be permitted to operate an airplane at night, at an airport with an operating control tower, at an altitude of more than 10,000 feet MSL or 2,000 feet AGL, whichever is higher, on an international flight or when the flight or surface visibility is less than three statute miles.

Subpart D - Recreational Pilots.

Proposed 61.103 Eligibility requirements.

The minimum age for a recreational pilot certificate has been set at 16 years. In most states, this is the minimum age for a license to operate a motor vehicle. This age should also be appropriate for the recreational pilot. As with the student recreational pilot, a medical certificate is not required as long as the pilot certifies that he/she has no known medical defect that would make him/her unable to safely operate the airplane. This pilot certificate would limit the holder to the operation of airplanes. An FAA written test of aeronautical knowledge appropriate to a recreational pilot would be required, as would a certification oral and flight test.

61.107 Operational experience.

This section, referred to in the current regulations as Aeronautical experience, presents a new concept for the certification of pilots. There has been no effort made to specify a minimum number of flight-hours, but rather, certain minimum number of flights to gain operational experience are required. The student would be required to receive dual instruction and solo flights during which maneuvers and procedures as specified would be demonstrated and practiced. The proposal recognizes the advances made in recent years in airplane simulation. There is no prohibition against the use of a simulator or training device in teaching or in evaluating a student's performance. The limit of the use is only dictated by the sophistication of the device. and the ingenuity of the instructor. The proposed cross-country training would also be different from the FAA's historical method of regulating. The proposal would not specify a minimum number of hours or minimum distances for each leg, but would specify the number of flights, the number of legs for each flight and the number of airport/landing areas that must be visited. A review of recent accidents indicates that the enroute phase, other than adverse weather encounters, is not the accident producing phase of flight for the new pilot, but rather, take-offs and landings, both at the home airport/landing area and at other airports/landing areas. More emphasis will be placed on the proper procedures when arriving and departing airports.

It is estimated that it will require an average student at least 40 hours to complete a course of instruction and solo practice and satisfactorily demonstrate the ability to safely operate the airplane. The regulation will continue to require the logging of flight time for recency and for recording the number of flights for certification eligibility.

61.109 Recreational pilot privileges and limitations.

This class of pilot certificate, as the name implies, is for the pilot who desires to fly a small factory or homebuilt airplane. It may also be appropriate for the person who wishes to fly an ultralight. The proposal would limit the holder to airplanes certified for not more than two occupants with a powerplant of not more than 200 horsepower. The certificate holder may carry a passenger and may share the expenses of the flight with that passenger. He/she may not act as pilot in command of another category of aircraft, such as a rotorcraft, nor act as pilot in command of an airplane with more than one engine. The holder may not carry passengers for compensation or hire nor may he/she be compensated for flying an airplane. The recreational pilot may not use the airplane in connection with any business or employment nor may he/she demonstrate the airplane to a prospective buyer. The recreational pilot may not carry a passenger in an airlift operation sponsored by a charitable organization for which the passenger has made a donation to the organization.

There is no requirement for night training and since many airplanes that would be flown by this class of pilot will not have an electrical system or navigation lights, the rule would prohibit night flying. For the same reason, the recreational pilot would not be given instruction in the use of radio for two-way communication and would be prohibited from operating at an airport with an operating control tower.

A review of student and private pilot accidents shows that flight into adverse weather conditions constitutes a large percentage of the accidents involving this class of pilot. This rule would specify a minimum flight or surface visibility requirement of not less than three statute miles. The term surface and landing area is used in this proposal as there is no prohibition against a recreational pilot flying either a land or a sea plane. Because of the limited experience requirements for the recreational pilot, international flight would not be permitted.

Subpart E - Student pilots other than student recreational pilots.

This pilot certificate is for the individual who desires to progress toward a private pilot certificate so that he/she may fly airplanes certified for more than two occupants or with an engine of more than 200 horsepower. It would also be for the person who wishes to fly other categories of aircraft such as rotorcraft or gliders. The recreational pilot may at a later date, desire to upgrade his/her certificate to a private pilot certificate. Before such a person flies solo in an airplane certified for more than two occupants, with an engine of more than 200 horsepower, at night or at an airport with a control tower, he/she must have a medical certificate and a student pilot certificate. He/she could then be endorsed for solo flight by an authorized instructor. Upon completion of all the requirements for a private pilot certificate, the applicant would surrender the recreational pilot certificate, the student pilot certificate and be issued a private pilot certificate.

61.113 Eligibility requirements.

This section specifies that the minimum age for a student pilot certificate issuance would be 15 years. The student pilot certificate is the counterpart of the learner's permit issued in many states to operate a motor vehicle. The student pilot certificate carries many of the same limitations as a learner's permit. The student pilot must remain under the supervision of a flight instructor, thus minimizing the risks in reducing the minimum age.

61.115 Application.

There are no changes proposed from that specified in existing section 61.85.

61.117 Requirements for solo flight.

Proposed paragraph (a) is identical to that contained in current Section 61.87 (a).

Proposed paragraph (b) has been amended to require the satisfactory completion of a written examination administered and graded by the flight instructor who is to endorse the certificate for solo. A pre-solo written is not required by the current rule.

Paragraph (c) of current section 61.87, Flight Proficiency Training, describes the training that students are to receive but there is no requirement for the student to demonstrate proficiency. In proposed paragraph (c), the title has been changed to Pre-solo Flight Training to better describe the intention of the paragraph. The listing of maneuvers and procedures has been upgraded to place emphasis on the areas of flight training in need of improvement to reduce accidents. The lead-in sentence of the new paragraph requires that the student demonstrate proficiency to an acceptable performance level as judged by the flight instructor. Prior to adoption, an Advisory Circular must be developed and published to provide guidance to instructors in evaluating student performance.

Proposed paragraph (d) contains only a minor change from existing paragraph (d) of 61.87 in that it is made clear that only an instructor who has flown with the student may sign the certificate for solo flight.

61.119 Cross-country flight requirements.

Proposed paragraph (a) has been reworded from that found in current paragraph (a) of 61.93. to simplify the language and to eliminate the minimum distance requirements. The student is required to demonstrate proficiency to an acceptable performance level. The instructor is responsible to provide instruction and evaluate the student's performance. This can only be accomplished by flying a distance from the local practice area. The cruising speed differences between aircraft currently used in flight training makes an arbitrary minimum distance requirement to describe a cross-country no longer valid. For simplicity, the maneuvers and procedures that are appropriate to all categories of aircraft are contained in paragraph (b)(1) followed by the maneuvers and procedures unique to the particular category and class being used. The wording to describe the maneuvers and procedures that must be accomplished has been changed. For example, current Section 61.93 requires the recognition of critical weather situations but does not require the procurement and analysis of aeronautical reports and forecasts. This lack of knowledge has been a factor in a number of accidents that have occured following flight into adverse weather. In like manner, the current regulations do not discuss aircraft cross-country performance or limitations or the recognition of operational problems associated with terrain features in the geographical area in which the flight is to be flown.

Paragraph (c) Flight Instructors Endorsements, contains minor corrections for clarity and the last sentence has been changed to delete the mileage limitations for repeated solo cross-country flights. It is the instructor's responsibility to evaluate the student's performance level before authorizing repeated solo cross-country flights.

61.121 Limitations.

Proposed section 61.121 (a) has been changed from that contained in

61.89 by adding a new (5) to specify a flight or surface visibility minimum for day and for night. Accidents involving student pilots as the result of involvement in adverse weather requires that visibilty minimums be established.

61.123 Aircraft limitations: Pilot in command.

Proposed section 61.123 is identical to existing 61.91.

Subpart F - Private Pilots

61.127 Eligibility requirements.

Proposed 61.127 (a) has been changed from existing 61.103 (a) in that the minimum age to be eligible for a private pilot certificate has been lowered from 17 years to 16 years. Most states permit 16 year olds to receive a driver's license to operate a private vehicle and there is no accident data that would justify not allowing a 16 year old to operate a private aircraft.

There are no changes in paragraph (b), (c), (d), (e) or (f) from the existing sections of 61.103.

61.129 Aeronautical knowledge.

Proposed 61.129 introductory sentence has been changed from existing 61.105. Applicants for a private pilot certificate must receive instruction from an authorized instructor in the specified areas of aeronautical knowledge and successfully complete a written examination. The wording in the proposal has been changed to be more specific as to the scope of the knowledge for all aircraft and for specific aircraft.

61.131 Operational experience.

Proposed 61.131 replaces existing 61.109, 61.113, 61.115, and 61.117, all currently called aeronautical experience. The new concept as discussed under the recreational pilot certification has been applied here. The flight hours to acquire the knowledge and skill necessary to pass the oral and flight test for certification will exceed the time currently specified for certification. The cross-country requirements are designed to provide the student with more experience in landing area arrival and departure, where a high frequency of accidents occur, rather than the enroute phase. The minimum distances described in the current rules requires the student to fly excessively long cross-country flights, sometimes causing pilot fatigue.

61.133 Cross-country flights: Pilots based on small islands.

Proposed 61.133 is identical to existing 61.111.

61.135 Private pilot privileges and limitations: Pilot in command.

Proposed 61.135, currently 61.118, has been amended to correct problems with the existing rule.

Proposed paragraph (a) has been added to require that a private pilot must receive flight instruction and a log book endorsement prior to acting as pilot in command of an airplane that has a powerplant of more than 200 horsepower, or one with retractable gear or controllable pitch propeller. The instruction is to be required in each make and model of this category of airplane. Private pilots have been involved in accidents in high performance airplanes and their knowledge and skill has been questioned.

Proposed paragraph (b) has been included in this section to specify new requirements for the private pilot with less than 400 hours of flight time. A review of private pilot accidents has shown that there has been an inordinate number of accidents by pilots who have logged less than 400 hours. The proposal would require that a pilot, who has less than 400 hours and who had not flown an aircraft as pilot in command within the preceding 180 days, may not act as pilot in command until he/she has received flight instruction and a log book endorsement that he/she is competent to pilot the aircraft.

Proposed paragraph (c) has been taken from the recency requirements of section 61.57 and it again addressed the private pilot with less than 400 hours. Such pilots would be required to complete a flight review each 12 months. After logging 400 hours, the pilot would be required to meet the biennial flight review requirements of section 61.57.

Proposed paragraph (d) is a rewrite of the flush paragraph contained in current section 61.118.

Proposed paragraph (e) provides for a flight or surface visibility minimum for the private pilot who has logged less than 400 hours.

Proposed paragraphs (f) and (g) are identical to existing paragraphs (a) and (b) of section 61.118.

Proposed paragraph (h) states that a private pilot may not act as a salesperson if he/she has logged less than 400 hours of flight time.

Proposed paragraph (i) has been amended from that contained in paragraph (d) of section 61.118 to require the private pilot used in a passenger carrying airlift to have logged in excess of 400 flight hours.

The remaining paragraphs have been taken from existing Part 61. Your comments and rationale for recommended changes, including recommended language for the change is solicited.

The Proposed Amendment

Accordingly, we petition the Administrator to amend Part 61 of the Federal Aviation Regulation (14 CFR Part 61) as follows:

Subpart C - Student Recreational Pilots

61.81 Applicability.

This subpart prescribes the requirements for the issuance of student recreational pilot certificates, the conditions under which those certificates are necessary, and the operating rules and limitations for the holders of those certificates.

61.83 Eligibility Requirements.

To be eligible for a student recreational pilot certificate, a person must be:

(a) Be at least 14 years of age: and,

(b) Hold at least a current third-class medical certificate issued under Part 67 of this chapter, or certify that he/she has no known medical defect that makes him/her unable to safely pilot an airplane.

61.85 Application.

An application for a student recreational pilot certificate is made on a form and in a manner provided by the Administrator and is submitted to an FAA operations inspector or designated pilot examiner, accompanied by a valid medical certificate or a certification by the applicant that he/she has no known defect that makes him/her unable to safely pilot an airplane.

61.87 Requirements for Solo Flight.

(a) General. A student recreational pilot may not operate an airplane in solo flight until he/she has complied with the requirements of this section. As used in this section, the term solo flight means that flight times during which the student pilot is the sole occupant of the airplane.

(b) Aeronautical knowledge. The student must demonstrate satisfactory knowledge of the appropriate portions of Parts 61 and 91 of this chapter that are applicable to student recreational pilots. This demonstration must include the satisfactory completion of a written examination that is administered and graded by the flight instructor who is to endorse the student's pilot certificate for solo flight. The written examination must include questions on the applicable regulations and the flight characteristics and operational limitations of the make and model airplane to be flown.

(c) Pre-solo flight training. The student must have received and logged instruction in at least the following maneuvers and procedures and must demonstrate proficiency to an acceptable performance level as judged by the instructor who endorses the student's pilot certificate. The maneuvers and procedures must include:

(1) Flight preparation procedures;

(2) Taxiing or surface operations;

(3) Take-offs including normal and crosswind;

(4) Climbing turns;

(5) Level flight shallow, medium and steep banked turns;

(6) Flight at various airspeeds from cruising speed to minimum controllable speed;

(7) Stall entries from various flight attitudes with recovery initiated at the first indication of a stall and immediately following the stall;

(8) Descents in straight flight and in turns;

(9) Ground reference maneuvers;

(10) Landing traffic patterns;

(11) Approaches to the landing area with engine power off and with partial power;

(12) Landings including normal and crosswind;

(13) Go-arounds from final approach and from the landing flare;

(14) Forced landing procedures initiated on take-off, during initial climb, cruise, descents and in the landing pattern; and

(15) Appropriate emergency procedures.

The required instruction must be given and the log book endorsed by a flight instructor who is authorized to give flight instruction in airplanes. When instruction is given in a simulator or training device, such training shall be given and the log book endorsed by a flight or ground instructor.

(d) Flight instructor endorsements. A student recreational pilot may not operate an airplane in solo flight unless his/her student pilot certificate is endorsed for the specific make and model airplane to be flown. Additionally, his/her log book must have been endorsed for solo flight within the preceding 90 days. These endorsements must be made by the flight instructor who has flown with the student and the instructor's endorsement certifies that he/she:

(1) Has given the student instruction in the make and model of airplane in which solo flight is to be made;

(2) Finds that the student has met the flight training requirements of this section; and

(3) Finds that the student is competent to make safe solo flights in that airplane.

61.89 Cross-country flight requirements.

(a) A student recreational pilot may not operate an airplane in solo cross-country flight unless his/her student pilot certificate has been endorsed for solo cross-country. By an endorsement in the student's log book, an instructor may authorize a student to practice take-offs and landings at airports other than the home airport.

(b) Flight training. In addition to the pre-solo flight training maneuvers and procedures, a student recreational pilot must have received and logged instruction from an authorized instructor in at least the following items prior to being endorsed for solo cross country flight. The student must demonstrate proficiency to an acceptable performance level as judged by the instructor who is to endorse the student's pilot certificate. The maneuvers and procedures must include:

(1) The use of aeronautical charts for VFR navigation using pilotage and dead reckoning with the aid of a magnetic compass;

(2) Airplane cross-country performance and limitations;

(3) The procurement and analysis of aeronautical weather reports and forecasts including the recognition of critical weather situations;

(4) Short field and soft field take-offs, approaches, and landing procedures;

(5) Cross-country emergency procedures including lost procedures, adverse weather encounters, and precautionary off airport approach and landing procedures;

(6) Normal landing area arrival and departure traffic pattern procedures; and

(7) Recognition of operational problems associated with terrain features in the geographical area where the cross-country flight is to be made.

(c) Flight instructor endorsements. No student recreational pilot may conduct a solo cross-country flight unless:

(1) His/her student certificate contains an endorsement stating that he/she has received instruction in cross-country flight and the applicable training requirements of this section and has been found competent to make solo cross-country flights in the make and model airplane involved; and,

(2) His/her log book is endorsed certifying that the instuctor has reviewed the flight planning and preparation for the specific crosscountry. Such endorsement may contain the circumstances and conditions that the instructor believes are necessary for the student to conduct the cross-country safely. An instructor may endorse a student's log book for repeated solo cross-country flights and specify minimum requirements that must be met by the student.

61.91 Limitation.

(a) A student recreational pilot may not act as pilot in command of an airplane:

(1) Certificated for more than two occupants;

(2) With a powerplant of more than 200 horsepower;

(3) That is carrying a passenger;

(4) That is carrying property for compensation of hire;

(5) For compensation of hire;

(6) In furtherance of a business;

(7) At night;

(8) At an airport or landing area with an operating control tower;

(9) At an altitude of more than 10,000 feet MSL or 2,000 feet AGL, whichever is higher;

(10) With a flight or surface visibility of less than 3 statute miles; and,

(11) On an international flight.

Subpart D - Recreational Pilots

61.101 Applicability.

This subpart prescribes the requirements for the issuance of a recreational pilot certificate, the conditions under which the certificate is necessary, and the operating rules and limitations for the holders of these certificates.

61.103 Eligibility Requirements.

To be eligible for a recreational pilot certificate, a person must -

(a) Be at least 16 years of age;

(b) Hold at least a current third-class medical certificate issued under Part 67 of this chapter or certify that he/she has no known medical defect that would make him/her unable to safely pilot an airplane;

(c) Pass a written test on the subject areas on which instruction is required by 61,105; and,

(d) Pass an oral and flight test on maneuvers and procedures selected by the FAA inspector or designated examiner to determine the applicant's competency in the flight training maneuvers and procedures of sections 61.87(c) and 61.89(b).

61.105 Aeronautical Knowledge.

(a) An applicant for a recreational pilot certificate must have received instruction from an authorized instructor and must demonstrate satisfactory knowledge by successfully completing a written examination covering at least the following areas of aeronautical knowledge -

(1) The Federal Aviation Regulations applicable to recreational

privileges, limitations and flight operations;

(2) The accident reporting requirements of the National Transportation Safety Board;

(3) The information contained in applicable Advisory Circulars;

(4) The use of aeronautical charts for VFR naviation;

(5) The procurement and analysis of aernautical weather report and forecasts;

(6) The effects of density altitude on take-off and climb performance; and,

(7) Collision avoidance and wake turbulence precautions.

61.107 Operational experience.

An applicant for a recreational pilot certificate must have logged flight instruction and solo flight as follows:

(a) Dual instruction -

(1) At least ten flights during which the maneuvers and procedures described in section 61.87(c) are performed;

(2) At least three flights following the first solo cross-country in preparation for the flight test; and,

(3) At least two cross-country flights, each containing four legs with landings at three or more airports/landing areas, in addition to the departure (home) airport/land area, and during which the maneuvers and procedures of 61.89(b) are performed.

(b) As sole occupant -

(1) At least ten flights during which the maneuvers and procedures as authorized by the instructor and as described in section 61.87(c) are performed; and,

(2) At least three solo cross-country flights, each containing four legs with landings at three or more airports/landing areas, in additon to the departure (home) airport/landing area.

61.109 Recreational pilot privileges and limitations.

(a) A recreational pilot may act as pilot in command of a single-engine airplane that is certificated for not more than two occupants and that has a powerplant of not more than 200 horsepower and he/she may -

(1) Carry a passenger; and,

(2) Share the operating expenses of the flight with that passenger.

(b) A recreational pilot may not act as pilot in command of an airplane

(1) With more than one engine;

(2) Certificated to carry more than two occupants;

(3) With a powerplant of more than 200 horsepower;

(4) That is carrying passengers or property for compensation or hire;

(5) For compensation of hire;

(6) In furtherance of a business;

(7) As a salesperson nor may he/she demonstrate an airplane to a prospective buyer;

(8) Used in a passenger carrying airlift sponsored by a charitable organization and for which the passenger made a donation to the organization;

(9) At night;

(10) At an airport or landing area with an operating control tower;

(11) At an altitude of more than 10,000 feet MSL or 2,000 feet AGL,whichever is higher;

(12) When the flight or surface visibility is less than 3 statute miles; or,

(13) On an international flight.

(c) A recreational pilot may not act as pilot in command of an airplane carrying a passenger unless he/she has made three take-offs and landings as sole manipulator of the controls within the preceding 90 days.

(d) A recreational pilot who has logged less than 400 flight hours and who has exceeded 180 days without having made at least 3 take-offs and landings in an airplane, shall not act as a pilot in command until he/she received flight instruction from an authorized flight instructor and that instructor certifies that he/she is competent to pilot the airplane.

(e) A recreational pilot who has logged less than 400 flight hours may not act as pilot in command of an airplane unless -

(1) Within the preceding 12 calendar months he/she accomplishes a flight review given to him/her in an airplane by an appropriately certificated flight instructor or other person designated by the Administrator; and,

(2) The pilot's log book has been endorsed by that instructor certifying that he/she has satisfactorily accomplished the flight review.

A recreational pilot who has logged more than 400 flight hours need not comply with the requirements of (d) and (e) of this section but shall meet the requirements of section 61.57 of this part.

Subpart E - Student Pilots - Other than student recreational pilots.

61.111 Applicability.

This subpart prescribes the requirements for the issuance of a student pilot certificate for other than student recreational pilot, the conditions under which those certificates are necessary, and the operating rules and limitations for the holders of those certificates.

61.113 Eligibility requirements.

To be eligible for a student pilot certificate for other than a student recreational pilot certificate, a person must -

(a) Be at least 15 years of age, or a least 14 years of age for a student pilot certificate limited to the operation of a glider or free balloon;

(b) Be able to read, speak and understand the English language or have such operating limitations placed on his/her pilot certificate as are necessary for the safe operation of the aircraft, to be removed when he/she shows that he/she can read, speak and understand the English language; and,

(c) Hold at least a current third-class medical certificate issued under Part 67 of this chapter, or in the case of glider or free balloon operations, certify that he/she has no known medical defect that makes him/her unable to safely pilot a glider or free balloon.

61.115 Application.

An application for a student pilot certificate for other than student recreational pilot certificate is made on a form and in a manner provided by the Administrator and is submitted to -

(a) A designated aviation medical examiner when applying for an FAA medical certificate; or,

(b) An FAA operations inspector or designated pilot examiner, accompanied by a current FAA medical certificate, or in the case of an application for a student pilot certificate limited to gliders or free balloons, accompanied by a certification by the applicant that he/she has no known medical defect that makes him/her unable to safely pilot a glider or free balloon.

61.117 Requirements for solo flight.

(a) General. A student pilot may not operate an aircraft in solo flight until he/she has complied with the requirements of this section. As used in this subpart, the term solo flight means that flight time during which a student pilot is the sole occupant of the aircraft or that flight time during which a student pilot acts as pilot in command of an airship requiring more than one flight crewmember.

(b) Aeronautical knowledge. The student must demonstrate satisfactory knowledge of the appropriate portions of Parts 61 and 91 that are applicable to student pilots. This demonstration must include the satisfactory completion of a written examination to be administered and graded by the instructor who is to endorse the student's pilot certificate for solo flight. The written examination must include questions on the applicable regulations and the flight characteristics and operational limitations of the make and model of aircraft to be flown.

(c) Pre-solo flight training. The student must have received and logged instruction in at least the following maneuvers and procedures and must have demonstrated proficiency to an acceptable performance level as judged by the instructor who endorses the student pilot's certificate. These maneuvers and procedures must include -

(1) For all aircraft (As appropriate to the aircraft being flown)

(i) Flight preparation procedures;

(ii) Taxiing or surface operations;

(iii) Take-offs including normal and cross-wind;

(iv) Climbing turns;

(v) Level flight shallow, medium and steep banked turns;

(vi) Stall entries from various flight attitudes with recovery initiated at the first indication of a stall and immediately following the stall;

(vii) Descents in straight flight and in turns;

(viii) Flight at various airspeeds from cruising to minimum controllable airspeed.

(ix) Proper use of the radio for two-way communication when solo flight is to be conducted at an airport with an operating control tower.

(2) For airplanes. In addition to (1)-

(i) Ground reference maneuvers;

(ii) Landing traffic patterns;

(iii) Approaches to the landing area with power off and with partial power;

(iv) Landings including normal and cross-wind;

(v) Go-rounds from final approach and from the landing flare;

(vi) Forced landing procedures initiated on take-off and during climb, cruise, descents and in the landing pattern; and,

(vii) Emergency procedures appropriate to the airplane being flown.

(3) For rotorcraft. In addition to (1)-

(i) Hovering and air taxiing;

(ii) Landing area traffic patterns;

(iii) Maneuvering by ground reference;

(iv) Autorotational descents initiated from hover, take-off, climb, cruise and descent;

(v) Go-arounds from landing hover and from final approach; and,

(vi) Emergency procedures appropriate to the rotorcraft being flown.

(4) For single place gyroplanes. In addition to the appropriate items in (1) that can be performed in gyroplanes -

(i) At least three successful flights in a gyroplane towed from the ground under the observation of the instructor who is to endorse the student's pilot certificate.

(5) For gliders. In addition to (1) -

(i) Preflight of the towline, principles of glider disassembly and assembly, review of signals and release procedures to be used.

(ii) Aero or ground tow procedures;

(iii) Procedures and techniques for thermalling, convergence lift or ridge lift as appropriate to the training area;

(iv) Landings including normal, cross-wind and downwind; and,

(v) Emergency operations including towline break conditions.

(6) For airships. In addition to the appropriate items in (1) -

(i) Rigging, ballasting, controlling pressure in balloonet and superheating;

(ii) Landings with positive and negative static balance;

(iii) Normal approaches to landing; and,

(iv) Emergency procedures.

(7) For free balloons. In addition to the appropriate items of (1) -

(i) Operation of hot air or gas source, ballast, valves and rip panels as appropriate;

(ii) Liftoffs and ascents;

(iii) Descents, landings and emergency use of rip panels;

(iv) The effects of wind on climb and approach angles; and,

(v) Normal landing procedures.

The required instruction must be given and the log book endorsed by a flight instructor who is authorized to give instruction in the particular category and class of aircraft used. When instruction is given in a simulator or training device, such training shall be given and the log book endorsed by a flight or ground instructor. In free ballons, the holder of a commercial pilot certificate with a lighter-than-air category and free balloon class rating may give the appropriate instructions.

(d) Flight instructor endorsements. A student pilot may not operate an aircraft in solo flight unless his/her student pilot certificate is endorsed for the specific make and model of aircraft to be flown. Additionally, his/her log book must have been endorsed for solo flight within the preceding 90 days. These endorsements must be made by the flight instructor who has flown with the student and the instructor's endorsement certifies that he/she -

(1) Has given the student instruction in the make and model aircraft in which the solo flight is to be made;

(2) Finds that the student has met the flight training requirements of this section; and,

(3) Finds that the student is competent to make safe solo flights in the aircraft.

61.119 Cross-country flight requirements.

(a) General. A student pilot may not operate an aircraft in solo cross-country flight unless his/her student pilot certificate has been endorsed for solo cross-country. By log book endorsement, the instructor may authorize a student to practice take-offs and landings at airports other than the home airport.

(b) Flight training. In addition to the pre-solo flight training maneuvers and procedures, a student pilot must have received and logged instruction from an authorized instructor in at least the following prior to being endorsed for solo cross-country flight. The student must demonstrate proficiency to an acceptable performance level as judged by the instructor who is to endorse the certificate. The maneuvers and procedures for solo cross-country must include -

(1) For all aircraft - (As appropriate to the aircraft flown)

(i) The use of aeronautical charts for VFR navigation using pilotage and dead reckoning with the aid of a magnetic compass;

(ii) Procurement and analysis of aeronautical weather reports and forecasts including recognition of critical weather situations;

(iii) Aircraft cross-country performance and limitations;

(iv) Cross-country emergency procedures including lost procedures, adverse weather encounters and precautionary off airport approaches and landing procedures;

(v) Normal landing area arrival and departure traffic pattern procedures; and,

(vi) Recognition of operational problems associated with terrain features in the geographical area in which the cross-country is to be flown.

(2) For airplanes. In addition to (1) -

(i) Short and soft field take-off, approach and landing procedures;

(ii) Take-off climbs at best angle and best rate;

(iii) Control and maneuvering solely by reference to flight instruments including climbs and descents and the use of radio aids or radar directives;

(iv) Use of radio for VFR navigation and for two-way communication; and,

(v) Night flying including take-offs, landings, go-arounds and VFR navigation.

(3) For rotorcraft. In addition to (1) -

(i) High altitude take-off and landing procedures;

(ii) Steep and shallow approaches to a landing hover;

(iii) Rapid decelerations; and,

(iv) Use of radio for VFR navigation and two-way communication.

(4) For gliders. In addition to the appropriate items of (1) -

(i) At least one off airport landing at a site away from the airport of take-off;

(ii) Principles of the use of a radio for two-way communication;

(iii) Recognition of weather conditions for cross-country soaring; and,

(iv) Landings accomplished without the use of the altimeter from at least 2,000 feet above the surface.

(5) For airships. In addition to the appropriate items of (1) -

(i) Control of the airship solely by reference to flight instruments; and,

(ii) Control of gas pressure with regard to superheating and altitude changes.

(c) Flight instructor endorsements. No student pilot shall conduct a solo cross-country flight unless -

(1) His/her student pilot certificate contains an endorsement stating that he/she has received instruction in cross-country flying and the applicable training requirements of this section and has been found competent to make solo cross-country flights in the aircraft involved; and,

(2) His/her log book contains an endorsement certifying that the instructor has reviewed the flight planning and preparation for the particular solo cross-country flight. Such endorsement may contain the circumstances and conditions that the instructor believes are necessary for the student to conduct the cross-country safely. The instructor may endorse the student's log book authorizing repeated specific solo cross-country flights and specify minimum requirements that must be met by the student.

61.121 Limitation.

(a) A student pilot may not act as pilot in command for an aircraft -

(1) That is carrying a passenger;

(2) That is carrying property for compensation or hire;

(3) For compensation or hire;

(4) In the furtherance of a business;

(5) With a flight or surface visibility of less than 3 statute miles during daylight hours or 5 statute miles at night; or,

(6) On an international flight, except that a student pilot may make solo training flights from Haines, Gustavus, or Juneau, Alaska to White Horse or Yukon, Canada and return, over the province of British Columbia.

(b) A student pilot may not act as a required pilot flight crewmember on any aircraft for which more than one pilot is required, except when receiving flight instruction from an authorized instructor to board an airship and no person other than a required flight crewmember is carried on the aircraft.

(61.123) Aircraft limitations. Pilot in command.

A student pilot may not serve as pilot in command of any airship requiring more than one flight crewmember unless he has met the pertinent requirements prescribed in Sections 61.117(c)(1) and (c)(6).

Subpart F - Private Pilots

61.125 Applicability.

This subpart prescribes the requirements for the issuance of private pilot certificates and ratings, the conditions under which those certificates and ratings are necessary and the operating rules and limitations for the holders of those certificates and ratings.

61.127 Eligibility requirements.

To be eligible for a private pilot certificate, a person must -

(a) Be at least 16 years of age;

(b) Be able to read, speak, and understand the English language, or have such operating limitations placed on his/her pilot certificate as are necessary for the safe operation of aircraft, to be removed when he/she shows that he/she can read, speak and understand the English language;

(c) Hold at least a current third-class medical certificate issued under Part 67 of this chapter, or, in the case of a glider or free balloon, certify that he/she has no known medical defect that makes him/her unable to safely pilot a glider or free balloon, as appropriate;

(d) Pass a written test on the subject areas on which instruction is required by Section 61.129;

(e) Pass an oral and flight test on maneuvers and procedures selected by the FAA inspector or designated pilot examiner to determine the applicant's competency in the flight training maneuvers and procedures of Sections 61.117(c) and 61.119(b); and,

(f) Comply with the sections of this part that apply to the rating(s) he/she seeks.

61.129 Aeronautical knowledge.

An applicant for a private pilot certificate must have instruction from an authorized instructor and must demonstrate satisfactory knowledge by successfully completing a written examination covering at least the following areas of aeronautical knowledge appropriate to the category and class of aircraft for which a rating is sought -

(a)   For all aircraft -

(1) Federal Aviation Regulations applicable to private pilot privileges, limitations and flight operations;

(2) Accident reporting requirements of the National Transportation Safety Board;

(3) The information contained in applicable Advisory Circulars;

(4) The use of aeronautical charts for VFR navigation using pilotage and dead reckoning with the aid of a magnetic compass;

(5) The use of radio for VFR navigation and two-way communication;

(6) The procurement and analysis of aeronautical weather reports and forecasts and recognition of critical weather situations;

(7) The safe and efficient operation of aircraft including high density airport operations and collision avoidance and wake tubulence precautions; and,

(8) Elementary principles of aerodynamics.

(b) For gliders. In addition to (a) -

(1) Principles of air mass lift generation;

(2) Glider performance in various air masses;

(3) Cross-country techniques and safety considerations;

(4) Ground handling techniques; and,

(5) Glider instrumentation and their proper use.

(c) For airships and balloons. In addition to (a) -

(1) The effects of superheating and positive and negative lift; and,

(2) Operating principles and procedures of balloon operation, including gas and hot-air inflation systems.

61.131 Operational experience.

An applicant for a private pilot certificate must have logged the minimum number of flight as specified under this section as applicable to the category and class of aircraft.

(a) For airplane -

(1) Dual instruction -

(i) At least fifteen flights during which the maneuvers and procedures described in Section 61.117(c)(1) and (c)(2) are performed;

(ii) At least two cross-country flights, each containing four legs with landings at three or more airports/landing areas in addition to the departure/arrival airport/landing area during which the maneuvers and procedures in Section 61.119(b)(1) and (b)(2) are performed; and,

(iii) At least three flights following the first solo cross-country in preparation for the flight test.

(2) As sole occupant -

(i) At least ten flights during which the maneuvers and procedures authorized by the instructor for solo flight and as described in Section 61.117 (c)(1) and (c)(2) are performed; and,

(ii) At least four solo cross-country flights, each containing four legs with landings at three or more airports/landing areas in addition to the departure/arrival airport/landing area.

(b) For rotorcraft-helicopter -

(1) Dual instruction -

(i) At least fifteen flights during which the maneuver and procedures described in Sections 61.117 (c)(1) and (c)(3) are performed;

(ii) At least two cross-country flights, each containing four legs with landings at three or more airports/heliports in addition to the departure/arrival airport/heliport and during which the maneuvers and procedures described in Sections 61.119 (b)(1) and (b)(3) are performed;

(iii) At least three flights following the first solo cross-country in preparation for the flight test.

(2) As sole occupant -

(i) At least ten flights during which the maneuvers and procedures authorized by the instructor and as described in Sections 61.117 (c)(1) and (c)(3) are performed; and,

(ii) At least four solo cross-country flights, each containing four legs with landings at three or more airports/heliports in addition to the departure/arrival airport/heliport.

(c) For rotorcraft-gyroplane -

(1) Dual instruction -

(i) At least ten flights during which the appropriate maneuvers of 61.117 (c)(1) and (c)(4) are performed;

(ii) At least two cross-country flights, each containing four legs with landings at three or more airports in addition to the departure/arrival airport and during which the maneuvers and procedures described in 61.119 (b)(1) and (b)(3) are performed; and,

(iii) At least three flights in preparation for the flight test.

(2) As sole occupant -

(i) At least ten flights during which the maneuvers and procedures authorized by the instructor and as described in Section 61.117 (c)(1) and (c)(4) are performed; and,

(ii) At least four solo cross-country flights, each containing four legs with landings at three or more airports other than the departure/arrival airport.

(d) For gliders -

(1) Dual instruction -

(i) At least 25 flights during which the maneuvers and procedures described in Sections 61.117 (c)(1) and (c)(5) and 61.119 (b)(1) and (b)(4) are performed; and,

(ii) At least three flights in preparation for the flight test.

(2) As sole occupant -

(i) At least 25 flights (aero tow) with 20 or more having a release point at least 2,000 feet AGL during which the maneuvers and procedures authorized by the instructor and as described in 61.117 (c)(1) and (c)(5) are performed; or;

(ii) At least 50 flights (ground tow) with 40 or more having a release point at least 500 feet AGL during which the maneuvers and procedures authorized by the instructor and as described in 61.117 (c)(1) and (c)(5) are performed; and,

(iii) At least one soaring flight (duration as permitted by conditions) after release from the tow.

(e) For airships -

(1) Dual instruction -

(i) At least 25 flights during which the maneuvers and procedures described in Section 61.117 (c)(1) and (c)(6) are performed; and,

(ii) At least two cross-country flights during which the maneuvers and procedures described in 61.119(b)(1) and (b)(5) are performed.

(2) As sole occupant or performing the functions of the pilot in command of an airship for which more than one pilot is required -

(i) At least five flights during which maneuvers and procedures authorized by the instructor and as described in 61.117 (c)(1) and (c)(6) are performed; and,

(ii) At least two cross-country flights, each containing at least four legs.

(f) For free balloons -

(1) Dual instruction -

(i) At least 6 flights under the supervision of a person holding at least a commercial pilot certificate with a free balloon rating and during which the maneuvers and procedures described in Section 61.117 (c)(1) and (c)(7) are performed; and,

(ii) At least one cross-country flight during which the maneuvers and procedures described in Section 61.119 (b)(1) are performed.

(2) As sole occupant -

At least two flights with at least one flight to an altitude of at least 3,000 feet.

61.133 Cross-country flight: Pilots based on small islands.

(a) An applicant who shows that he is located on an island form which the required cross-country flights cannot be accomplished without flying over water more than 10 nautical miles from the nearest shoreline need not comply with the cross-country requirements of Section 61.131. However, if other airports that permit civil operations are available to which a flight may be made without flying over water more than 10 nautical miles from the nearest shoreline, he/she must show that he/she has completed two round trips in solo flights between those two airports that are farthest apart, including a landing at each airport on each flight.

(b) The pilot certificate issued to a person under paragraph (a) of this section contains an endorsement with the following limitations which may be subsequently amended to include another island if the applicant complies with paragraph (a) of this section with respect to that island: "Passenger carrying prohibited on flights more than 10 nautical miles from (appropriate island)".

(c) If an applicant for a private pilot certificate under paragraph (a) of this section does not have at least the solo cross-country requirements of 61.131 appropriate to the category of aircraft being flown, his/her pilot certificate is also endorsed as follows: "Holder does not meet the cross-country flight requirements."

(d) The holder of a private pilot certificate with an endorsement described in paragraph (b) or (c) of this section is entitled to removal of the endoresment, if he/she presents satisfactory evidence to an FAA inspector or designated pilot examiner that he/she has complied with the applicable solo cross-country requirements and has passed a practical test on cross-country flying.

61.135 Private pilot privileges and limitations: Pilot in command.

(a) A private pilot may not act as pilot in command of an airplane that has more than 200 horsepower or that has a retractable landing gear and/or a controllable pitch propeller unless he/she has received flight instruction in that particular make and model of airplane from an authorized flight instructor and that instructor has certified in his/her log book that he/she is competent to pilot that airplane.

(b) A private pilot may not act as pilot in command of an aircraft carrying passengers unless within the preceding 90 days he/she has made three take-offs and landings as sole manipulator of the flight controls in an aircraft of the same category and class and if a type rating is required, in that type. If the pilot is to act as pilot in command of an aircraft in daylight hours, the take-offs and landings must have been made during daylight hours. If he/she is to act as pilot in command during nighttime hours, the take-offs and landings must have been made at night. If the flight is to be made in a tailwheel airplane, the take-offs and landings must have been made to a full stop in a tailwheel airplane.

(c) A private pilot who has logged less than 400 flight hours and who has not flown as pilot in command of an aircraft within the preceding 180 days, may not act as pilot in command of an aircraft until he/she has received flight instruction in an aircraft for which he/she is rated. Such instruction must have been given by an authorized instructor and that instructor must certify in the pilot's log book that he/she is competent to pilot an aircraft.

(d) A private pilot who has logged less than 400 flight-hours may not act as pilot in command of an aircraft unless -

(1) Within the preceding twelve calendar months, he/she accomplishes a flight review given to him/her in an aircraft for which he/she is rated by an appropriately rated flight instructor or other person designated by the Adminstrator; and,

(2) The pilot's log book has been endorsed by the instructor certifying that he/she has satisfactorily accomplished the flight review. A private pilot who has logged more than 400 flight-hours need not comply with the requirements of (c) and (d) of this section but must meet the requirements of Section 61.57 of this Part.

As used in this section, a flight review shall have the same meaning as contained in Section 61.57 of this Part.

(e) Except as provided in paragraph (g) through (j) of this section, a private pilot may not act as pilot in command of an aircraft that is carrying passengers or property for compensation or hire; nor may he/she for compensation or hire, act as pilot in command of an aircraft.

(f) A private pilot who has logged less than 400 flight hours may not act as pilot in command of an aircraft when the flight or surface visibility is less than 3 statue miles during daylight hours or 5 statute miles at night, except that a private pilot who holds an instrument rating and who is conducting a flight under an instrument flight plan need not comply with this section.

(g) A private pilot may, for compensation or hire, act as pilot in command of an aircraft in connection with any business or employment if the flight is only incidental to that business or employment and the aircraft does not carry passengers or property for compensation or hire.

(h) A private pilot may share the operating expenses of a flight with his passengers.

(i) A private pilot who is an aircraft salesperson and who has more than 400 hours of logged flight time may demonstrate an aircraft in flight to a prospective buyer.

(j) A private pilot may act as pilot in command of an aircraft used in passenger carrying airlifts sponsored by a charitable organization and for which the passengers make a donation to the organization, if -

(1) The sponsor of the airlift notifies the FAA district office having jurisdiction over the area concerned, at least 7 days before the flight, and furnishes any essential information that the office request;

(2) The flights are conducted from a public airport adequate for the aircraft used, or from another airport that has been approved for the operation by an FAA inspector;

(3) The pilot has logged at least 400 hours of flight time;

(4) No aerobatic or formation flights are conducted;

(5) Each aircraft used is certificated in the standard category and complies with the 100-hour inspection requirements of Section 91.169 of this chapter; and,

(6) The flights are made under VFR conditions during the daylight hours.

For the purpose of paragraph (j) of this section, a "charitable organization" means an organization listed in Publication No. 78 of the Department of the Treasury called the "Cumulative List of Organization described in Section 170(c) of the Internal Revenue Code of 1954", as amended from time to time by published supplemental lists.

61.137 Free balloon rating: Limitations.

(a) If the applicant for a free balloon rating takes the flight tests in a hot air balloon with an airborne heater, his/her pilot certificate contains an endorsement restricting the exercise of the privileges of that rating to hot air balloons with airborne heaters. The restriction may be deleted when the holder of the certificate obtains the pilot experience required for the rating on a gas balloon.

(b) If the applicant for a free balloon rating takes the flight test in a hot air balloon without an airborne heater, his/her pilot certificate contains an endorsement restricting the exercise of the privileges of that rating to hot air balloons without airborne heaters. The restriction may be deleted when the holder of the certificate obtains the pilot experience and passes the tests required for a rating on a free balloon with an airborne heater or a gas balloon.

61.139 Private pilot privileges and limitations: Second in command of aircraft requiring more than one required pilot.

Except as provided in paragraphs (g) through (j) of Section 61.135 a private pilot may not, for compensation or hire act as second in command of an aircraft that is type certificated for more than one required pilot, nor may he/she act as second in command of such an aircraft that is carrying passengers or property for compensation or hire.

Amend 61.57 as follows:

61.57 Recent flight experience: Pilot in command, except private and recreational pilots with less than 400 flight-hours.

(a) Flight review. No person may act as pilot in command of an aircraft unless, within the preceding 24 calendar months, he/she has -

(The remaining portions of existing 61.57 to continue as written.)

Amend Subparts E,F, and G to redesignate them as Subparts G,H, and I and renumber all Sections in these Subparts.

A-3

Certification and Operation of Amateur-Built Aircraft

1. Purpose. This advisory circular (AC) provides guidance and information relative to the airworthiness certification and operation of amateur-built aircraft.

2. Cancellations.

a. AC 20-27B, Certification and Operation of Amateur-Built Aircraft, dated April 20, 1972.

b. AC 20-28A, Nationally Advertised Construction Kits Amateur-Built Aircraft, dated December 29, 1972.

3. Background.

a. The FAA has received many requests from amateur aircraft builders for information relative to the construction, certification, and operating of amateur-built aircraft. This AC provides guidance concerning the building certification, and operation of amateur-built aircraft of all types; defines the eligibility of nationally advertised kits; defines how much construction the amateur builder must do to have the aircraft eligible for airworthiness certification; and describes the FAA role in the certification process.

b. The Federal Aviation Regulations (FAR) provide for the issuance of experimental certificates to permit the operation of amateur-built aircraft. FAR § 21.191(g) defines an amateur-built aircraft as an aircraft, the major portion of which has been fabricated and assembled by person(s) who undertook the construction project solely for their education or recreation. The FAA has interpreted this rule to require that more than 50 percent of the aircraft must have been fabricated and assembled by the individual or group. Commercially produced components and parts which are normally purchased for use in aircraft may be used, including engines and engine accessories, propellers, tires, spring steel landing gear, main and tail rotor blades, rotor hubs, wheel and brake assemblies, forgings, castings, extrusions, and standard aircraft hardware such as pulleys, bellcranks, rod ends, bearings, bolts, rivets, etc.

4. Definition. As used herein, the term "District Office" means the FAA General Aviation (GADO), Flight Standards (FSDO), or Manufacturing Inspection (MIDO) District Office that will perform the airworthiness inspection and certification of an amateur-built aircraft.

5. FAA Inspection Criteria.

a. In the past, the FAA has inspected amateur-built aircraft at several stages during the construction of the aircraft. These inspections are commonly referred to as precover inspections. The FAA also inspected the aircraft upon completion (prior to the initial issuance of the special airworthiness certificate necessary to show compliance with FAR 91.42(b)), and again prior to the issuance of the unlimited special airworthiness certificate. In the interest of streamlining operations within the government, and utilizing FAA inspection resources in areas most affecting safety, the FAA has reassessed its position concerning the need for all of these inspections. The following reflects the results of this assessment:

(1) The amateur-built program was designed to permit any person to build and operate an aircraft solely for educational and recreational purposes. The FAA has always maintained that the amateur builder may select his/her own design and should not be inhibited by any overly stringent FAA requirements. The FAA does not approve these designs since it would not be practicable to develop design standards for the multitude of unique design configurations that are generated by amateur builders.

(2) FAA inspections of these aircraft are limited to ensuring the use of acceptable workmanship methods, techniques, and practices; verification of flight tests to ensure that the the particular aircraft is controllable throughout its normal range of speeds and throughout all the maneuvers to be executed; and determination of operating limitations necessary to protect persons and property not involved in this activity.

(3) In recent years, amateur builders have adopted a practice whereby they call upon a person having expertise with aircraft construction techniques (such as Experimental Aircraft Association (EAA) designees, reference paragraph 7d(1)), to inspect particular components, e.g., wing assemblies, fuselages, etc., prior to covering, and conduct other inspections, as deemed necessary. This practice has been highly successful in ensuring construction integrity.

(4) There are many instances where the FAA has found that precover inspections were unnecessary, since in some cases the areas requiring inspection were readily acessible when the aircraft was completed. In other instances, precover inspections were found to be neither meaningful nor feasible, such as in cases involving aircraft constructed from composite materials.

(5) The FAA inspection previously performed after successful completion of the flight test, and prior to issuance of an unlimited certificate, was determined to be redundant in that any workmanship discrepancies would be detected during inspections performed prior to the issuance of the initial special airworthiness certificate.

b. In view of the foregoing considerations, the FAA has concluded that safety objectives, relative to the amateur-built program, can be best accomplished, with no derogation of safety, by the use of the following criteria:

(1) Amateur builders should continue the practice of having knowledgeable persons (i.e. EAA designees, FAA certificated mechanics, etc.) perform precover inspections and other inspections as appropriate. In addition, builders should document construction using photographs taken at appropriate times prior to covering. The photographs should clearly show methods of construction and quality of workmanship. Such photographic records should be included with the builder's log or other construction records.

(2) The FAA will conduct an inspection of the aircraft prior to the issuance of the initial special airworthiness certificate to enable the applicant to show compliance with FAR 91.42(b). This inspection will include a review of the information required by FAR 21.193, the aircraft builder's log books, and an examination of the completed aircraft to ensure that proper workmanship has been used in the construction of the aircraft. Appropriate operating limitaitons will also be prescribed at this time.

(3) Upon completion of the required flight test, the FAA will review the results of the tests accomplished, as recorded in the aircraft log book. Upon a determination that compliance has been shown with FAR 91.42(b), the FAA will issue the limited special airworthiness certificate with expanded operating limitations.

6. Certification Steps. The following procedures are in the general order to be followed in the certification process:

a. Initial Step. The prospective builder should contact the nearest District Office to dicuss his plans for building the aircraft with an FAA inspector. During this contact, the type of aircraft, its complexity and/or materials should be discussed. The FAA will provide the prospective builder with any guidance necessary to ensure a better understanding of applicable regulations.

b. Registration. Prior to completion of the aircraft, the builder may apply for an identification number and register the aircraft. Detailed procedures are in paragraph 7a. This must be done before submitting an Application for Airworthiness Certificate, FAA Form 8130-6, under FAR § 21.173.

c. Marking. The identification number (N-number) assigned the aircraft, and an identification plate must be affixed in accordance with FAR § 21.182 and FAR Part 45, Identification and Registration Marking. Detailed procedures are in paragraph 7b.

d. Application. The builder may apply for an experimental certificate by submitting the following documents and data to the nearest District Office:

(1) Application for Airworthiness Certificate, FAA Form 8130-6.

(2) Enough data (such as photographs) to identify the aircraft.

(3) An Aircraft Registration Certificate, AC Form 8050-3, or the pink copy of the Aircraft Registration Application, AC Form 8050-1.

(4) A statement setting forth the purpose for which the aircraft is to be

used; i.e. "operating an amateur-built aircraft, FAR 21.191(g)."

(5) A notarized statement that the applicant fabricated and assembled the major portion (reference paragraph 7e) of the aircraft, for education or recreation, and has evidence to support the statement available to the FAA upon request (see Appendix 3 for sample.)

(6) Evidence of inspections, such as a log book entry signed by the builder describing all inspections conducted during construction of the aircraft. This will substantiate that the construction has been accomplished in accordance with acceptable workmanship methods, techniques, and practices, in addition to photographic documentation of construction details.

e. FAA Inspection and Issuance of Airworthiness Certificate.

(1) After inspection of the documents and data submitted with the application, the FAA will inspect the aircraft, and upon a determination that the aircraft has been properly constructed will issue an experimental certificate together with operating limitations that specify the flight test area. The inspector will verify that all required markings are properly applied, including the following placard which must be displayed in the cabin or the cockpit at a location where it is in full view of all the occupants:

"PASSENGER WARNING—THIS AIRCRAFT IS AMATEUR-BUILT AND DOES NOT COMPLY WITH FEDERAL SAFETY REGULATIONS FOR STANDARD AIRCRAFT"

(2) Details concerning flight test areas are contained in paragraph 7c. The operating limitations are a part of the experimental certificate and must be displayed with the certificate when the aircraft is operated. It is the responsibility of the pilot to conduct all flights in accordance with the operating limitations, as well as the General Operating and Flight Rules in FAR Part 91.

(3) Upon satisfactory completion of operations in the assigned test area, the owner of the aircraft may apply to the FAA for amended operating limitations by submitting to the nearest District Office an Application for Airworthiness Certificate, FAA Form 8130-6. Prior to issuance of the amended limitations, the FAA inspector will review the applicant's flight log to determine whether corrective actions have been taken on any problems encountered during the testing and that aircraft condition for safe operation has been established.

7. General Information

a. Aircraft Registration. The FAR require that all U.S. civil aircraft be registered, before an airworthiness certificate can be issued. FAR Part 47, Aircraft Registration, prescribes the requirements for registering civil aircraft. The basic procedures are as follows:

(1) Before an amateur builder can register his aircraft he must first obtain an identification number which will eventually be displayed on the aircraft. It is not necessary to obtain an identification number at an early

stage in the project, especially if the builder intends to obtain a special number of his choice. Under FAR Part 47, a special identification number costs $10.00 and may be reserved for no longer than one year. Although this reservation does not apply to numbers assigned at random by the Aircraft Registry, the best time to request identification number assignment in either case is in the later stages of construction.

(2) To apply for either a random identification number or special identification number, the owner of an amateur-built aircraft must provide information required by the FAA Aircraft Registry by completing an Affidavit of Ownership for Amateur-Built Aircraft, AC Form 8050-88. The affidavit establishes the ownership of the aircraft. If the aircraft is built from a kit, the builder should also submit a signed bill of sale from the manufacturer of the kit as evidence of ownership. Any communication sent to the FAA concerning aircraft registration should be mailed to the FAA Aircraft Registry, Department of Transportation, P.O. Box 25504, Oklahoma City, Oklahoma 73125.

(3) After receipt of the applicant's letter requesting identification number assignment, the FAA Aircraft Registry will send a form letter giving the number assignment, a blank Aircraft Registration Application, AC Form 8050-1, and other registration information. All instructions must be carefully complied with to prevent return of the application and delay in the registration process. The Aircraft Registration Application white original and green copy should be returned to the FAA Aircraft Registry within 90 days prior to the estimated completion date of the amateur-built aircraft, accompanied by a fee of $5.00 payable by check or money order to the Federal Aviation Administration. The pink copy of the application should be retained by the applicant to be carried in the aircraft as a temporary registration until the Certificate of Registration is issued.

b. Identification Marking. When a builder applies for an airworthiness certificate for his amateur-built aircraft, he must show in accordance with FAR § 21.182 that his aircraft bears the identification and registration markings required by FAR Part 45. The following summary of the pertinent rules is provided for guidance.

(1) The aircraft must be identified by means of a fireproof plate that is etched, stamped, engraved, or marked by some other approved fireproof marking as required by FAR 45.11. The identification plate must include the information required by FAR 45.13.

(2) The identification plate must be secured in such a manner that it will not likely be defaced or removed during normal service, or lost or destroyed in an accident. It must be secured to the aircraft at an accessible location near an entrance, except that if it is legible to a person on the ground it may be located externally on the fuselage near the tail surfaces.

(3) The builder's name on the data plate must be the amateur builder, not the designer, plans producer, or kit manufacturer. The model is whatever the builder wishes to assign, provided it will not be confused with other commercially built aircraft model designations.

330

(4) The required registration marks on most amateur-built airplanes must be displayed on either the vertical tail surfaces or the sides of the fuselage. However, the builder should refer to FAR § 42.25, which defines specific requirements for the location of marks on fixed-wing aircraft. The location of registration marks for rotorcraft, airships, and balloons is specified in FAR § 45.27. These registration marks must be painted on or affixed by any other means insuring a similar degree of permanence. Decals are also acceptable. The use of tape which can be peeled off or water soluble paint, such as poster paint, is not considered acceptable.

(5) Most fixed-wing amateur-built aircraft are eligible to display registration marks with a minimum height of three (3) inches. However, if the maximum cruising speed of the aircraft exceeds 180 knots (207 miles per hour), registration marks at least twelve (12) inches high must be displayed. The builder should refer to FAR § 45.29, which defines the minimum size and proportions for registration marks on all types of aircraft.

(6) The identification marks displayed on the aircraft must consist of the Roman capital letter "N" (denoting United States registration) followed by the registration number of the aircraft. Any suffix letter used in the marks must also be a Roman capital letter. In addition, the word "experimental" must also be displayed on the aircraft near each entrance to the cabin or cockpit in letters not less than 2 inches nor more than 6 inches in height.

(7) If the configuration of the aircraft prevents the aircraft from being marked in compliance with any of the above requirements, the builder should contact the FAA regarding approval of a different marking procedure. It is highly recommended that any questions regarding registration marking be discussed and resolved with a local FAA Inspector before the marks are affixed to the aircraft.

c. Flight Test Areas.

(1) Amateur-built airplanes and rotorcraft will initially be limited to operation within an assigned flight test area for at least 25 hours when a type certificated (FAA-approved) engine/propeller combination is installed, or 40 hours when an uncertified (not FAA-approved) engine/propeller combination is installed. Amateur-built gliders, balloons, dirigibles and ultralight vehicles built from kits evaluated by the FAA and found eligible to meet requirements of FAR 21.191(g), for which original airworthiness certification is sought will be limited to operation within an assigned flight test area for at least 10 hours of satisfactory operation, including at least five takeoffs and landings.

(2) The desired flight test area should be requested by the applicant, and if found acceptable by the FAA Inspector will be approved and so specified in the Operating Limitations. It will usually encompass the area within a twenty-five (25) statute mile radius from the aircraft's home base. The FAA will ensure that the area selected is not over densely populated areas or in congested airways so that the flight testing, during which passengers may not be carried, would not likely impose any hazard to persons or

property not involved in this activity. The shape of the flight test area selected may need to be modified to satisfy these requirements.

(3) The carrying of passengers or other crewmembers will not be permitted unless they are necessary to the conduct of the flight test while the aircraft is restricted to the flight test area.

(4) When it is shown in accordance with FAR § 91.42(b) that the aircraft is controllable throughout its normal range of speeds and all maneuvers to be executed, and has no hazardous operating characteristics or design features, and the time period in the flight test area has been completed, the owner may apply for operation outside the assigned flight test area.

d. Design and Construction.

(1) Many individuals who desire to build their own aircraft have little or no experience with respect to aeronautical practices, workmanship or design. An excellent source for advice in such matters is the Experimental Aircraft Association (EAA) located in Hales Corners, Wisconsin. The EAA is an organization established for the purpose of promoting amateur building and giving technical advice and assistance to its members. The EAA has implemented a designee program, whose aim is to ensure the safety and dependability of amateur-built aircraft. Most EAA designees are willing to inspect amateur-built aircraft projects and offer constructive advice regarding workmanship and/or design. The FAA strongly encourages the use of such designees.

(2) Any choice of engines, propellers, wheels, and other components, and any choice of materials may be used in the construction of an amateur-built aircraft. However, it is recommended that FAA-approved components and established aircraft quality material be used, especially in fabricating parts constituting the primary structure, such as wing spars, critical attachment fittings, and fuselage structural members. Inferior materials whose identity cannot be established, should not be used.

(3) The design of the cockpit or cabin of the aircraft should avoid, or provide for padding on, sharp corners or edges, protrusions, knobs and similar objects which may cause injury to the pilot or passengers in event of an accident.

(4) An engine installation should be such that adequate fuel is supplied to the engine in all anticipated flight attitudes. Also, a suitable means, consistent with the size and complexity of the aircraft, should be provided to reduce fire hazard wherever possible, including a firewall between the engine compartment and the fuselage. When applicable, a system providing for carburetor heat should also be provided to minimize the possibility of carburetor icing.

(5) Much additional information and guidance concerning acceptable fabrication and assembly methods, techniques, and practices are provided in FAA Advisory Circular (AC) No. 43.1301A "Acceptable Methods, Techniques, and Practices - Aircraft Inspection and Repair," and AC No. 43.13-2A, "Acceptable Methods, Techniques and Practices - Aircraft Inspection and Repair," and AC No. 43.13-2A, "Acceptable Methods,

Techniques and Practices - Aircraft Alterations." These publications are available from the Government Printing Office.

(6) In the areas of engineering design, the builder should obtain the services of a qualified aeronautical engineer, or consult the seller of purchased plans or construction kits, as appropriate.

e. Construction Kits.

(1) Construction kits containing raw materials and some prefabricated components may be used in building an amateur-built aircraft; however, aircraft which are assembled from kits composed of completely finished prefabricated components and parts, and precut, predrilled materials are not considered to be eligible for certification as amateur-built aircraft, since the major portion of the aircraft would not have been "fabricated and assembled" by the builder.

(2) An aircraft built from a kit may be eligible for certification, provided that the major portion (more than 50 percent) has been "fabricated and assembled" by the amateur builder. The major portion of such a kit may consist of raw stock such as lengths of wood, tubing, extrusions, etc., which may have been cut to an approximate length. A certain quantity of prefabricated parts such as heat treated ribs, bulkheads or complex forms made from sheet metal, fibre-glass, or polystyrene would also be acceptable, provided it still meets the major portion of "fabrication and assembly" requirement and the amateur builder satisfies the FAA Inspector that completion of the aircraft is not merely an assembly operation.

(3) Various material/part kits for the construction of aircraft are available nationally for use by amateur aircraft builders. Advertisements tend to be somewhat vague and may be misleading as to whether a kit is eligible for amateur-built certification. It is not advisable to order a kit prior to verifying with a FAA Inspector that the aircraft, upon completion, would be eligible for certification as amateur-built under existing rules and established policy.

(4) It should be noted that the FAA does not certify aircraft kits or approve kit manufacturers; however, the FAA does perform evaluations of kits that have potential for national sales interest, but only for the purpose of determining whether an aircraft built from the kit can meet the "major portion" criteria. Appendix 2 provides a listing of current eligible amateur aircraft kits.

f. Safety Precaution Recommendations.

(1) All Aircraft

(a) The pilot should thoroughly familiarize himself with the ground handling characteristics of the aircraft by conducting taxi tests before attempting flight operations.

(b) Before the first flight of an amateur-built aircraft, the pilot should take precautions to ensure that emergency equipment and personnel are readily available in the event of an accident.

(c) Violent (acrobatic) maneuvers should not be attempted until sufficient flight experience has been gained to establish that the aircraft is satisfactorily controllable throughout its normal ranges of speeds and maneuvers. Those maneuvers successfully demonstrated while in the test area may continue to be permitted by the FAA when the operating limitations are expanded.

(2) **Rotorcraft.**

(a) The pilot should be prepared to cope with a nonconventional aircraft which has flight characteristics unlike that of an airplane.

(b) The effect of the collective pitch and cyclic pitch control movements should be thoroughly understood by the pilot.

(c) Operators of rotorcraft having fully articulated rotor systems should be particularly cautious of "ground resonance." This condition of rotor unbalance, if maintained or allowed to progress, can be extremely dangerous and usually results in structural failure.

(d) Tests showing that stability, vibration, and balance are satisfactory should normally be completed with the rotorcraft tied down, before beginning hover or horizontal flight operations.

g. **Documentation Requirements.**

(1) To preclude any problems or questions concerning source or specification of materials, parts, etc., used in fabricating the aircraft, it would be helpful if the builder kept copies of all invoices or other shipping documents.

(2) A construction log maintained by the builder for the project, including photographs taken as major components are completed will be acceptable substantiation that the builder constructed the major portion of the aircraft.

(3) The aircraft's flight history should be recorded in an aircraft log book. The nature as well as duration of each flight should be documented. If the aircraft is considered acrobatic, the acrobatic maneuvers should be demonstrated in the flight test area and recorded in the aircraft log book.

8. **Recurrent Airworthiness Certification.** When an amateur-built aircraft has completed operations in the assigned test area, it is eligible for an UNLIMITED duration airworthiness certificate. With the issuance of the unlimited airworthiness certificate, an operating limitation requiring a condition inspection at 12 month intervals is imposed. The aircraft builder can be certified as a repairman to enable him to perform the condition inspection. Specific information regarding repairman certification can be found in AC No. 65-23, Certification of Repairman (Experimental Aircraft Builders).

9. **Reference Material.**

a. **Federal Aviation Regulations.**

Part 21 — Certification Procedures for Product and Parts.

Part 45 — Identification and Registration Marking.

Part 47 — Aircraft Registration.

Part 65 — Certification: Airmen Other than Flight Crew Members.

Part 91 — General Operating and Flight Rules.

Part 101 — Moored Balloons, Kites, Unmanned Rockets, and Free Balloons.

Part 103 — Ultralight Vehicles.

b. Advisory Circulars

20-90 — Address List for Engineering and Manufacturing District Offices (Now redesignated Manufacturing Inspection District Offices).

* 43.13-1 — Acceptable Methods, Techniques and Practices Aircraft Inspection and Repair.

* 43.13-2 — Acceptable Methods, Techniques and Practices Aircraft Alterations.

65-23 — Certificaiton of Repairmen (Experimental Aircraft Builders). Builders).

* 91-23 — Pilot's Weight and Balance Handbook.

10. How To Get Publications. The FAR and those ACs for which a fee is charged (marked with an asterisk (*) in paragraph 9(b)) may be obtained from the Superintendent of Documents, U.S. Government Printing Office, Washington, D.C. 20402. A listing of FARs and current prices is in AC 00-44, Status of Federal Aviation Regulations, and a listing of all ACs is in AC 00-2, Advisory Circular Checklist. These two ACs may be obtained free of charge from:

Department of Transportation
Publications Section, M-442.32
Washington, D.C. 20590

Publications

1. To request free advisory circulars:

> U.S. Department of Transportation
> Publications Section, M-442.32
> Washington, D.C. 20590

2. To be placed on FAA's mailing list for free advisory circulars:

> U.S. Department of Transportation
> Distribution Requirements
> Section, M-481.1
> Washington, D.C. 20590

3. To purchase for sale advisory circulars and FARs:

> Superintendent of Documents
> U.S. Government Printing Office
> Washington, D.C. 20402

SAMPLE NOTARIZED STATEMENT

Amateur Builder's Name _____

Address _____

City _____ State _____ Zip _____

Telephone No. Residence   Business _____

Aircraft Information

Model _____ Engine(s) Make _____

Assigned Serial No. _____ Engine(s) Serial No. _____

Registration No. _____ Propeller(s) Make _____

Aircraft Fabricated: ☐ Plan ☐ KitPropeller(s) Serial No. _____

Statement

I have fabricated and assembled the major portion of the aforementioned aircraft for my education and/or recreation and have evidence to support this statement available to the FAA upon request.

_____
_____

                        Signature of Builder

Notarization Statement:

A-4
FAA Aircraft Registration Information and Forms

Form Approved: Budget Bureau No. 04-R076.2

UNITED STATES OF AMERICA
DEPARTMENT OF TRANSPORTATION
FEDERAL AVIATION ADMINISTRATION

AIRCRAFT REGISTRATION INFORMATION

An aircraft is eligible for registration only: (1) if it is owned by a citizen of the United States and it is not registered under the laws of any foreign country; or (2) if it is owned by a governmental unit. Operation of an aircraft that is not registered may subject the operator to a civil penalty.

PREPARATION: Prepare this form in triplicate. Except for signatures, all data should be typewritten or printed. Signatures must be in ink. The name of the applicant should be identical to the name of the purchaser shown on AC Form 8050-2, Aircraft Bill of Sale, its equivalent, or conditional sales contract, whichever is applicable.

If an individual owner or co-owners are doing business under a trade name, each owner must be shown along with the trade name on the proof of ownership. This application must be signed by the owner or by each person who shares title as co-owner, whichever is applicable.

When a partnership submits an application, it must: (1) state the full name of the partnership on the application; (2) state the name of each general partner; (3) have a general partner sign the application.

If the application is signed by an agent, he must indicate that he is signing as an agent or attorney-in-fact. In addition to submitting FAA forms to the FAA Aircraft Registry, he must also submit a signed power of attorney or copy thereof certified as a true copy of the original. Persons signing on behalf of corporations should see Section 47.13 of the Federal Aviation Regulations.

PROOF OF OWNERSHIP: The applicant for registration of an aircraft must submit proof of ownership that meets the requirements prescribed in Part 47 of the Federal Aviation Regulations. AC Form 8050-2, Aircraft Bill of Sale, or its equivalent may be used as proof of ownership. If the applicant did not purchase the aircraft from the last registered owner, he must submit conveyances completing the chain of ownership from the last registered owner to himself.

The purchaser under a CONTRACT OF CONDITIONAL SALE is considered the owner for the purpose of registration and the contract of conditional sale must be submitted as proof of ownership. A BILL OF SALE SHOULD NOT BE SUBMITTED.

REGISTRATION AND RECORDING FEES: The fee for issuing a certificate of aircraft registration is $5.00. An additional fee of $5.00 is required when a conditional sales contract is submitted as proof of ownership along with the application for aircraft registration. ($5.00 for the issuance of the certificate, and $5.00 for the recording of the lien evidenced by the contract.) The fee charged for recording a conveyance is $5.00 for each aircraft listed therein. (There is no fee for issuing a certificate of aircraft registration to a governmental unit or for recording a bill of sale that accompanies an application for Aircraft Registration and the proper registration fee.)

CHANGE OF ADDRESS: An aircraft owner must notify the FAA Aircraft Registry of any change in his permanent address. This form may be used to submit a new address.

Please send the WHITE original and GREEN copy of this application to the FAA Aircraft Registry, P.O. Box 25082, Oklahoma City, Oklahoma 73125; RETAIN PINK COPY which is authority to operate the aircraft when carried in the aircraft with an appropriate and current airworthiness certificate or a special flight permit. (See note on pink copy.)

AC Form 8050-1 (11-69) (0052-628-9002)

ADDRESSES

Experimental Aircraft Association, Inc.
Mailing: P.O. Box 229
             Hales Corners, Wisconsin 53130

Street: 11311 West Forest Home Avenue
             Franklin, Wisconsin

(Phone: Area Code (414) 425-4860

Federal Aviation Administration
Mailing: Airmen and Aircraft Registry
             Department of Transportation
             P.O. Box 25504
             Oklahoma City, Oklahoma 73125

Street: 6500 South MacArthur Boulevard
             Oklahoma City, Oklahoma

(Phone: Area Code (405) 686-4331)

A-5

FAA Aircraft Bill of Sale Information and Forms

Before purchasing an aircraft, the buyer should make, or have made, a search of the records and encumbrances affecting ownership at the FAA Aircraft Registry, FAA Aviation Records Building, Aeronautical Center, P.O. Box 25082, Oklahoma City, Oklahoma 73125. A list of title search companies, AC Form 8050-55, will be furnished upon request.

Do not submit a bill of sale as proof of ownership when an aircraft is purchased under a contract of conditional sale since a bill of sale transfers all right, title, and interest. However, under a contract of conditional sale the seller retains title. The purchaser under a contract of conditional sale is considered the owner for the purpose of registration and the contract of conditional sale must be submitted as proof of ownership.

The use of a typewriter in the preparation of registration documents is not mandatory, but is preferred. Prepare this form, or an equivalent bill of sale, in duplicate, with all signatures IN INK. When a bill of sale (or other proof of ownership) shows a trade name as the purchaser or seller, the name of the individual owner or co-owners must be shown along with the trade name. In addition, when necessary for clarification, it is requested that the bill of sale indicate that such individual(s) is doing business under the trade name.

If the bill of sale is signed by an agent, he must show the name of the person for whom he is signing and indicate whether he is signing as agent or attorney-in-fact. A signed power of attorney (or a certified true copy of the original) must be submitted. Persons signing on behalf of a corporation should see Section 47.13 of the Federal Aviation Regulations.

The name of the applicant on an Aircraft Registration Application (AC Form 8050-1) must be the same as the name of the purchaser as shown on this bill of sale, its equivalent, or other proof of ownership.

The fee for issuing a certificate of aircraft registration is $5.00. An additional fee of $5.00 is required when a conditional sales contract is submitted as proof of ownership along with the application for aircraft registration. ($5.00 for the issuance of the certificate, and $5.00 for the recording of the lien evidenced by the contract.) The fee charged for recording a conveyance is $5.00 for each aircraft listed therein. There is no fee for issuing a certificate of aircraft registration to a governmental unit. Neither is there a fee for recording a bill of sale that accompanies an Aircraft Registration Application and the proper registration fee.

Mail the original signed in black ink to the FAA Aircraft Registry, P.O. Box 25082, Oklahoma City, Oklahoma 73125. Retain the purchaser's copy for your records.

FORM APPROVED
OMB NO. 04-R0076

DO NOT WRITE IN THIS BLOCK
FOR FAA USE ONLY

UNITED STATES OF AMERICA
DEPARTMENT OF TRANSPORTATION
FEDERAL AVIATION ADMINISTRATION

AIRCRAFT BILL OF SALE

FOR AND IN CONSIDERATION OF $ THE UNDERSIGNED OWNER(S) OF THE FULL LEGAL AND BENEFICIAL TITLE OF THE AIRCRAFT DESCRIBED AS FOLLOWS:

AIRCRAFT MAKE AND MODEL

MANUFACTURER'S SERIAL NUMBER

NATIONALITY & REGISTRATION MARKS

DOES THIS   DAY OF   19

HEREBY SELL, GRANT, TRANSFER AND DELIVER ALL RIGHTS, TITLE, AND INTERESTS IN AND TO SUCH AIRCRAFT UNTO:

PURCHASER

NAME AND ADDRESS
(IF INDIVIDUAL(S), GIVE LAST NAME, FIRST NAME, AND MIDDLE INITIAL.)

AND TO   EXECUTORS, ADMINISTRATORS, AND ASSIGNS TO HAVE AND TO HOLD SINGULARLY THE SAID AIRCRAFT FOREVER, AND WARRANTS THE TITLE THEREOF.

IN TESTIMONY WHEREOF   HAVE SET   HAND AND SEAL THIS   DAY OF   19

NAME (S) OF SELLER (TYPED OR PRINTED)	SIGNATURE (S) (IN BLACK INK.) (IF EXECUTED FOR CO-OWNERSHIP, ALL MUST SIGN.)	TITLE (TYPED OR PRINTED)

SELLER

ACKNOWLEDGMENT   (NOT REQUIRED FOR PURPOSES OF FAA RECORDING; HOWEVER, MAY BE REQUIRED BY LOCAL LAW FOR VALIDITY OF THE INSTRUMENT.)

ORIGINAL: TO FAA

AC FORM 8050-2 (4-71)(0052-629-0002)

340

A-6

FAA Application for Airworthiness Certificate

Form Approved
Budget Bureau No. 04-R0058

DEPARTMENT OF TRANSPORTATION
FEDERAL AVIATION ADMINISTRATION

APPLICATION FOR AIRWORTHINESS CERTIFICATE

INSTRUCTIONS—Print or type. Do not write in shaded areas; these are for FAA use only. Submit original only to an authorized FAA Representative. If additional space is required, use an attachment. For special flight permits complete Sections II and VI or VII as applicable.

I. AIRCRAFT DESCRIPTION

1. REGISTRATION MARK	2. AIRCRAFT BUILDER'S NAME (make)	3. AIRCRAFT MODEL DESIGNATION	4. YR. MFG	FAA CODING
5. AIRCRAFT SERIAL NO.	6. ENGINE BUILDER'S NAME (make)	7. ENGINE MODEL DESIGNATION		
8. NUMBER OF ENGINES	9. PROPELLER BUILDER'S NAME (make)	10. PROPELLER MODEL DESIGNATION		11. AIRCRAFT IS

NEW	USED	IMPORT

II. CERTIFICATION REQUESTED

APPLICATION IS HEREBY MADE FOR: (Check applicable items)

A	1	STANDARD AIRWORTHINESS CERT. (Indicate category)	NORMAL	UTILITY	ACROBATIC	TRANSPORT	GLIDER	BALLOON

| B | | SPECIAL AIRWORTHINESS CERTIFICATE (Check appropriate items) |

	2	LIMITED					
	5	PROVISIONAL (Indicate class)	1	CLASS I			
			2	CLASS II			
	3	RESTRICTED (Indicate operation(s) to be conducted)	1	AGRICULTURE & PEST CONTROL	2	AERIAL SURVEYING	3	AERIAL ADVERTISING
			4	FOREST (Wild life conservation)	5	PATROLLING	6	WEATHER CONTROL
			0	OTHER (Specify)			
	4	EXPERIMENTAL (Indicate operation(s) to be conducted)	1	RESEARCH AND DEVELOPMENT	2	AMATEUR BUILT	3	EXHIBITION
			4	RACING	5	CREW TRAINING	6	MKT. SURVEY
			0	TO SHOW COMPLIANCE WITH FAR			
	8	SPECIAL FLIGHT PERMIT (Indicate operation to be conducted then complete Section VI or VII as applicable on reverse side)	1	FERRY FLIGHT FOR REPAIRS, ALTERATIONS, MAINTENANCE OR STORAGE			
			2	EVACUATE FROM AREA OF IMPENDING DANGER			
			3	OPERATION IN EXCESS OF MAX. CERTIFICATED TAKE-OFF WEIGHT			
			4	DELIVERING OR EXPORT	5	PRODUCTION FLIGHT TESTING	

C	6	MULTIPLE AIRWORTHINESS CERTIFICATE (Check appropriate Restricted Operation and Standard or Limited as applicable above)

III. OWNER'S CERTIFICATION

A. REGISTERED OWNER (As shown on Certificate of Aircraft Registration) IF DEALER, CHECK HERE →

NAME	ADDRESS

B. AIRCRAFT CERTIFICATION BASIS (Check applicable blocks and complete items as indicated)

AIRCRAFT SPECIFICATION OR TYPE CERTIFICATION DATA SHEET (Give No. and Revision No.)	AIRWORTHINESS DIRECTIVES (Check if all applicable AD's complied with and give latest AD No.)
AIRCRAFT LISTING (Give page No(s.))	SUPPLEMENTAL TYPE CERTIFICATE (List number of each STC incorporated)

C. AIRCRAFT OPERATION AND MAINTENANCE RECORDS

CHECK IF RECORDS IN COMPLIANCE WITH FAR 91.173	TOTAL AIRFRAME HOURS—Enter for used aircraft only	3	EXPERIMENTAL ONLY—Enter hours flown since last certificate issued or renewed

D. CERTIFICATION—I hereby certify that I am the owner (or his agent) of the aircraft described above; that the aircraft is registered with the Federal Aviation Administration in accordance with Section 501 of the Federal Aviation Act of 1958, and applicable Federal Aviation Regulations; and that the aircraft has been inspected and is airworthy and eligible for the airworthiness certificate requested.

DATE OF APPLICATION	NAME AND TITLE (Print or type)	SIGNATURE

IV. INSPECTION AGENCY VERIFICATION

A. THE AIRCRAFT DESCRIBED ABOVE HAS BEEN INSPECTED AND FOUND AIRWORTHY BY: (Complete this section only if FAR 21.183 (d) applies)

2	FAR PART 121 OR 127 CERTIFICATE HOLDER (Give Certificate No.)	3	CERTIFICATED MECHANIC (Give Certificate No.)	6	CERTIFICATED REPAIR STATION (Give Certificate No.)
5	AIRCRAFT MANUFACTURER (Give Name of Firm)				

DATE	TITLE	SIGNATURE

V. FAA REPRESENTATIVE CERTIFICATION

(Check ALL applicable blocks) I find that the aircraft described in Section I or VII meets the requirements for: ☐ The certification requested, or ☐ Amendment or modification of its current airworthiness certificate. Inspection for a special flight permit under Section VII was conducted by: ☐ FAA Inspector; certificate holder under ☐ FAR 65, ☐ FAR 121 or 127, or ☐ FAR 145.

DATE	DISTRICT OFFICE	DESIGNEE'S SIGNATURE AND NO.	FAA INSPECTOR'S SIGNATURE

FAA Form 8130-6 (7-70)

	A. MANUFACTURER	
	NAME	ADDRESS

<table>
<tr><td rowspan="13" style="writing-mode: vertical-lr">VI. PRODUCTION FLIGHT TESTING</td><td colspan="2">B. PRODUCTION BASIS (Check applicable item)</td></tr>
</table>

VI. PRODUCTION FLIGHT TESTING

A. MANUFACTURER

NAME	ADDRESS

B. PRODUCTION BASIS (Check applicable item)

	PRODUCTION CERTIFICATE (Give production certificate number)
	TYPE CERTIFICATE ONLY
	APPROVED PRODUCTION INSPECTION SYSTEM

C. GIVE QUANTITY OF CERTIFICATES REQUIRED FOR OPERATING NEEDS:

DATE OF APPLICATION	NAME AND TITLE (Print or type)	SIGNATURE

VII. SPECIAL FLIGHT PERMIT PURPOSES OTHER THAN PRODUCTION FLIGHT TEST

A. DESCRIPTION OF AIRCRAFT

REGISTERED OWNER	ADDRESS
BUILDER (Make)	MODEL
SERIAL NUMBER	REGISTRATION MARK

B. DESCRIPTION OF FLIGHT

FROM	TO	
VIA	DEPARTURE DATE	DURATION

C. CREW REQUIRED TO OPERATE THE AIRCRAFT AND ITS EQUIPMENT

PILOT	CO-PILOT	NAVIGATOR	OTHER (Specify)

D. THE AIRCRAFT DOES NOT MEET THE APPLICABLE AIRWORTHINESS REQUIREMENTS AS FOLLOWS:

E. THE FOLLOWING RESTRICTIONS ARE CONSIDERED NECESSARY FOR SAFE OPERATION (Use attachment if necessary)

F. CERTIFICATION—I hereby certify that I am the registered owner (or his agent) of the aircraft described above; that the aircraft is registered with the Federal Aviation Administration in accordance with Section 501 of the Federal Aviation Act of 1958, and applicable Federal Aviation Regulations; and that the aircraft has been inspected and is airworthy for the flight described.

DATE	NAME AND TITLE (Print or type)	SIGNATURE

VIII. AIRWORTHINESS DOCUMENTATION (FAA use only)

A. Operating Limitations and Markings in Compliance with FAR 91.31 as Applicable	G. Statement of Conformity, FAA Form 317 (Attach when required)
B. Current Operating Limitations Attached	H. Foreign Airworthiness Certification for Import Aircraft (Attach when required)
C. Data, Drawings, Photographs, etc. (Attach when required)	I. Previous Airworthiness Certificate Issued in Accordance with FAR _____ CAR _____ (Original attached)
D. Current Weight and Balance Information Available in Aircraft	
E. Major Repair and Alteration, FAA 337 (Attach when required)	J. Current Airworthiness Certificate Issued in Accordance with FAR _____ (Copy attached)
F. This Inspection Recorded in Aircraft Records	

C   FAA AC 72-0771

A-7
Aircraft Registration Application

Cert. Iss. Date: FORM APPROVED BUDGET BUREAU NO. 04-R076.2

UNITED STATES OF AMERICA
DEPARTMENT OF TRANSPORTATION — FEDERAL AVIATION ADMINISTRATION

AIRCRAFT REGISTRATION APPLICATION

TYPE OF REGISTRATION (Check one box) ☐ 1. Individual
☐ 2. Partnership ☐ 3. Corporation ☐ 4. Co-Owner ☐ 5. Gov't.

NATIONALTY AND REGISTRATION MARKS N	AIRCRAFT MAKE AND MODEL

AIRCRAFT SERIAL No.

NAME(S) OF APPLICANT(S)

FOR FAA USE ONLY

(Must be same as Purchaser on Bill of Sale; if individual(s), give last name(s), first name(s), and middle initial(s).)

RESS (Number and Street; P. O. Box; or Rural Route.)

☐ CHECK HERE IF ADDRESS CHANGE ONLY	CITY	STATE	ZIP CODE

(No fee required for revised Certificate of Registration)

ATTENTION!   Read the following statement before signing this application. A false or dishonest answer to any question in this application may be grounds for punishment by fine and/or imprisonment (U.S. Code, Title 18, Sec. 1001).

CERTIFICATION

I/WE CERTIFY that the above described aircraft (1) is owned by the undersigned applicant(s), who is/are citizen(s) of the United States as defined in Sec. 101(13) of the Federal Aviation Act of 1958; (2) is not registered under the laws of any foreign country; and (3) legal evidence of ownership is attached or has been filed with the Federal Aviation Administration.

TE: If executed for co-ownership all applicants must sign. Use reverse side if necessary.

EACH PART OF THIS APPLICATION MUST BE SIGNED IN INK.	SIGNATURE	TITLE	DATE
	SIGNATURE	TITLE	DATE
	SIGNATURE	TITLE	DATE

NOTE: Pending receipt of the Certificate of Aircraft Registration, the aircraft may be operated for a period not in excess of 90 days, during which time the PINK copy of this application must be carried in the aircraft.

AC Form 8050-1 (11-69) (0052-628-9002)

A-8
The National Association of Sport Aircraft Designers

ABOUT NASAD

The National Association of Sport Aircraft Designers is an independent, non-profit organization of aircraft designers and enthusiasts, dedicated to the development and improvement of aircraft and related components.

The charter meeting of NASAD was held at EAA Headquarters in Hales Corners, Wisconsin on October 23, 1971 and was hosted by EAA's president Paul Poberenzy. Thirty-two designers joined NASAD at that time as charter members. Steve Wittman and the late Stan Dzik wrote the organization's charter. Although every member of NASAD was a member of EAA, headquarters wanted NASAD to be a separate and independent group to eliminate any possible conflict of interests. This permitted NASAD to tackle the knotty task of analyzing the quality of drawings, plans, and kits offered for sale on the market to amateur builders. The entire field of available "homebuilt" aviation merchandise was surveyed, and the "Status Report" on it was prepared and distributed on confidential basis to NASAD members. This information served as the basis for the formulation of NASAD "Standards of Quality" for homebuilt aircraft. The Standards were later accepted by its membership as the yardstick of minimum data to be supplied in commercially sold plans and kits to amateur builders possessing several levels of skill. A Compliance Board was named, consisting of 3 highly respected professional aeronautical engineers with more than 100 years of design experience between them, not presently involved in any commercial activities. They analyze the Plans submitted to them by designers, on voluntary basis, for compliance with the Standards in specified classes of skills. If they pass, a Certificate of Compliance is issued to the submitted design, giving its designer the right to display NASAD's copyrighted "Seal of Quality."

WHAT DOES NASAD DO?

1. NASAD has set up a system of standards to evaluate the commercially available aircraft plans, drawings and kits for amateur-built aircraft.
2. NASAD's panel of experts has, at the request of the designers,

evaluated many designs. Of these, seventeen have complied with the minimum standards, and have been awarded a "Certificate of Compliance."

3. NASAD makes available its evaluations free to its members, and to the public at a nominal fee, in order to promote excellence in all phases of aircraft design and construction.

4. NASAD provides a forum for the free exchange of new ideas and latest technology among its fellow members and helps designers to improve their designs.

5. NASAD coordinates with other national aviation organizations efforts to achieve regulations which will deal fairly with Sport Aviation.

Memberships are open to all aviation enthusiasts. Send $25 dues and inquiries to: NASAD Secretary, 1756 Hanover St., Cuyahoga Falls, Ohio 44221. You will receive the NASAD Standards of Quality Manual and List of Approved Airplanes and Engines, as well as a newsletter of significant events.

Definition of Classes

Class 1: Plans are rated for "Average Amateur" level of skill, or higher. The builder may have no previous experience in aircraft construction. Has moderate amount of previous experience in mechanical assembly, operation and maintenance of motor-powered vehicles. Knows how to use common hobby shop power tools and hand tools. Has access to professional machine shop capable of turning out work within 1-mil (0.001 inch) tolerances, or can do it himself. First aircraft building project. No flying experience required. This Class has 44 compliance requirements.

Class 2: Rated for "Experienced Amateur." **Aircraft building experience required.** Second or third aircraft building project. Previous aircraft building project was completed, including successful flight test. Flying experience as a pilot in command in similar aircraft is required. This Class has 25 compliance requirements.

Class 3: Rated for "Experienced Experimenter." This builder is qualified and expected to do his own aerodynamic calculations and stress analysis, or stress tests. Capable of examining potentially dangerous areas which may exist, but for which not enough data are given to be detected by the Compliance Board. Third or fourth aircraft building and flying project. Familiar with aircraft style hardware, design practices and preventive maintenance. Extensive flight experience as pilot in command in similar aircraft is required. This Class has 16 compliance requirements.

Other Definitions

Major Modifications - those design modifications which could adversely affect and/or alter aerodynamic performance or structural integrity of the aircraft.

V-g Limits - literally, "velocity-gravity" information prepared by the designer showing the maximum tested or proven limits of airspeed (V) and "g" acceleration loads. Information should include: (1) Calculated design limits, and/or (2) Limits obtained by static tests, if any, and (3) Limits obtained by flight tests, supported by test records.

Test Records - originals or photocopies of data taken during actual tests. Must include: the date and description of test, location, equipment used, name of operator(s) performing tests, results obtained and operator's signature.

Qualitative Ratings
A. Quality of Plans:
1. Completeness .... Adequate - excellent - superior
2. Clarity .... Adequate - excellent - superior

B. Quality of Design:
3. Complexity of construction .... Simple - medium - high
4. Complexity of Piloting .... Basic skills - advanced skills

C. Quality of Parts and Kits:
5. Completeness of kit .... Partial - complete
6. Quality of parts supplied .... Adequate - excellent - superior

GUEST RECORD AND AGREEMENT

Aircraft Built by: _____ Model: _____ Registration No.: _____

This is to certify that the Experimental Aircraft identified above is sole property of the Owner whose signature appears below. It is further certified that the Owner hereby grants permission to the Guest signed below, and the Guest agrees, (for himself, his heirs, administrators and assigns) to operate this Aircraft in accordance with the following stipulations:

1. The Guest is aware of risks and potential dangers involved when flying Experimental aircraft and knows that this type of "amateur-built" aircraft does not, nor is it required to, comply with Federal Aviation Administration's safety standards for commercially sold aircraft, nor with any other standards.

2. The Guest agrees and understands that the builder of said Aircraft has the sole responsibility for its manufacture, design and workmanship. He also understands and agrees that no warranties, neither explicit nor implied, neither verbal nor written are given by the Builder, nor the Owner, nor by their suppliers, as to the performance expectations and safety of this Experimental equipment. The Guest acknowledges that he has read and agrees to comply to the letter with all instructions of the Owner as well as of those contained in the Manuals of Vendors' parts and components. The Guest states without reservation that he/she possesses the skills and knowledge necessary to operate said Aircraft, and that he/she is currently in compliance with all requirements of the FAA and will operate said Aircraft pursuant to all applicable instructions and flight rules governing said flight.

3. **FOR THE PRIVILEGES AND COURTESIES EXTENDED TO THE GUEST WHILE OPERATING, OR RIDING IN, OR BEING EXPOSED TO THE SUBJECT EXPERIMENTAL AIRCRAFT, THE GUEST AGREES TO ASSUME THE RISK AND TO HOLD (FOR HIMSELF, HIS HEIRS, ADMINISTRATORS AND ASSIGNS), THE OWNER, BUILDER, DESIGNER, MATERIALS OR PLAN SUPPLIERS, AND ANY OTHER THIRD PARTIES ASSOCIATED IN ANY WAY WITH THE CONSTRUCTION, DESIGN, APPROVAL, LICENSING AND/OR OPERATION OF SAID AIRCRAFT, ITS PLANS OR ANY PART THEREOF, HARMLESS FROM AND IDEMNIFY THEM AGAINST ANY AND ALL LIABILITIES, DEMANDS, CLAIMS, SUITS, LOSSES, DAMAGES, CAUSES OF ACTION, FINES OR JUDGMENTS, INCLUDING ALL COSTS OF LITIGATION, AND EXPENSES INCIDENT THERETO, CAUSED OR OCCASIONED BY OR ARISING FROM THEIR ACTS, NEGLIGENCE AND/OR OMISSION, OR FROM ANY OTHER CAUSE IN ANY INCIDENT RELATED CONSEQUENTIALLY OR INCONSEQUENTIALLY TO HIS USING OR BEING EXPOSED TO THIS AIRCRAFT.**

4. The Guest also agrees to replace, repair or adequately compensate the Owner and/or third parties for any equipment or materials which he may consume, wear out, lose, damage or destroy in the course of his using, acting upon and/or operating said Aircraft. He also agrees to use all reasonable care and precautions to prevent accidents, and to obey safety rules, regulations and instructions of the FAA, local officials and of local Airport management.

5. No one is authorized to modify or waive these conditions, and the Owner admits no liability by accepting this Release. The Guest shall carry one executed copy of this Release with him while operating the Aircraft, and the Owner shall file the second copy in his records.

6. The Owner further certifies that he grants this permission, and the Guest receives it, of their free will and accord, and no compensation in any form for it has been exchanged or promised between them. This permit is valid only for the date(s) shown below.

Additional Owner's Instructions: _____

_____

_____	_____	_____
Guest	Date	Owner
_____		_____
Guardian, if under legal age		Guardian, if under legal age

SYMBOLS IN THE TABLE: ● -- Must comply.   O -- Critical items only; involving primary structure and those members whose failure or incorrect fabrication would lead to catastrophic hazard (fatal or serious injuries to the occupants.)

A. GENERAL SPECIFICATIONS:

		Class 1	Class 2	Class 3
1.	Designer's name and Model designation given	●	●	●
2.	Design Gross Weight and Maximum Weight permissible given	●	●	●
3.	Design Engine and propeller hp plus minimum and maximum allowable engine horsepower and weight given	●	●	●
4.	The fuel capacity, and if two-cycle engine is used, the oil grade and oil-in-fuel ratio given	●		
5.	Overall and major essential dimensions given	●	●	●

B. PLANS & DRAWINGS:

		Class 1	Class 2	Class 3
1.	Statement and description of the NASAD's Class of minimum required building and flying skills given	●	●	●
2.	Builder-fabricated parts dimensioned	●	O	O
3.	Builder-fabricated parts identified by Part or Drawing No.	●	O	
4.	Fasteners (bolts, rivets etc.) specified and identified by SAE, ASTM, AN or MIL numbers	●	O	
5.	Revisions marked and dated on Drawings	●	O	O
6.	Full-size templates of critical parts shown	●	O	
7.	Exploded views, sketches or photos of critical assemblies shown	●	O	
8.	Tolerances of builder-fabricated parts given	●	O	
9.	Lists of Materials and Hardware given	●	O	
10.	Material Specifications given	●	O	O
11.	"Non-aircraft" parts and materials used where specified	●	●	●
12.	Shopping sources for materials and hardware given	●		
13.	Flight Controls, Powerplant, Electrical, Hydraulic etc. (as applicable) Systems depicted	●	●	O
14.	Limits of motion of control surfaces and positive stops limiting travel of controls provided, specified and shown	●	O	
15.	Seat belt and shoulder harness anchoring structure specified	●	●	●
16.	Customers promptly notified when critical and mandatory fixes are required	●	●	●

C. MANUALS:

		Class 1	Class 2	Class 3
1.	Description of Design and Performance Manual supplied	●	●	●
2.	Construction and Assembly Manual supplied	●	O	
3.	Pilot's Manual supplied	●		
4.	Inspection and Maintenance Manual supplied	●	O	
5.	Lubricants for each lube joint and time interval for each lube joint specified	●	●	
6.	Overhaul & service periods specified for all vital components	●	O	
7.	Weight and balance procedure given	●	●	
8.	C.G. travel limits given	●	●	●
9.	Pre-maiden-flight ground test procedures specified	●	●	
10.	Maiden flight test procedure specified	●	●	
11.	Stall speed and Vne specified, supported by Test Records	●	●	●
12.	Check list for routine Pre-Flight and Post-Flight inspections given	●		
13.	Systems' pressures, loads and capacities given	●	O	
14.	Inspection Manual available	●	●	O

D. HISTORY OF EXPERIENCE:
(Supported by Test Records available on request).

		Class 1	Class 2	Class 3
1.	The Prototype has logged a total of 150 accident-free hours of test and development flight time	●		
2.	The Prototype has logged more than 50 hours on certified engine or 75 hours on uncertified engine of accident-free flight since the last Major Modification prior to offering the Plans and/or Kits for sale	●	●	
3.	Using the aircraft built exactly to the Drawings, the designer has performed a minimum of 5			

flight test hours of engineering evaluation establishing the V-g limits, without encountering flutter or any aero-elastic instabilities... • • •

4. Minimum Rate of Climb of 300 ft/min, or angle of climb of 1/12 or higher, to at least 1000-foot altitude above ground level and engine-out glide to landing, were achieved in standard air at rated Gross Weight .... • • •

5. The Prototype has completed at least the flight program outlined in Paragraphs D.3 and D.4 before "information data pack", "brochure", or any other material is advertized for sale to the public.. • • •

6. Stress analysis and/or tests of critical components performed and recorded in Test Records • ○

7. Full throttle climb tests at most critical attitude were performed without fuel starvation or engine malfunction .... • • •

8. Time limit for full throttle operation at minimum airspeed given... • • •

9. Stalls, power on and off, climbing, gliding and turning, performed safely, and characteristics described in the Manual... • •

10. On spinnable aircraft, spin tests performed and characteristics described in the Manual, or design placarded prohibiting spins .... • • •

E. PARTS AND KITS:

1. Parts manufactured to the specified dimensions and tolerances.. •
2. Materials, parts and workmanship of the specified quality and quantity............................ •
3. Parts identified by Part or Drawing No.. •
4. Fastener of the required quantity and quality (AN, MIL as per Drawings and Specifications) •
5. The latest revision of the Drawings incorporated in the Parts and Kits (where interchange-ability is affected, special note required) .... •
6. The completeness of the materials, parts and kits is as advertised
   a) Airframe (wing, fuselage, tail including fasteners).. •
   b) Control system (cables, rods and hardware).. •
   c) Landing gear (shocks, wheels, brakes and accessories)... •
   d) Fuel system (tank, lines, drains etc.) .... •
   e) Instruments and accessories.. ○
   f) Electric system (wires, fuses, switches, lights etc.)... ○
   g) Engine (complete with carburetor, prop flange, magnetos or equivalent, spark plugs, starter and generator when applicable)... ○
   h) Engine installation (baffles, exhaust with heat mufflers, attachments, air boxes and filter, etc.)..
   i) Propeller to the specifications .... ○
   k) Fairings to the specifications and in accordance to those tested .... •
7. If Drawings not approved, are the supplied instructions adequate?..................................... •
8. If parts or assemblies not approved by designer, is adequate service experience available to NASAD or does the designer have valid objections? .... •

NASAD Seal of Quality means:

The parts supplied conform to above criteria which assure the builder he is using the right quality. It is also an attempt to judge the completeness of the kit.

Note: This label must be affixed to both sides of the aircraft cockpit, in conjunction with having your guest pilot sign the above agreement.

N.A.S.A.D.
NATIONAL ASSOCIATION OF SPORT AIRCRAFT DESIGNERS

AIRCRAFT BILL OF SALE

FOR EXPERIMENTAL-AMATEUR BUILT AIRCRAFT. THIS FORM SUPPLEMENTS & DOES NOT REPLACE FAA

FORM AC8050-2. N NUMBER (IF ASSIGNED:) **N** _____

SERIAL NUMBER (OF BUILDER'S CHOICE:) _____ THIS AIRCRAFT IS A FACSIMILE

OF AN AIRCRAFT KNOWN AS A: _____

This aircraft is not designed or built to meet any standards of airworthiness as with a certificated aircraft. This aircraft does not have a FAA Form 317 Statement of Conformity on file, since there is no FAA approved data to conform to. This is an experimental aircraft and the registered owner is the experimenter. The aircraft was not built in a permanent jig and parts are not interchangeable with any other aircraft of the same facsimile. FAA records list the registered owner as the manufacturer of an experimental-amateur built aircraft. The registered owner is free to make any modifications or changes he so wishes. The aircraft is an example of the owners creative ability. The new owner of an experimental-amateur built aircraft becomes it's manufacturer, when it is registered to him. He becomes responsible for it's aerodynamic and structural concept. The new owner is responsible for the performance and fit for purpose of every part and piece on the aircraft. Warranty is not expressed or implied for any feature or part of this experimental-amateur built aircraft.

I accept the terms of this **Bill of Sale** and all responsibility for the aircraft described herein.

PURCHASER

NAME: _____

ADDRESS: _____

_____

SIGNATURE: _____

SIGNATURE OF SPOUSE: _____

I this _____ day of _____ 19 _____ , do hereby sell, grant, transfer, and deliver all rights, title, and interest in and to such aircraft.

SELLER

NAME OF SELLER: _____

ADDRESS: _____

_____

SIGNATURE: _____

NOTARY SEAL SPACE

This **Bill of Sale** must be signed by both parties. The seller keeps the original and gives a copy to the new owner. Send a copy of the original to FAA with the canceled registration (if registered.) Sign before a notary if required by the state where the transaction occurs. FAA dropped the requirement for notarizing in 1972.

ARV Related Organizations and Publications

MAGAZINE PUBLISHERS

Air Progress Ultralights
7950 Deering Avenue
Canoga Park, CA 91304

Canadian Ultralight News
P.O. Box 563
Station "B"
Ottawa, Ont. KIP 5P7

Ultralight and The Lightplane
Wittman Field
Oshkosh, WI 54903

Glider Rider
P.O. Box 6009
Chattanooga, TN 37401

Sportsman Pilot
P.O. Box 2768
Oshkosh, WI 54903

Ultralight Aircraft Magazine
16200 Ventura Blvd.
Suite 201
Encino, CA 91436

Ultralight Flyer Newspaper
P.O. Box 98786
Tacoma, WA 98499

Ultralight Pilot,
Including Lightplane Pilot
P.O. Box 5800
Bethesda, MD 20814

Whole Air Magazine
P.O. Box 144
Lookout Mtn., TN 37350

ORGANIZATIONS

AOPA Air Safety Foundation
421 Aviation Way
Frederick, MD 21701
(301) 695-2000

Experimental Aircraft Assn.
Wittman Field
Oshkosh, WI 54903
(414) 426-4800

BOOK PUBLISHERS

AViation Publishers
P.O. Box 234
Hummelstown, PA 17036
1-800-441-7527 (only for credit card orders or our FREE Catalog)

Canadian Dist. for above
Acfield Aviation Supplies, Ltd.
7040 Torbram Rd. (14)
Mississauga, Ont. L4T 3Z4
(416) 677-4717

COMPOSITE CONSTRUCTION
For Homebuilts, Ultralights, and ARVs
Jack Lambie
240p/195il......$15.95

This is the only book that covers the field of composite kitplanes. You'll learn how you can build the fast, beautiful, and unique aircraft of your dreams - without expensive tooling or a lot of time. Discover why they're so popular and practical for you. This manual shows you the techniques of working with plastics, and the basics of structural and aerodynamic design.

Some important topics presented include:

- Using foam/fiberglass matrixes, paper cores, Kevlar, S-glass, graphite, polyester and epoxies.
- Mold making techniques, attaching other materials and fittings, inspection and repair procedures, and safety and health precautions.
- The reasoning behind lay-ups and composite sandwich designs.
- A complete catalog of supplies, costs, tools, materials, definitions, shop facilities, and equipment requirements.

Complete construction details and pilot reports are included on: Quickie Q2/200, Dragonfly, VariEze, Long-EZ, Goldwing ST, Mini-Imp, Bullet, Polliwagen, Glassair, Sea Hawk, KR-1 & 2, and WAR replicas.

It's all here...the aircraft, materials, and methods. Learn how to work with the newest material - Molt Taylor's new "paper/glass" composites. The book shows you the subtle differences in style and construction philosophy of the 14 most popular composite airplanes. Let it help you decide which is best for you.

Jack Lambie, the author, has built airplanes for movies, made gliders, and flown self-modified aircraft for over 30 years. He was on the Gossamer Condor design/construction team. He has written over 130 aviation magazine articles, and two books on building and flying kitplanes.

COMPOSITE CONSTRUCTION **takes the "mystery" out** of plastic kitplanes. Whether you're thinking of building a kit, or considering an original design, this book's for you. If you want to make modifications to improve your present airplane, or simply keep current on the use of these new wonder materials, this is your guide.

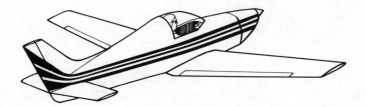